ODYSSEY OF A FRIEND

ODYSSEY OF A FRIEND

Whittaker Chambers
Letters to William F. Buckley, Jr.
1954-1961

Edited With Notes by William F. Buckley, Jr.

FOREWORD BY LANCE MORROW
EPILOGUE BY RALPH de TOLEDANO

REGNERY BOOKS
Washington, D.C.

Library of Congress Cataloging-in-Publication Data

Chambers, Whittaker.
  Odyssey of a friend.

    Reprint. Originally privately printed by
National Review, 1969.
    Includes bibliographical references and index.
    1. Chambers, Whittaker—Correspondence.
2. Buckley, William F. (William Frank), 1925–   —
Correspondence. 3. Spies—United States—Correspondence.
4. Journalists—United States—Correspondence.
5. United States—Politics and government—1953–1961.
6. Communism—United States—1917–   . 7. Hiss,
Alger.   I. Buckley, William F. (William Frank),
1925–   . II. Title.
E743.5.C46   1987   973.921′092′4   87–23252

        ISBN 0–89526–567–2 (cloth)
        ISBN 0–89526–788–8 (pbk.)

    Published in the United States by
        Regnery Gateway
      1130 17th Street, NW
      Washington D.C. 20036

    Distributed to the trade by
    Kampmann & Company, Inc.
        9 E 40th Street
      New York NY 10016

    10 9 8 7 6 5 4 3 2 1

Contents

Those of us who knew him, who shared his trust or had a sometime view of the life he saw through those laughing, prescient eyes, can reread his letters and weep and know the cold edge of our loss. Why write of him when he has so much better written of himself?

—RALPH DE TOLEDANO, July, 1961

That pointed finger, leveled at his friend, electrified our age and will haunt our history. It revealed, like a stab of lightning, this century's underworld of lost hopes and breeding terrors. And the life that ended in such a moment of truth will never end. Tricked by life, he succeeded in tricking death. Sunday's victory was deceptive; when death called, he had already gone. But while we live, and until the eclipse of the West, this figure stands central and alive, living still his death of demonstration; bearing witness.

—RICHMOND *News Leader*, July, 1961

The witness is gone, the testimony will stand.

—ARTHUR KOESTLER, July, 1961

Introduction

"ALGER HISS STILL SEEKING VINDICATION" is a headline which
might appear anywhere, any time. I most recently saw it, in
exactly that form, in the New York *Post,* on June 3, 1968. The
story was filed in London, where Alger Hiss was visiting, and
the reporter spoke of lawyers who were still tracking down leads
"which they hope will establish that Hiss was an innocent
victim of the McCarthy era of American politics." Alger Hiss
was quoted directly, "My trial concerns me vitally and continually. My lawyers and I are still following leads and evidence
and I remain as convinced as ever of my ultimate vindication."

If Mr. Hiss is ever vindicated—the circle-squaring ambition
of his friends and supporters—he will clearly owe them a great
deal. They are a true Lobby. It seems as if ever since the
conviction of Hiss a year never goes by without either the publication of a book supporting Alger Hiss, or news of a book
in preparation supporting Alger Hiss. We have had Alistair
Cooke, Lord Jowitt, Fred Cook, Alger Hiss himself, Meyer
Zeligs, and now one hears that a Mr. Rubin is about to publish.
What he will find new to say it is interesting to speculate about.
Dr. Zeligs showed in his psychobiography that there are no
limits to human ingenuity bent upon historical revisionism.

Shortly after Hiss's conviction, Messrs. Ralph de Toledano
and Victor Lasky published their extremely useful and dramatic best seller, *Seeds of Treason,* which concluded that when
Hiss was convicted, justice had been done. Two years later,
Whittaker Chambers spoke for himself in *Witness.* That was a

9

very long time ago (1952), two years before Hiss was released from prison and the counteroffensive was launched. Chambers died in 1961, and his *Cold Friday,* a tapestry of essays, was brought out posthumously in 1964. Between the appearance of *Witness* and his death, Chambers spoke publicly only once on Alger Hiss, in an article published (May 9, 1959) in *National Review,* in which he opposed the effort to deny Hiss a passport to travel abroad. But he made many references to Hiss and to the Hiss case in letters to me (and presumably to other friends). These letters are, to say the least, illuminating.

The facts in the Hiss case have proved very balky to Chambers' detractors. Court after court has listened to Hiss's remonstrances, without flinching. Thus it is that the case for Hiss relies increasingly on efforts to discredit Chambers personally, the most egregious of which has been the volume of the said Dr. Zeligs, which sought by the use of psychiatric expressionism to reduce Whittaker Chambers to a tangled, contemptible, neurotic mess. It strikes me under the circumstances that it is long overdue to publish letters sent to me over the years by Chambers which clearly belong to the public. They are not a schematic on the Hiss case—that would be redundant. They are spontaneous personal and philosophical reflections which will help the reader to judge the plausibility of the attacks on Whittaker Chambers' character. Mr. Peter Collier, reviewing Zeligs' book (favorably) in *Ramparts* magazine, sighed that that book would undoubtedly have several effects. "William Buckley, Chambers' Boswell, will launch anathemas against Zeligs, sublime in their arrogance, from his pulpit in the National Review." "Sublime" is exactly the right word to describe what will have issued in response to Zeligs' attack in the judgment of this reader of the following correspondence—it was I who opened the envelopes that brought these communications, finding in them a sublimity which I most frankly acknowledge as having been as much influential as the goddamn Woodstock typewriter in convincing me of the credentials of Whittaker Chambers. "Arrogant," I doubt any reader will find these letters to be, or any of the anathemas which, to be sure, are here and there loosed in them. The letters are intact except that an occasional reference has been obscured. Boswell did not edit Johnson.

Because so many years have gone by, and because there are so many who never knew the story line of the Hiss case. I publish as an epilogue an account of that case written by Mr. Ralph de Toledano for a book I edited several years ago, *The Committee and Its Critics*. It is an excellent account, and illuminates several references to the case that come up in Whittaker Chambers' letters.

I am most grateful for the encouragement of four very old friends of Whittaker Chambers: Mr. Toledano himself, Mr. Henry Grunwald, Mr. Duncan Norton-Taylor, and Mr. John Chamberlain, none of whom, however, is in any way responsible for the editorial presentation. And I wish to thank Miss Agatha Schmidt for her heroic assistance in checking some of the references in the letters, and in getting translations of the German and the Russian phrases.

W.F.B.

Stamford, Connecticut
July 1, 1969

Foreword

At the beginning of *Witness,* Whittaker Chambers addressed his children. "As long as you live," he wrote, "the shadow of the Hiss case will brush you. In every pair of eyes that rests on you, you will see pass, like a cloud passing behind a wood in winter, the memory of your father. . ."

But there is also the cloud of forgetfulness. The Hiss case was a long time ago. *Witness,* Chambers' record of the matter, was published in 1952. The copy that lies on my desk now is one that I bought in a used-book store in Port Washington, N.Y., a dozen years ago. The hard covers are gone from the volume, the spine exposed. The book is a derelict, like a rusted Plymouth from the early fifties. I imagine that Chambers might have liked the idea of having his life arrive upon another generation's doorstep in somesuch form, roadweary, but with his words stepping out of the vehicle still sonorous and doomy and alive.

Chambers is a sort of orphan of historical memory. But the passage of time has if anything improved his reputation. In 1984, President Reagan awarded a posthumous Medal of Freedom to Chambers. The citation read: "At a critical moment in our Nation's history, Whittaker Chambers stood alone against the brooding terrors of our age. Consummate intellectual, writer of moving majestic prose, and witness to the truth, he became the focus of a momentous controversy in American history that symbolized our century's epic struggle between freedom and totalitarianism, a controversy in which the solitary figure of Whittaker Chambers personified the mystery of human redemption in the face of evil and suffering. As long as humanity speaks of virtue and dreams of freedom, the life and writings of Whittaker Chambers will ennoble and inspire. The words of Arthur Koestler are his epitaph: 'The witness is gone; the testimony will stand.' " It may be another generation before the poisons are dissipated and one can appreciate him clearly.

The American memory of the Hiss case retains mostly a few vivid objects—a pumpkin in a Maryland field, a Woodstock typewriter, another old car (roadster, Ford, 1929, should you look it up)—without being able to say precisely what they signified (whose guilt, whose innocence), or why such guilt or innocence should matter. What exactly was the Hiss case? Prehistory: an old war from the time when Richard Nixon was young and Josef Stalin was an active malignancy—an ancient, primordial rumble of the Cold War. It was a matter of opinion which figure in the Hiss-Chambers case represented the Dark Side. Still is, although the tribe of those who can knowledgeably discuss the case is dwindling. My own view is that the facts were pretty much as Chambers stated them. A few years ago, I saw Alger Hiss walking up Madison Avenue in Manhattan, an old man, the threadbare ghost of the case. Even at that late date in the century, so long after the trials, I wanted to confront Hiss and say, "There is no one else here: Tell me." Alistair Cooke wrote in 1950 that in the Hiss case, an entire generation was on trial. Chambers said that the case epitomized a basic conflict. "And Alger and I were archtypes."

Yes, but each generation has its drama. It is a source of wonder when one discovers that the defining tragedy of one's own life is, to the next generation, a gray, receding business. It is hard for the young to take in the truth that their fathers were passionate long ago, were great lovers and haters, and once may even have killed someone. Viet Nam was the defining drama of a later generation. I was shocked not long ago when a young man of draft age looked at me blankly when I mentioned the Tet offensive of early 1968. It might as well have been Cold Harbor or the Somme. Surprised and irritated, I thought, how could anyone not know about Tet? All right: How could anyone not know about the Hiss case?

One carries in memory the vivid image of Whittaker Chambers from the days of his testimony. He was, as he knew, spectacularly unprepossessing. I first saw his picture when I was a child in Washington D.C. and the sad smudge of his form arrived in the morning on the front page of the Washington Times-Herald. That line of poetry to his children ("like a cloud passing behind a wood in winter,/ the memory of your father. . .") is perfect: austerely rueful, self-knowing, but also prescient and exact, as Chambers often was. A small, complicated transaction: Chambers floated himself out into the region of the American future where he would be remembered, and described the bleak afterlife he would have there. He exactly imagined his own ghost, an orphan in the winter of the future. Chambers did seem at the time of his fame—and would seem in the American memory of him—to be as gray and dissheveled as a January cloud seen behind bare black trees. The sad sack vanishing.

That was a stratagem, I have sometimes suspected. Whittaker Chambers was a far more interesting man than most Americans ever understood—a wonderful writer, heroically self-possessed, a complicated figure full of doom and an amazing tenderness and poetry. His intelligence was sometimes melodramatic and melancholy, but it was always alive. The mental ecology of Whittaker Chambers was one of nature's mostly hidden wonders.

Writing is either alive, or it is a simulation of life, the words making their way across the page as best they can, even in orderly file, but with no brain attached. One always knows. Chambers' sentences are alive, with a curious force and a remarkable equilibrium. He became famous because of a spy case; the case was his destiny, he believed, and it more or less exhausted him. In his last letter to William Buckley, Chambers wrote, "Weariness, Bill—you cannot yet know literally what it means . . . History hit us with a freight train." The freight train passed. The Hiss case was a moment in history. One wishes that Chambers had survived to comment on China and the Soviet Union now.

Presumptuously, one also wishes that Chambers had been spared his necessity to stand in the middle of that track—wishes that he had been pardoned to go on writing and living. Suppose that Chambers had been a cherished son, and a golden boy of

American letters, full of Pulitzer Prizes and six-figure book contracts. Suppose he had become a celebrity, an iridescence showing up from time to time in *People* magazine. It is obnoxious to go on with the fantasy, but I find myself sometimes inventing a counter-life, as if the life he had were a mistake somehow. But Chambers was a great man for inevitabilities. In that sense, he was most un-American.

His imagination was intensely visual, moral, and apocalyptic in a way that may have been, at bottom, artistic. He had many sides, and one side was saint and martyr. He wrote in one of these letters: "At its own level, *Witness*, too, is chiefly a poem. I am more and more convinced that it is the force of this that people feel; but few know it; they read into it the meanings they choose." He enacted ideas, gave himself over to them, which is the saint's—or the fanatic's—business. The Christian theme of renunciation sounds through his work and life. One hears Gerard Manley Hopkins there: "No worst, there is none./ Pitched past pitch of grief/ pangs will, schooled of forepangs,/ wilder ring." That is the sound of a long experience in a spiritual struggle that the world mostly cannot understand and, more deeply, cannot tolerate. And yet as Buckley writes at the end of this book, "I never knew a man who so enjoyed laughing." That also makes sense, but as always with Chambers, one must think about it a little.

In *Witness,* Chambers has a wonderful scene in which he describes running away from home and going to work helping to lay new streetcar tracks in Washington D.C. "There was one job that every man dreaded," he wrote. A man would have to lie prone in a shallow tunnel, with the deadly third rails two inches above his shoulders, all the electricity of the Washington transit system jolting through that steel, and he would have to chip out concrete with a cold chisel. "A sudden turn of my head, a slip of the hammer or chisel would have brought me in contact with the rail. It was an invaluable experience."

Chambers had an almost bizarre genius for doubling and vanishing himself simultaneously—assertion and abnegation somehow twinned in his mind. Going through these splendid letters for the first time, I was appalled to come upon lines written on

January 3, 1956: "Thus, for me, success always was negative, and lay in my firmness in destroying almost everything I wrote as fast as I wrote it. I have burned a book half the size of *Witness,* and consider it one of my best deeds."

Consider: *Witness* runs to just over 800 printed pages. Did Whittaker Chambers, who published little in his life, really destroy 400 pages of his prose? A reader who knows Chambers chiefly on the basis of *Witness* and these letters senses on the surface here an annihilating romantic gesture of an almost adolescent kind. But that romantic impulse, which Chambers surely had, was not working alone. For all of the deeply depressive shadows that crossed his life, the betrayals and vanishings and the terrible nights (terrible is a word Chambers used often), Chambers seems to me to have had an amazingly steady set of spiritual instruments.

He dramatized himself: He proclaimed himself witness and martyr. "I am the witness on whom it all still swings," he wrote to Buckley on February 7, 1954. "The enemy is tirelessly seeking to discredit me . . . My reactions are a kind of public trust."

He sometimes displayed grandiosity and asceticism simultaneously. One begins to feel one is in the presence of an elemental struggle, in Chambers' own mind, between life and death. What is astonishing was the courage with which Chambers accepted and endured the struggle. His younger brother refused all of it, and committed suicide as a young man. Whittaker sent his brother off to be embalmed. He wrote: "I thought that he had acted quickly and bravely to destroy his life before the world could destroy it . . . I made my decision: No, I will live. There is something in me, there is some purpose to my life which I feel but do not understand. I must go on living until it is fulfilled. I added to myself, I shall be sorry that I did not go with my brother." When I read the first sentence of that passage ("quickly and bravely to destroy his life"), red lights and alarms went off in my mind. They still do. I wonder at the deep wistfulness of the thought. In Chambers' life, the third rail was always just an inch above, and one had to go on banging concrete.

Chambers' rhetoric makes one think sometimes of Alexander

Solzhenitsyn's warning to the West in the commencement address at Harvard in June of 1978. Solzhenitsyn almost scornfully contrasted the spiritual depths of his Russian homeland with what he regarded as the frivolous shallows of the West. In Russia, said Solzhenitsyn, "through intense suffering our country has now achieved a spiritual development of such intensity that the Western system in its present state of spiritual exhaustion does not look attractive . . . Life's complexity and mortal weight have produced stronger and more interesting characters than those generated by standardized Western well being."

Whittaker Chambers was a character of formidable "complexity and mortal weight." He had a Slavic gravitas about him, a sort of authenticity of suffering, that was somehow startling in an American. One thought of the Archpriest Avvakum, the prophet of the Old Believers. Avvakum was a sort of Jonathan Edwards of Russian Orthodoxy in the 17th century, and through him ran the thin, pure note, the vibration, sometimes extraterrestrial, one hears in Solzhenitsyn, say, or the old age of Malcolm Muggeridge. There is a form of ranting that in old age purifies itself into a clear blue light.

I have sometimes thought that Chambers' character was a sort of violent dialectic. He became as Russian as he was American. He claimed his roots in the Narodniki, savoring the idea of a repudiation that would fire him out of America so violently that he would overshoot Europe entirely and land in Russian terrorism. He comes back to America to subvert and destroy it, and then, rather touchingly, he ends by writing to Buckley about the doings of Wall Street.

In many ways, Chambers seems to me to have been profoundly American. The first 200 pages of *Witness* is one of the greatest and most harrowing of American autobiographies—a heartbreaking, terrifying record of his childhood and youth on Long Island. It would be presumptuous and silly to go at Chambers in a merely Freudian way; the role of conscious thought and will and historical judgment was powerful in his life, and he was not merely blown about by desolate gusts from his early years. He was a highly developed man, but also a man haunting and haunted.

I think it is difficult to understand Whittaker Chambers without reading the first quarter of *Witness* and all of these letters. The first quarter of *Witness* is to me haunting in its loneliness, its almost infantile desolation—the mother beset, the father gone, the brother dying, the grandmother mad, wandering around the house at night flashing a knife. The letters, dealing with the other end of his life, suggest a sweetness of friendship, and the resignation of aftermath.

William Buckley and Whittaker Chambers became friends only after the storm of the Hiss case had passed. One of the charms of these letters is the way that they mingle great public issues and small private business—the fate of the West one moment and then news of the farm: "I worked the hay load last night against the coming rain." The letters have surprises (Chambers' attitude toward Joseph McCarthy and Richard Nixon, for example), humor, and Chambers' learning and weirdly pertinent take on things ("one of the great moral moments in current U.S. writing is the quarry scene in *From Here to Eternity*—the scene in which one of the prisoners takes his crowbar and, on request, breaks the arm or leg of a fellow prisoner.") They have Chambers' occasional bombast, his lyricism, and beyond that, a finer, stranger sound. As he wrote, "It seems as if, by the fretting of the raw edges, there arises a peculiar music: we do not know how."

There is enduring music in these letters—the music of Chambers' soul toward the end of a densely complicated life. Chambers' emotional and cultural range was amazing, his concentration was spookily absolute.

LANCE MORROW
Essayist, *Time* magazine

I

January to April, 1954

In December of 1953, Senator Joseph R. McCarthy was given to read the galleys of McCarthy and His Enemies, *by William F. Buckley and L. Brent Bozell, which would be published the following March by the Henry Regnery Company of Chicago. Senator McCarthy reported back that he found the book to be hypercritical and that some of his friends thought it would do him net damage. Henry Regnery sent a set of galleys, along with the Senator's comments, to his friend Whittaker Chambers, who replied:*

Jan. 14, 1954

Dear Henry,

Please take my order for the co-authors' book right away.

In my opinion, the Senator hasn't got a leg to stand on. I don't see how, in the end, he can fail to realize that the book does him the great service of stating his case with understanding, clarity, cogency, good humor, knowingness and more generosity than many would be inclined to indulge simply on the face of some of the cited facts. Besides, the authors have managed to make it all readable from start to end. This is a feat. For, as the picture unfolds, the awful sense begins to invade you, like a wave of fatigue, that the Senator is a bore, for the same reason that Rocky Marcinano (if that is his name) is a bore to people who are not exclusively interested in fist-throwing. The Senator is not, like Truman, a swift jabber who does his dirty work with a glee that is infectiously impish; nor, like F. D. Roosevelt, an artful and experienced ringmaster whose techniques may be studied again and again and again. (This is the weakness at the root of the authors' defense of McCarthy in terms of the others' skulduggery—as they are aware.) The

23

Senator, the authors make it all too clear, is a heavy-handed slugger who telegraphs his fouls in advance. What is worse, he has to learn from consequences or counselors that he has fouled. I know he thinks this is a superior technique that the rest of us are too far behind to appreciate. But it is repetitious and unartful, and, with time, the repeated dull thud of the low blow may prove to be the real factor in his undoing. Not necessarily because the blow is low, or because he lacks heart and purpose, but because he lacks variety, and, in the end, simply puts the audience to sleep. Very likely he senses this and that may be part of his distaste for the book. He may also feel as I do (perhaps without knowing just what it is he feels) that the real value and interest of the book lies less in what it tells about McCarthy than in the detailed picture it gives (for the first time, so far as I know) of the Tydings Committee episode. That, in fact, is why I want it in my library. But I should not hesitate to tell the Senator that I think the book is a real job in his behalf and that he owes the authors a loud well-done and thank you. I cannot think of anybody but Buckley and his partner who could have brought it off so effectively—who could have brought it off at all.

I begin much farther up the valley in my thoughts about much of the context they explore, so that I come out by a different pass and have a somewhat different view of the landscape below, including the Senator. But I think they have chosen their road wisely and followed it admirably, and that it is the shortest road from A to Z. Tucking the Marshall episode into the Appendix is a shrewd tactic. I expect, though, that that will be a point of attack on their position, which will be justified for the same reasons that justify their tactic.

The Senator's field of choice is strictly limited in the nature of the case. What can he choose between except an all-out eulogium, which would be self-defeating and which nobody but a hack would undertake, and this knowingly moderate, carefully reasoned, generally sympathetic appraisal? Of course, the Senator wants the former. Wants is too weak a word. He craves it, not only because he is at bottom a naïve and simple-hearted man, but because even a slugger gets very, very tired. That he should let his craving show is perfectly natural. That he should let it get in the way of the good this book can do him marks one line of his limitation. I said long since that the crucial question about Senator McCarthy was not whether his aims are ultimately good or bad, but whether his intelligence is equal to his energy. That includes all other questions. And I think that the best augury for him, and perhaps the most flattering thing that need be said, is that there are a lot of people who still believe that the answer is worth waiting for.

I remain of the same opinion still about the Foreword. If anything, more so. Its prose should be as direct and uncluttered as the text of the book. Its only possible justification, as I see it, is to shed more light on what follows by putting the subject on even higher ground in a wider context. If it does not do that with a clarity that matches the clarity of the text, the effect is like groping into a brightly lit house through a dimly lit vestibule with too many chairs piled along the walls.

None of this is, of course, for the Senator's eyes or ears. Except as you might want me to give him my opinion, which I shall gladly do.

As always,
Whittaker

Henry Regnery showed me the letter, and I prevailed on the promotion manager to wire Whittaker Chambers to ask whether he would be willing to write a blurb on the book for promotional use. He replied by telegram that he did not want his name to be used in any way. And followed with a letter.

Feb. 7, 1954

Dear Mr. Buckley,

I am deeply concerned that my refusal to write a blurb for your book should not offend or wound you; that you should understand the reasons for it and for my bluntness. You may be sure that they have nothing to do with my regard for you. They involve considerations beyond you and me, which I find overriding.

The first of these is the Hiss Case. I suppose we can agree, in general, that the Hiss Case is still the heart of the anti-Communist fight here, and that by it most of the rest stands or falls. At least, I am sure that the enemy has few doubts about it. Nor need anyone else who stops for a moment to think what would happen if that case were in any serious way compromised or impaired. Do you doubt that, with the center crushed, the wings would quickly be rolled back and routed?

To that end the enemy works tirelessly and implacably. You may or may not know that, within the last two months, the Hiss defense again sought a retrial. The point is not that they failed again, but that they are ceaselessly at work. The Hiss Case is a permanent war; and the forces and money behind the enemy effort are formidable. In my opinion, we shall not know how formidable until Alger Hiss leaves prison. Then the guns will begin to go off.

In that critical case, I am not really a free agent and scarcely even an individual man. I am the witness on whom, to a great degree, it still all swings. The enemy is tirelessly seeking to discredit me. How I conduct myself, what I say and do, what forces and people I publicly associate myself with, are matters to be governed by no whim of mine. My reactions are a kind of public trust. They call for the most vigilant intelligence and careful judgment.

One way whereby I can most easily help Communism is to associate myself publicly with Senator McCarthy; to give the enemy even a minor pretext for confusing the Hiss Case with his activities, and rolling it all into a snarl with which to baffle, bedevil and divide opinion. That is why I told Senator McCarthy, when he asked me to keynote his last Wisconsin campaign, that we were fighting in the same war, but in wholly different battles, and that the nature of the struggle at this time enjoins that we should not wage war together. I do not think that the Senator really grasps this necessity. For it is more and more my reluctant opinion that he is a tactician, rather than a strategist; that he continually, by reflex rather than calculation, sacrifices the long view for the short pull.

Perhaps this is getting wordy. But I hope it will suggest why, as the Government witness in the Hiss Case, I cannot move in the McCarthy controversy even by endorsing publicly a book which is of necessity a function of that controversy.

That is the tactical consideration. There is another quite as decisive. You must be aware from Henry Regnery how good I think your book is. This for two reasons. First, it presents the case for the Senator as I have not seen it presented and as he is clearly incapable of presenting it for himself. It commands for him a literate, reasoned hearing, which he has not had and which the national intelligence owes it to itself to see that he gets. It seems to me to make the best possible case for him (as, at Henry Regnery's request, I have written and told him). It also seems to me that, like any other man, the Senator is entitled simply in justice to have the best possible case made for him. Since neither justice nor humanity are mere mechanisms, making such a case inevitably involves accenting those points that are naturally strong and favorable and de-emphasizing those points that are inherently weak (the Marshall episode, for example). Every lawyer does this; it is part of the protection that justice affords. The Senator has a right to claim it and find it. The fact that he has not found it heretofore gravely impairs a true understanding of him; and that lapse, in turn, covers, and even condones, certain lapses of his own. Further, I admire the professional competence with which you have done so difficult a job. In short, I hold that the Senator has a right to have the job done for him and that you have done it as few others could.

That said, I must add that I by no means share all your conclusions. This is in part because I do not evaluate all the evidence as you do. In part it is because I believe that I have other evidence gleaned from my own first-hand observations of the Senator, or from the observations of others who are peculiarly well posted to observe him. None of us are his enemies. All of us would like to be his partisans, if only because all are engaged in the same war. As it is, most of us make an effort to overlook certain matters or to give him the benefit of most doubts. But, all of us, to one degree or another, have slowly come to question his judgment and to fear acutely that his flair for the sensational, his inaccuracies and distortions, his tendency to sacrifice the greater objective for the momentary effect, will lead him and us into trouble. In fact, it is no exaggeration to say that we live in terror that Senator McCarthy will one day make some irreparable blunder which will play directly into the hands of our common enemy and discredit the whole anti-Communist effort for a long while to come. For myself, I must say that the Bohlen episode, insofar as he involved me in it (together with certain other matters), was a shock more educative than ten years of merely reading the Senator's remarks.[1] Thereafter, I could not possibly view anything he does with my initial simplicity or without tacit caveat. I never publicly criticize the Senator. Whenever necessary, I defend him insofar as I find him defensible and bearing in mind the Hiss Case restrictions.

Thus, I believe your book is a good and necessary book, and I admire the way you have done it. But I could not write a blurb for it without making qualifications so strong that they would undo the purpose of the blurb, and would be in effect the very kind of criticism of Senator McCarthy which I do not wish to make.

My wire to Mr. Strube was so emphatic because I was afraid that, if I said anything less blunt, his publishing enthusiasm,

[1] Senator McCarthy had stoutly opposed the confirmation of Charles Bohlen as ambassador to the Soviet Union. At a crucial moment in the Senate debate, when it was expected that Senator McCarthy would document his case against Bohlen, he suddenly disappeared from Washington, and leaked to the press that he had gone to Westminster, Maryland, to consult with Whittaker Chambers. At Westminster, McCarthy did not bring up Bohlen's name. But the Senator's visit had had the desired effect.

obvious from his wire, might lead him to do something that would publicly embarrass us all.

These things are much more easily talked out than written about in a letter, and I look forward to a time when we may talk about them. Meanwhile, I hope you fully realize my personal regard for you and my gratitude for your kindness to me.[2] My refusal is poor requital. But the situation is bigger than any of us.

Sincerely,

Whittaker Chambers

I wrote to say that I would greatly like to go to see him, and would bring along a friend, a professor of political science at Yale, Willmoore Kendall, who had actively defended Chambers on the campus during the Hiss trial and continued to do so as the occasion arose.

Feb. 25, 1954

Dear Mr. Buckley:

It is you who must bear with my wavy[3] script (and in pencil, to boot), for I am in bed for a while. Your letter greatly relieved me: I had been afraid of wounding you. By all means come on March 11 and bring Professor Kendall. Poor man! I don't think that he should endanger or exasperate his situation at Yale for my sake. The score, as the points are chalked up, clearly and boldly, more and more convinces me that the total situation is hopeless, past repair, organically irremediable. Almost the only position of spiritual dignity left to men, therefore, is a kind of stoic silence, made bearable by the amusement of seeing, hearing and knowing the full historical irony that its victims are blind and deaf to, and disciplined by the act of withholding comment on what we know. This may well be more of a

[2] I do not recall what kindness WC alluded to. I had never met him.
[3] WC wrote mostly by typewriter, but occasionally by hand. Some words are very difficult to decipher and, as in "wavy," are not rendered with full confidence.

posture than a position, and, happily, none of us will be permitted to assume it, or could, without violating our own articulate imperative. By August, 1952, I was so certain that this was the proper course that I had made a decision not to write again (or only under exceptional circumstances) and had begun to re-assemble a dairy herd with the intention henceforth of dividing my talents between milking and mastitis. At that point, and in the cow barn itself, a fist came down on my head and I went down with this heart that makes it impossible for me to milk cows exclusively (or otherwise) again. And from that hour to this that indignity and defect has rankled every moment and raised the corrosive question: Why? But all this reminiscence was brought on by Professor Kendall, to whom my thanks, but whom I still counsel to silence as the better course.

Let me tell you how to get here from Washington. I assume you will drive. Drive out Wisconsin Ave. to Bethesda. From Bethesda to Rockville, from Rockville to Gaithersburg. Then to Damascus, Mt. Airy, Taylorsville, Westminster. A road map will give you the route numbers. Route 140 is Main Street, Westminster. Drive out 140 (toward Pennsylvania) for three miles beyond Westminster. There a concrete road comes in to 140, but does not cross it. This is Route 496, the only concrete road you will meet above Westminster. Drive out 496 two and 7/10 miles. We are there, on your left, we are back from 496 on a hill; you have to turn left down a dirt country road for a short distance; then right at the mailbox into our lane. At the corner of 496 and that country road, there is one of those metal Guernsey Cattle Club signs which says: Chambers. In addition, anybody in the county can tell you where.

I look forward to seeing you.

Sincerely,
Whittaker Chambers

Come anytime of the day. If you will take potluck, I am sure we can find some scraps of old ham or eggs or something to eat.

We spent several hours together. I wrote and thanked him effusively, and (evidently) raised a point or two concerning the nature of the opposition to Senator McCarthy (this was during the Army-McCarthy hearings).

April 7, 1954

Dear Buckley,

What follows is almost a textbook example of all that I hold a letter should not be—long, prolix and subjective. It should not be sent. But I shall send it because you must be answered, and I do not feel up to writing another. Perhaps you will file it among your curiosa.

It is not really a letter at all, but an effort to hold an urgent conversation. This I find most interesting. In general, I make friends with grudging slowness, and my true intimates are few. But perhaps four times in my life I have had this experience: I have sat down with a stranger, and, with the first words, had the sense, not of beginning, but of resuming a conversation that had been going on for years, and might well go on without effort for the rest of our lives. It happened to me first in my teens with a woman musician, half German, half Russian. We met by the improbable chance that we sat next to each other in a high school auditorium. World War I was on, and we began to talk about Middle European and Balkan politics as if we had always been talking about them. She died during World War II, but her shaping influence upon me will end only with my own death.

Much the same thing happened with Henry Regnery. He walked into my hotel room in Milwaukee not quite two years ago. In ten minutes, I felt as if I had known him always and that there was nothing that we could not discuss with complete trust and understanding. I am afraid that I had somewhat the same feeling about you. The fourth instance you might guess. It was Alger and Priscilla Hiss. That is why no day passes without my dying a little at the thought of what befell them through me. To me (and to my wife) they remain essentially what they were—the friends for whom our feeling never changes, but whom history forced me to make suffer. Judge Murphy [4] was right about this too. "I have always said," he wrote me a year or so ago, "that, if they were to change tomorrow, you would be friends with them again."

Thank you for the Butterfield [5] which I shall look for presently. I have been trying in vain to get a book called *The Rebel*, by Albert Camus, published by Knopf earlier this year. If you come across it anywhere, will you be good enough to send it on? I know the price and will send you a check for it.

Sincerely,
Whittaker Chambers

April 6, 1954

Dear Buckley,

There are two Apparats, as you know—the Communist and the socialist. I believe that it is prevailingly the displeasure of the second Apparat that you are now suffering. It can be stated, simply as an objective fact, that Senator McCarthy is a Communist target, set up on a worldwide scale. Their aim in recognizing the possibilities of this target is, as so often with Communists, not merely negative (the destruction of an enemy), but positive (an issue and activity around which to recruit mass support). Incidentally a similar appraisal helps to determine my "neutralism" in the matter. Precisely because the Communists do not have the American masses with them on this issue, they must, to be effective, work up the "classes" to a pitch. Fortunately for the CP, the first Apparat, that is easy to do. The second Apparat (socialism) is self-starting to a high degree, and the law of inertia can be counted on to do the rest with only a nudge now and then from the multitongued Agitprop. The

---

[4] Charles Murphy, the prosecutor at the Hiss trial.
[5] Herbert Butterfield's *Man on His Past: The Study of the History of Historical Scholarship.*

socialist Apparat will eagerly do the rest. And almost every-where and always, it is these people, rather than the masses, who have been the effective agents of Communist advance. Even when they are not the "classes" by origin, the socialists adapt themselves to the classes, and share their tone, habitats and superior venom. They are cobras, not pit vipers, like the Communists. They strike with some precision and grace; and their bite produces paralysis, rather than the agonized swelling and mortification of the rattlers. (There may always be a point, of course, at which the masses become decisive for the CP, but that is another story, though it would be a mistake not to bear it in mind.)

Now, the Communists recognized at once (or, more probably, after they had stirred things up a bit) that Senator McCarthy is a political godsend. The socialists like to note this disin-genuously for their own political purposes, but the fact remains a fact. The reason is obvious. Not only does Senator McCarthy unite through fear the socialist Apparat and its far-flung free-masonry of fellow travelers (anybody who believes as an article of faith that a low voice is a sweet and modest thing in woman, and even in man; and that one does not bang one's spoon against one's cup whilst stirring one's tea). Equally important, Senator McCarthy *divides* the ranks of the Right. Historically, this is inevitable. There have been a series of these divisive leaders, varying in this or that set of details—Chiang Kai-shek, Syngman Rhee, General de Gaulle, etc. The Right, so long as it has vitality enough to fight back at all, must throw them up: they embody, inter alia, a way of fighting. Value judgments are not in point. The point is that their leadership never fails to divide the Right and unite the Left almost to the limits of its spectrum.

Senator McCarthy was almost made to order. He is a man, fighting almost wholly by instinct and intuition, against forces for the most part coldly conscious of their ways, means, and ends. In other words, he scarcely knows what he is doing. He simply knows that somebody threw a tomato and the general direction from which it came. His general tactic might be epitomized in Samson's bright thought of setting fire to the foxes' tails and sending them helter-skelter against the enemy.[6] A tactic not altogether ruled out in a minor skirmish in a guerrilla war—but it is not a strategy; and repetition dooms it, not only to defeat, but to boredom.

Yet the Senator represents the one force that all shades of the Left really fear. This does not contradict what I have written above about his tactical inadequacy. It results from the fact that, in the U.S., the Left must take power by deception. This is peculiarly true of the socialist Apparat. Deception and secrecy, for the Communist Apparat, are only certain methods, among others, of working. But for the socialist Apparat, deception and secrecy are prerequisites for the actual taking of power in the State, which they have held before (New and Fair Deals), and which they feel within an eyelash of taking, and permanently consolidating, soon again. That is, they stand within an inch of closing the capitalist phase of history in the U.S. (hence in the world), and of rooting their power in its vast, fertilizing dinosauric corpse. But there is one prime condition: they may not do it as socialists. They may do it only as something else, due to the ingrained American aversion to the word, socialism. By repeatedly lighting his foxes' tails and loosing them indiscriminately toward the Left, the Senator repeatedly calls the attention of the antisocialist masses to the fact that the socialist Apparat exists; and worse, that the socialist and Communist Apparats co-exist, blend at certain points of tactic and purpose; have been, and are, auxiliaries, although, no doubt, it is the socialist intention, as Franklin Roosevelt once noted for passing political effect, to lie in wait for the Communists on the day of reckoning. That day is the *Machtergreifung*, the seizure of power; and it is that seizure of power that the Senator constantly imperils. He alone on the Right, at this moment, *visibly* imperils it. So both Apparats, the cobras and the pit vipers, converge on him.

They also converge on anybody in any way associated with

[6] Book of Judges 15:4.

him: Where such association is nonexistent or demure, strategy calls for forcible association with the main target (real guilt by association) of anybody who can remotely be linked with him. See Granville Hicks' effort (a typical Stalinist "amalgam" device) in the *New Leader* week before last [March 22, 1954].

This presumptuous preface is my pedantic way of pointing out that, of course, your lectures and other appearances are being canceled.[7] You are articulate (rare on the Right) and, therefore, all the more nicked for proscription. This is why, to glance at smaller matters, the *Saturday Review* wired me to review your book, hoping, under the guise of a fraudulent fairness, to draw me toward the fangs with the coil thus generously looped out. This is why, too, even if no other considerations were in play, the situation enjoins me to stand clear of the McCarthy brawl.

But, as you know, I do not believe that the Senator has what it takes to win the fight for the Right. I believe that Richard Nixon may have some of what it takes. I believe it the more readily because the Left also believes it. Therefore, it sought to eliminate him at the start (of course, only as one detail of a wider strategy). Never suppose that the Left has finished with Nixon. But the Senator has proved a more available target; while Nixon has proved a more elusive strategist, and his methods and success are the more baffling (at least, momentarily) because they did not think he had it in him; and perhaps because they feel that they can eliminate him in the general wreck of the administration. For the present, that is sound tactics. But, once Senator McCarthy is pruned back, they will get on with the Vice President. As they will get on with me. One of the incidental values of Senator McCarthy as a target has been that he distracts attention from the Hiss Case, which remains the prime danger to the Left in that field. And this, both for what is past and because, if even one of the inner Hiss

---

[7] The reference is to a lecture or two which had been scheduled, and then, after the notoriety caused by the publication of *McCarthy and His Enemies*, canceled.

circle, say, Lee Pressman, should tell the truth, the political effect would be to blow the Left down for a season.

So, for a time, the Vice President is classified, while the Left offensive in the Hiss Case is waged subterraneously, out of public sight, in publishers' offices (including Random House: [8] see C. C. Wertenbaker's novel [9]) and lawyers' chambers (another attempt at a Hiss appeal was made, unknown to most citizens, at the end of 1953). Look for other detonations before the year is out, although, for the general political purposes of the Left, that might prove unwise. But, then, we must not suppose that the Left always acts wisely or as a unit. There are other factors, including Hiss's personal vindictiveness which, to some degree, brought the disaster of his case on the Left in the first place; and also the wider intention of the Communists to exploit his case for their own ends, at which point their purposes are not at one with the socialist Apparat.

Of course, in the larger sense, I believe that the bigger battle is lost in advance. This is nothing new with me. At heart, I have scarcely ever, if at all, believed anything else. My remark about "the losing side" aroused more concern among good folk than almost anything else in *Witness*. Moreover, I held this so strongly that in a passage, which so far as I know nobody has noticed, I said flatly that I felt that the cause I fought for was so powerless to help itself that even God had given up. This is the passage about my thoughts in the Wall Street district after the expert had mistakenly postdated the manufacture of the microfilm. I never really hoped to do more in the Hiss Case than give the children of men a slightly better, only slightly better, chance to fight a battle already largely foredoomed. I rejoice that I could make the effort, and I should rather never have lived than not have made it. But I had, and have, no illusion, or few. This is at the root of my endemic hopelessness, made deceptive to most people by my temperamental buoyancy. It is part of the climate that has taken vengeance on my heart—

8 Publishers of *Witness*, by Whittaker Chambers, in 1952.
9 *The Death of Kings*.

overweight and work are only incidental factors though of the kind that the secular world puts its faith in. This, too, was at the root of much of my vacillation in the past. I have, for years, been fascinated by the Book of Jonah, and I said to a few at the time that that was the pattern of the Hiss Case. Therefore, in a sense, I fled to Tarshish with the dread words in my ears: "Go up unto Nineveh, that great city, etc." But, when the tempest rose, and it became a question of myself or the crew, I had also to say: "Take me up and cast me into the sea, because it is for my sake that this trouble is come upon you." That is why Jonah's words in the belly of the whale [10] also appear in the Wall Street passage in *Witness*—by intention, the only Biblical quote in the book. But, in the end, I did go unto Nineveh, and when nothing really happened (nothing did), and when the ADA worms and others had eaten up the cucumber vine, and God had asked: "Do you well to be angry?" I answered and still answer: "I do well to be angry, even unto death." For I always knew that, as we would say, you cannot turn back the clock of history.

But that is why, too, the generosity behind your remark about original sin (so obviously untrue as not even to raise the issue of impiety) is, nevertheless, justified to this extent: that against the clear and forceful evidence of my own mind, I will always give my body to be burned if, by so doing, our children are given even that slightly better chance against the falling night. And the sure knowledge that that is what God is demanding of me in not permitting me to die is the seed of my private agony and the secret of my heart attacks. For only I know what God has said to me, and I have told no one, not even a priest. Those collapses which the world sees are due to the tension between my feeling that I do not have, as a man, the strength to do what will be laid on me, and the horror of knowing that, when it is laid on me, I shall do it. In sum, what

10 "The waters compassed me about even to the soul; the deep hath closed round about; the sea hath covered my head. I went down to the lowest parts of the mountains; the bars of the earth have shut me up for ever...."

have I to do with Senator McCarthy? What this cause must have is not a leader to lead it to success (historically, that is almost impossible), but a martyr to perpetuate what in it is alone worth preserving. Inevitably, that man must fight with the force of his human life against martyrdom. If, in that fight, he dies before his work is done, what he stood for will fail to that extent. If he is doomed to live, he will end more dreadfully, but what he stood for will live to the extent of his submissive agony. "Do you know," Judge Murphy wrote me, "that witness in Greek means martyr?" Of course, he knew that I knew; he knows me better than most living men. How odd that most of the world seems to have missed the point in *Witness;* that it seems to suppose that I said: "Destroy Communism and you can go back to business as usual." Of course, what I really said was: "This struggle is universal and mortal, and only *by means of* it, on condition that you are willing to die that your faith may live, can you conceivably recover the greatness which is in the souls of men. Therefore, I go a little in advance—to try to win for you that infinitesimal slightly better chance." If the bourgeoisie understood *Witness* aright, they would raise the war cry of their revolutionary heyday, and rush me "to the lantern." Of course, this is precisely what the socialists sense confusedly: hence, as the perpetuators of the bourgeois dream, their foam and fury.

These thoughts have been much re-inforced by the explosions in the Pacific,[11] which, like you, I cannot get out of my mind. I have long been convinced of that, too. Our faint hearts are all atremble with dread at the thought that what they are going to is a war. What they are really going to is the end of a civilization and an age. Now we see how. The solution lies with the Bombs, not with the arguments. But if it should not, if we should be so far gone in historical corruption as to outlaw the Bombs, gas, bacteria et al., the Communists will merely win over the slower haul. They will let us hang ourselves on our

[11] The hydrogen bomb tests at Eniwetok.

own base fears and parish-house morality. As Willi [Schlamm] says bitterly: "Malenkov will save civilization."

I wish I could close on a gayer note. But add it up again and again, I get no other answers. I am afraid that this letter is the penalty for your remark about original sin which touched certain secret springs that most people do not know of.

Meanwhile, may things look up for you currently. I offer you a quotation with which to bait and lure your opponents in controversy. Offer it in exhibit and ask them if they too believe this: "It goes without saying that only a planned economy can make intelligent use of *all* a people's strength." If they agree, the author is Adolf Hitler (*Hitler's Secret Conversations*, Farrar, Straus, & Young, page 15).

Sincerely,
Whittaker Chambers

II

August, 1954, to September, 1955

Dear Bill,

Thank you for the books, and, particularly, for your kindness in sending them. Camus is stunting in an intellectual glider, riding the currents of the tricky, upper air. I admire his skill in the qualified way with which we admire a skill we shall never be capable of, which seems to have little relevance to us, and which (perhaps because of our limitations) seems to have little to do with reality. But Butterfield has both feet firmly on the ground. I am reading him with interest. His grasp of what Marx means seems singular, coming from such a quarter; and my friend, John Chamberlain, should be made to read that chapter every morning before breakfast.

Of course, I wrote you a long letter as soon as Camus came, and added a few paragraphs with each Butterfield book. Yesterday, I did you the kindness to burn it. From it I shall pick up only one point, touched on by you in one of your letters. No, I no longer believe that political solutions are possible for us. I am baffled by the way people still speak of the West as if it were at least a cultural unity against Communism though it is divided not only by a political, but by an invisible cleavage. On one side are the voiceless masses with their own subdivisions and fractures. On the other side is the enlightened, articulate elite which, to one degree or other, has rejected the religious roots of the civilization—the roots without which it is no longer Western civilization, but a new order of beliefs, attitudes and mandates. In short, this is the order of which Communism is one logical expression, originating not in

Russia, but in the culture capitals of the West, reaching Russia by clandestine delivery via the old underground centers in Cracow, Vienna, Berne, Zurich and Geneva. It is a Western body of belief that now threatens the West from Russia. As a body of Western beliefs, secular and rationalistic, the intelligentsia of the West share it, and are therefore always committed to a secret emotional complicity with Communism of which they dislike, not the Communism, but only what, by the chances of history, Russia has specifically added to it—slave labor camps, purges, MVD et al. And that, not because the Western intellectuals find them unjustifiable, but because they are afraid of being caught in them. If they could have Communism without the brutalities of ruling that the Russian experience bred, they have only marginal objections. Why should they object? What else is socialism but Communism with the claws retracted? And there is positivism. What is more, every garage mechanic in the West, insofar as be believes in nuts and bolts but asks: "The Holy Ghost, what's that?" shares the substance of those same beliefs. Of course, the mechanic does not know, when he asks: "The Holy Ghost, what's that?" that he is simply echoing Stalin at Teheran: "The Pope—how many divisions has the Pope?" That is the real confrontation of forces. The enemy—he is ourselves. That is why it is idle to talk about preventing the wreck of Western civilization. It is already a wreck from within. That is why we can hope to do little more now than snatch a fingernail of a saint from the rack or a handful of ashes from the faggots, and bury them secretly in a flowerpot against the day, ages hence, when a few men begin again to dare to believe that there was once something else, that something else is thinkable, and need some evidence of what it was, and the fortifying knowledge that there were those who, at the great nightfall, took loving thought to preserve the tokens of hope and truth.

Sincerely,
Whittaker

Aug. 6, 1954

Dear Bill,

To underscore my rude slowness, your letter with its enclosures arrived this morning. I had already had an eyewitness account of the Hotel Astor meeting from one of the participating Minute Women, who quoted your speech. Who would not feel grateful? But I thought I should not have crept, even briefly, into Cohn's night.[1] Banquo's ghost could scarcely have been more out of place at another feast. Too many of the diners distrust and dislike me—and their instincts are sound. For my criticisms, at least my reservations about them, are deep-going, and they must distrust and dislike them since to do otherwise must enjoin a re-examination of their past, which has been harsh and bitter, of the present, which is shattering, and of themselves. Even before *Witness* was published, when the first few *SEP* [*Saturday Evening Post*] pieces had appeared, I listened to the assault of the Right on me, begun to my face by ———— and ————. I have met it since in other forms (————, ————, etc.). I withdrew at once and finally from such circles, since to stay could only widen a breach that could only serve and rejoice the Left. For the same reason, I have mentioned this matter only to two others, and not in full. Besides, I have my hands full with the assault from the Left, and it is simple tactics, if no more, not to acknowledge the true situation on my Right.

The Right can muster great forces. Potentially, it has a base of masses of Americans; potentially, it has all the brains, money and other resources it needs. But it can never mobilize them because it lacks one indispensable: it has no program. A distaste for Communism and socialism is not a program (this, inter alia, is what is wrong with Senator McCarthy). The Right has no program for one reason: it will not face historical reality. So

[1] The affair was a testimonial dinner tendered to Roy M. Cohn on his resignation as chief counsel of the Senate Investigating Committee of which Senator McCarthy was chairman.

even its occasional victories are invariably Pyrrhic. And its endemic defeats are glorious only in the Astor ballroom, after the third drink, the handy clichés, and the comfort of numbers. But by daylight, it is not glorious, and we see that there is a worm of truth in [Murray] Kempton's mean report; and the ring around the glass spells: sediment.

Will you tell Willi [Schlamm], when he comes to you, that I am eagerly expecting him, and that it is important that he telephone me from Washington since I do not know how to reach the Mandels. Occasionally, it is difficult to get through to us by telephone. So let Willi be persistent. I shall meet him in Washington. I shall also hear with interest your mutual plans.[2] For my sake, I am sorry you are going abroad, but, for your sake, glad. I should much like to talk with you.

W. C.

P.S. Bishop [Cuthbert] O'Gara spent hours here yesterday. We forgot time as we went, hour by hour, through his prison days and brainwashing. He simply wanted to talk to someone to whom his words were not words, but the blood drops of an understood experience. He is maimed for life.[3]

Aug. 19, 1954

Dear Bill,

As Willi will have told you, I am for a magazine. I am for it, that is, if its first and steadfast purpose is to succeed. Inevitably, that purpose must pretty narrowly define most editorial and organizational questions since they directly mesh with it. I surmise, subject to illumination, that there should be a market of some 500,000 readers who are now unserviced, or unsatisfactorily serviced. It is success in terms of that market, or even half of it, that alone interests me. Another *Freeman*, another crusade, does not interest me at all.

But the more I have thought about it, the clearer it becomes that I cannot commit myself to anything until you and I have

[2] To launch *National Review*.
[3] Bishop O'Gara had recently returned from China, where he had been imprisoned and tortured by the Communists.

talked it all out at length. For such a personal exchange, there is no substitute. No intermediary, clever, kind or enthusiastic, can do it for us. So I assume that it must wait until you return from Europe. By then, I shall have had to cross a dark river, perhaps two. The first is Willy Pogany's libel suit against me, whose implications, for me, go much farther than a libel action. They bear on people's indifference or animosity, and the general inability to protect me from harassment from the Left, which, if I must continue to sustain it absolutely alone, raises the question of why one should bother to. The second river concerns Alger Hiss' release from prison and what may happen then. I am surprised—not surprised, interested—at the number and kind of people who grow owlish and noncommittal when that point comes up. In any case, you and I could not talk to much purpose until I have crossed those streams. If I fail to, we shall not need to.

Have a good trip. If you come to Mont St. Michel *de la mer du péril,* bow your head for me and remember the [line] *Quae vocaris Stella Maris, Stella non erratica.*[4] Bishop O'Gara wrote me the other day about his visit here: "For me it was very like the experience of meeting a fellow missionary who spoke English, after a long stretch alone among the natives. The memory of that occasion shall always live in my heart." Mount St. Michael in peril of the Sea.

Sincerely,
Whittaker

Willi Schlamm met with Chambers and discussed the proposed magazine. Chambers wrote to him and sent me a copy of his letter without comment.

Aug. 30, 1954

Dear Willi,

Essences—a word I never permit myself to use—that is the right word. And that is why I never use it; because it is special,

---

[4] You who are called the Star of the Sea, the ever-constant Star.

and, like a jewel, not to be worn to work. And that is why you were right to use it. It is the essential affinity that can alone make such a project work. Editorially, I think it truly subsists between you, Buckley, [James] Burnham and me. I simply do not know about the others.[5] One of them I scarcely know. The other I have talked with only for an hour or so, and there certainly wasn't any essential affinity at work on that occasion. But I am an old soldier, and I know that, within the Staff, once an operation has been agreed on, discipline and command call for a devout effort to sink personality factors and to compromise as generously as can be up to the point of principle. I am also reasonably charitable, and when not, incline to remember that we are dust. I think that is a potentially brilliant staff—no, brilliant is a Woolworth word: it is a potentially effective staff of an order not readily duplicable in the sum of its parts. John C[hamberlain] for Special Features—fine!—if only he can be steeled to say no. Perhaps the trick is always to let him say yes where yes should be said; but to let a bouncer do his nay-saying. I must "buy" —— and —— on your credit, and Buckley's, accepting, in the absence of personal knowledge, your faith in their special competence in their special fields. Organizationally, it can be put this way: for working purposes, I shall lock away in Pandora's box any reservations I have about them until such time as experience has made them pointless, or until they themselves force up the lid. I realize now that, at the back of my mind, in each case, is something rather intangible that we did not talk about—tone, editorial tone. Tone seems to me of the first importance in this venture. All the others seem to me to be tone-conscious, particularly at the fine point where tone becomes a function of judgment. With the rest, total tone seems to me readily achievable as a merging of the quite individual tone of each. But in those two cases, I realize that what I fear is, in one instance, a tinkling, a play of caprice, which, in the past, has seemed to me a false note; and, in the other instance, I fear a tone-deafness, possibly due to the

[5] The other proposed editors.

fact that for him the problem of tone has scarcely existed, for somewhat the same reasons that Kansas has never produced a Bach. Nevertheless, if I am to be a part of this venture, I shall work loyally with those two, making more than a usual effort, unobtrusively, to collaborate easily with them.

If I am to be a part of this venture.... I *did* write Buckley, briefly, and not in a sense, I am afraid—I am certain—that would please you. I said that I was for the magazine, but that I could not commit myself until I had had a long talk with Buckley himself. I should have had sense enough to know that that must be true in time to say so to you while you were here. But, for reasons which I should be hard put to it to explain, it simply did not occur to me until I began to go over my mental notes after you had gone. Of course, it is obvious enough. What you say about areas of disagreement, or lack of congruence, refines the point. But I also accept, as a working premise, the possibility of compromise within the areas you mention—the Administration, the Senator. What we must try to establish is whether or not the difference is so radical in practice that, over the long haul, compromise could not keep the gap bridged, so that it would be kinder for everybody if I forbore in advance to identify myself with positions from which I might have ultimately to subtract myself. I fear this more in the case of the Senator than of the Administration. In fact, I am not clear wherein lie our differences about the Administration, except that I incline to say: "The returns are not all in yet"—and that there is an area of political maneuver still open to them, though, like you, I see little reason to suppose that they will maneuver, or know how to. This, in fact, was my original position on the Senator: Wait for the full returns. But, in his case, I now feel that the returns are in, or enough returns to plot the rest of the curve. Just as, in the case of the Senator, I forbore long after I had much adverse evidence, because I would not give anything to the common enemy, so, in the case of the Administration, my forbearance is pushed beyond the adverse evidence, by the fact that the alternative is the return to power of men I consider malign.

What is needed, ultimately, is a three-cornered conversation —you, Buckley and I—in which we test our common ground to make sure that we can go forward together since we must go in unison. But unison certainly does not mean lockstep. Nevertheless, since Buckley is abroad, and things seem to be moving so fast, I will hold my reservations in abeyance, and go along with you so far as you deem fitting. If, in the end, I must slip away, do you really feel that that is so important? I think I have a part among you, and that, together, we can prosper a common purpose. But your (and Buckley's) generous estimate of that part fills me with a kind of anxiety. I just wonder if I can live up to the billing.

In the last few years, my musical front has been crumbling. Before, I was a musical isolationist, almost impregnably a Bach through Beethoven man. Romantics (after Beethoven) I could not take. Schubert has been my slow undoing. And your Quartet is just the kind of Schubert I enjoy. You should not have sent it. And how nice that you did!

Also, please thank your wife for her kind letter to Esther, and for the mushroom data. It came just as our first big batch was liquifying. Now with Steffi's [6] help, we are doing better. But a new problem dogs us. We have had a fine crop of what we take to be the Parasol Lepiota and the Smooth Lepiota. Or they may not be. They may be crypto-toadstools. For the edible Parasol is easily mistaken for the Greengilled Lepiota, which is poisonous; while the Smooth Lepiota is easily mistaken for the Amanita Phalloides, known as the Destroying Angel. My little handbook begins, encouragingly, with this thought: "The best way not to be poisoned by mushrooms is not to eat them." But I have not much dilettante in me; I must eat or quit. I can even concede that eating an Amanita has its time and place (I see poor old Vargas chose a steel-jacketed quietus [7]). A man

6 Mrs. Schlamm.
7 Getulio Vargas had shot himself in Rio de Janeiro.

with a piece of Amanita no bigger than a quarter has quite the laugh of this world. But, then, this world is not all—there are, for us, other considerations.

We shall try to get up to you presently. But presently, as you know, means after a dark rendezvous. We shall see.

As always,
Whittaker

All my children are with us—and my grandson, a thoroughly remarkable boy. The southern contingent drove up all the night through the backlash of the hurricane off the Carolinas. I have long talks with my grandson, consisting, on both sides, of what my daughter calls: "Hoot-owl noises." Very gratifying.

Aug. 30, 1954

Dear Bill,

I thought in retrospect that my last letter to you had a kind of Cromwellian after-flavor—harsh and niggling. I wrote in haste, to try to catch you before you sailed. I was condensing a much longer letter to try to upraise a few points. Now I rather hope that my letter missed the boat and caught up with you only in Europe. I could write another, also dealing in more detail with more details. Instead, I mean to write something that may seem wholly irrelevant to matters in hand. But I don't think it is. I think it is not, because what has been proposed is first of all a relationship, and all stands or falls by that. So I think I shall pass, for the present, over all that has to do with editorial and organizational points and tell you about Ragozini-kova. For that bears on relationship; particularly on a relationship which, I fancy, has not even been thought about—it is so much taken for granted. But it is necessary to be aware of it. It is the true relationship between Willi and me, which, on the surface—on my part, and I believe, on his—is one of affectionate esteem. Yet between us, who have so much in common, there flows a deep quiet river whose headwaters rise far back in our revolutionary experience and determined the very different courses that experience took for each of us.

One of the great failures of *Witness* is that there was no time or place to describe the influences, other than immediate historical influences, that brought me to Communism. I came to Communism under the influence of the anarchists: Kropotkin, Tolstoi (the Tolstoi of *The Kingdom of God Is Within You*) and Edelstadt. But, above all, I came under the influence of the Narodniki (whose heirs are the Socialist Revolutionists). It has been deliberately forgotten, but, in those days, Lenin urged us to revere the Narodniki—"those who went with bomb or revolver against this or that individual monster." Unlike most Western Communists, who became Communists under the influence of Social Democracy, I remained under the spiritual influence of the Narodniki long after I became a Marxist. In fact, I never threw it off. I never have. It has simply blended with that strain in the Christian tradition to which it is akin. It shaped the particular quality of my revolutionary character that made me specially beloved (of course, it is wrong to say such things, but it is true) even among many of the crude, trifling American Communists; so that Ella Winter could say to a *Time* correspondent with whom she found herself junketing in East Germany after World War II: "I simply cannot believe that Whittaker Chambers has broken. I could believe it of anybody else, but not of him." To the Russians it made me seem a freak of nature—an American who was almost a Russian; a fact that endeared me to them while it perplexed and troubled them. And, of course, it was the revolutionary quality that bemused Alger—*mea culpa, mea maxima culpa.*

I remember how Ulrich, my first commander in the Fourth Section, once mentioned Vera Zasulitch and added: "I suppose you never heard that name." I said: "Zasulitch shot General Tropov for flogging the student, Bogomolsky, in the Paviak prison." And I remember the excited smile with which he answered (Ulrich was a Left Socialist Revolutionist, not a Communist): "That is true. But how do *you* know that?" For the spirit of the Narodniki, all that was soldierly and saintly in the revolution, found its last haven, O irony!, in the Fourth Section (one purpose of the Great Purge was to kill it out once for all).

Like Ulrich, I may presume in supposing that the name of Ragozinikova is unknown to you. But the facts are these. In 1907, the Russian government instituted a policy of systematically beating its political prisoners. One night, a fashionably dressed young woman called at the Central Prison in Petersburg and asked to speak with the commandant, Maximovsky. This was Ragozinikova, who had come to protest the government's policy. Inside the bodice of her dress were sewed thirteen pounds of dynamite and a detonator. When Maximovsky appeared, she shot him with her revolver and killed him. The dynamite was for another purpose. After the murder of Maximovsky, Ragozinikova asked the police to interrogate her at the headquarters of the Okhrana. She meant to blow it up together with herself; she had not known any other way to penetrate it. But she was searched and the dynamite discovered. She was sentenced to be hanged. Awaiting execution, she wrote her family: "Death itself is nothing. . . . Frightful only is the thought of dying without having achieved what I could have done. . . . How good it is to love people. How much strength one gains from such love." When she was hanged, Ragozinikova was twenty years old.

In *Witness*, I have told how Sazonov drenched himself with kerosene and burned himself to death as a protest against the mistreatment of others. And I have told what that meant to me at one moment; how, had my comrade, Sazonov, not done that, there would not have been a Hiss Case as we know it. This spirit persisted in the Fourth Section as late at 1938. Willi knows nothing of such people except as a legend. That is why, though Willi is transfixed with as many arrows as Sebastian, he simply does not understand the *source* of the glance that the saint bends upon the bowmen. I need scarcely underscore the point at which that strain of the revolutionary spirit blends with a Christian élan, or why it was imperative for Communism to kill it out. I labor this because my reaction to this difference between Willi and me underlies the tone of my last letter. It is also, above all, why you and I must talk at length.

Meanwhile, Willi has written me a generous and good letter. I have suggested that he send on my reply to you. It deals, in part, with necessary, but largely footling matters, and saves me going twice over them.

The Bach, which has just arrived—your parting thought—is magnificent in every sense. Only, you must really not send me anything else. I can make no return.

Sincerely,
Whittaker

If you should see André Malraux, will you convey to him my great esteem and most kind feelings? After *Witness* appeared, he wrote me: "You are one of those who did not return from Hell with empty hands." I never answered him because how is it possible to say to someone without seeming fantastic, and still remaining inadequate: "Great healing understanding"? When he was last in America I could not see him because I was then in bed.

Meanwhile, Willi Schlamm had answered Chambers, to whom he wrote once again, sending me a copy, with the notation: "Bill, this letter is really addressed to both of you."

Day after Labor Day whatever that is

Dear Willi,

Your letter rather sweeps my objections and reservations into a dustpan. Gratefully so, since the net effect is to tidy things up. My attitude would be intolerable if it were merely cranky. It is, instead, an effort to clear out of the way in advance those niggling points which, unforeseen, may wreck greater matters, but which, if charted in time, may be blasted out of

the way, or at least a channel be picked among them for all
good ships to sail in convoy, whatever their freights or eventual
ports. I do not think that Dwight [Eisenhower] and Richard
[Nixon] and Joseph [McCarthy] will be out of the way by next
April. I do incline to think that I did not make clear my
attitude about the first two members of that triad. For I simply
do not feel that we are seas apart about them. I chiefly say:
"Give them a little more rope."

What I suspect is something much more serious. It bears on
the concept that each of us holds of the Conservative Position.
That is why I raised the point when we talked. Somehow, it
seems to have got lost or blurred; or, more probably, I made a
poor job of my presentment. Briefly, I remain a dialectician;
and history tells me that the rock-core of the Conservative Position, or any fragment of it, can be held realistically only if
conservatism will accommodate itself to the needs and hopes of
the masses—needs and hopes, which, like the masses themselves,
are the product of machines. For, of course, our fight, as I
think we said, is only incidentally with socialists or other heroes of
that kidney. *Wesentlichen* [essentially], it is with machines. A
conservatism that cannot face the facts of the machine and mass
production, and its consequences in government and politics,
is foredoomed to futility and petulance. A conservatism that
allows for them has an eleventh-hour chance of rallying what is
sound in the West. All else is a dream, and, as [Helmuth] von
Moltke remarked about universal peace, "not a very sweet
dream at that." This is, of course, the Beaconsfield position.
Inevitably, it goads one's brothers to raise their knives against
the man who holds it. Sadder yet, that man can never blame
them, for he shares their feelings even when directed against
himself, since he, no less than they, is also a Tory. Only, he is a
Tory who means to live. And to live is not to hold the lost
redoubt. To live is to maneuver. The choices of maneuver are
now visibly narrow. They chiefly enjoin defying the enemy by
occupying (or capturing) that part of his position which reality
(many realities) have defined as settled for this historical period;

thereby splitting the enemy, immobilizing and confusing, if not winning, part of his forces. I should have stood with Lenin, not with Trotsky, Radek and Bukharin, about Brest-Litovsk. In the matter of social security, for example, the masses of Americans, like the Russian peasants in 1918, are signing the peace with their feet. The farmers are signing for a socialist agriculture with their feet.

Next Friday, eight of my neighbors, including one of my close personal friends, go on trial in federal court in Baltimore for various violations of the crop-control laws. Emotionally, I am with them to the point of fury. Yet, from any realistic viewpoint, their position is preposterous. First, because, by and large, the nation's farmers have voted for socialization in this form. Second, because even these farmers themselves are not invincibly against subsidies in the form of support checks. What they are against is government inspection of their crops to check the grain allotments. But, if you have voted for subsidies, or accepted $ checks, you have also voted for supervision. Who says A must also say B. Third, even if they were opposed on principle (as some are) to both subsidies and inspection, their position and reality have nothing in common because, in hard fact, in battling the government, they are battling a Boyg, a mirage. It is only in the second instance that they are battling the government. What, if they grasp reality, they are really battling is the 40-horsepower tractor, the self-propelled combine, the mechanical corn picker, the hay drier and 10-20-20 fertilizers which make possible those gigantic yields and that increased man-hour productivity whose abundance spells bankruptcy and crisis—or controls. This is not theory or little Arthur Schlesinger. This is what a man knows when he stands before the wheat harvest in the brimming granary bins, and knows that the grain he runs through his fingers is his contribution to an unsalable surplus—this terrene wealth, this bounty of his sweat and acres—which, uncontrolled, spells not wealth, but his undoing. Few farmers voted for socialism as such, or even the program of the Farmers Union, Clint Anderson or the

ADA, which, by and large, they loathe. They voted for a curb on their own incontinent productivity for the same reason that a fat man takes to diet—ultimately, to prolong his life.

The machine has done this. But every one of my indicted neighbors has sold off his horses and rides his tractor, and sends soil samples to the state college to learn how to up his yields. And not one of them has the slightest intention of smashing his machines or going back to horses and moderate yields—because machine farming is one reality that he can see and feel. Moreover, each knows how absurd it would be for him alone to buck the trend—he would be ploughed under by those who would not go along. The mass of farmers will keep their tractors and milk more and more cows until they drop of heart attacks. Only, they will not cut back. Therefore, the machine has made the economy socialistic. The government has only enacted one aspect of the fact into law. A conservatism that will not accept this situation must say: "We are reactionary in the literal sense. To be logical, we must urge you farmers to smash your machines (not sell them off, but smash them, and buy no more). For, otherwise, you will always get what you wanted; while what you do not want (restrictions, the end of the private domain) will be the literal reaping of what you sowed." But a conservatism that would say that is not a political force, or even a twitch: it has become a literary whimsy.

I loathe rural socialism. That is why I stopped growing wheat several years ago, and corn last year. I am trying to shape a workable farm economy that will slip around the socialist shackles; co-exist with it in, as John Chamberlain once said, "the interstices." But I am not a farmer in the general sense. I am the exception, not the rule. I prove nothing unless the possibility that a few men can still live amiably by bypassing, not by kicking against the pricks. I have by no means proved it as yet. Meanwhile, let the government men measure my fields and yields to their hearts' content. The very sight of them enrages me. I usually begin by treating them with formal courtesy and end by telling them to their faces that they are useless parasites. But, at worst, they stay only for a few hours, like a flock of crows; and, as I do not hunt crows when I am too busy with other things, though their clatter and marauding exasperates me, so I do not "run" (take a gun to) the agriculture inspectors, as some of my neighbors have done. For I know that the crows will be there so long as the corn attracts and feeds them. And, unlike the crows, the inspectors are better armed than I am. I will simply not plant corn though I have no illusion that that is more than a postponement. If it isn't corn, it will be some other crop.

Mind you, I hold that it is the duty of the intellectuals of the West to preach reaction. But that is from an absolute, an ideal standpoint. It is for books and posterity. It does not bear on tactics or daily life—or so indirectly as scarcely to matter here and now. In absolute terms, the *Maschinenstürmer* [Luddites] were right; their primitive instinct was right, and Marx was wrong to the same degree. He had only a rationale from observed data, which, to my way of feeling, even more than of thinking, were false data—false in the sense that they violate what is best in and for men. But that fact will not unhorse one farmer from his tractor or drive one worker from a factory. And, as you know, most factory workers are farmers manqués. Moreover, they flocked to the factories in the first place because even the industrial horrors of the nineteenth century seemed preferable to many than ten hours of haying in a shriveling sun, or cows going bad with garget. I worked the hay load last night against the coming rain—by headlights, long after dark. I know the farmer's case for the machine and for the factory. And I know, like the cut of hay-bale cords in my hands, that a conservatism that cannot find room in its folds for these actualities is a conservatism doomed to petulance and dwindling—first unreality and then defeat. Let Mr. ——— tie barley sacks behind the moving combine for even eight hours in a really good sun, and then load them, 100-, 150-pound bags, until midnight, and he will learn more about the realities of rural socialism (and about the realities of Conservatism) than he could ever glean from the late, ever to be honored Robert Taft.

It is at this point that I am tolerant of the Eisenhower Administration. It is not so much what they are doing that I quarrel with, as the stupid way it seems to me that they do it. It is, above all, on foreign policy and the Communist issue that I groan at them.

Naturally, it is not so simple as I have sketched it above. I know, too, that the 40-horsepower tractor is only one turn on the road that leads to the H-bomb and beyond. If I were a younger man, if there were any frontiers left, I should flee to some frontier because, when the house is afire, you leave by whatever hole is open for whatever area is freest of fire. Since there are no regional frontiers, I have been seeking the next best thing—the frontiers within, John's interstices. But I have no notion that my antics have a validity for anybody else except a handful of similar escapists. Escapism is laudable, perhaps the only truly honorable course for humane men—but only for them. Those who remain in the world, if they will not surrender on its terms, must maneuver within its terms. That is what conservatives must decide: how much to give in order to survive at all; how much to give in order not to give up the basic principles. And, of course, that results in a dance along a precipice. Many will drop over, and, always, the cliff dancers will hear the screaming curses of those who fall, or be numbed by the sullen silence of those, nobler souls perhaps, who will not join the dance.

When I wrote "a conversation with you and Buckley," obviously that is not to be taken in the singular. It presupposes many conversations—a new causeries (if that is not too cosy a word) de St. Peterbourg. It is possible that the conversations can have no end. But we do feel the same things, however we may differ as to whether we should march our elephants over the Alps, more even whether there are any passes to march over, and where we are marching to.*

Tell your wife that I am not really cavalier about toadstools.

I am bold, but fairly prudent as in: *Sei kühn, sei kühn, aber nicht zu kühn.*[8] But it is as well to learn to know poison when one sees it: the noblest minds have found it a blessing at need.

What a harangue.

As always,
Whittaker

* Zama, the world usually forgets, was reached by way of Cannae—so must the General Staffs of the world—notoriously apolitical, even the Great German G.S.—have all along been studying the magnificent detour to disaster. Perhaps the truth is Delenda est Chicago.

Sept. 29, 1954

Dear Bill,

Your letter did me a lot of good at the right moment. So when I go into court with the litigious Mr. W. Pogany three days hence, I shall not feel, as until now I have had to feel, that I am just as alone in 1954 as in 1948. It is a somewhat freezing feeling. For everybody's sake, I hope that I can handle this myself. But just your generous offer to stand by rallies my will.

Come to Westminster, if you will, when you return. We shall be delighted to have you. But, after your travels, the trip may seem a hardship; and there is no reason now why I should not go to N.Y. to talk with you. I shall leave until then most of the points that chiefly fatten letters without clarifying meaning. I doubt that, in principle, we have much to discuss. Here I shall merely touch on the point you say we shall not discuss; namely, certain aspects of your role. Don't you know that you are the indispensable man who alone may make a crew out of the individualistic mob which is Schlamm, Burnham and Chambers? Burnham and I could drop out, and it would make no real

[8] Be bold, be bold, but not too bold.

difference. But not you, and perhaps not Willi. Heaven help you. I am sure that rest of us will try to.

But never believe that Willi would become a Catholic if only the Church would strike Prudence from among the virtues. The very formulation suggests a deeper problem, though I am smiling as I say so. Fancy Willi (if it is not irreverent) in a confession box. Poor Father O'Toole! But I think that even Fr. O'T., not to speak of my good friends and battle companions, Fathers Bazinet and McSweeney, would ask Willi a question after the first hour on the subject of "certified gentility." I think they would ask: "Just what is your soul hankering after, my son?"

In your letter, you say something to the effect that the liberals have managed to convince the world that they are, among other things, morally right. It seems to me that you are shouldering something of first importance there. Your magazine is, above all, a moral apologetic; and it had better be good. For a morality is never stronger than the reality it speaks for. To my grotesque way of thinking, one of the great moral moments in current U.S. writing is the quarry scene in *From Here to Eternity*—the scene in which one of the prisoners takes his crowbar and, on request, breaks the arm or leg of a fellow prisoner. That is the moment for which the great muck heap of that book exists; and that is why I told a leading Quaker that *From Here to Eternity* is essentially a moral book. I shall long remember the expression of surprise and shock on his face. He had read Genesis, but he had not realized, in the way we feel dirt by taking it in our hand, that it was out of mud and primal ooze that God created the world. And when he had read that "the light shines in darkness," he had thought only about the light; he had not grasped that darkness is as much a clotted reality as illumination is real. Our dear, good, fatuous, mischief-making Quakers who need nothing so much as a touch of humanizing sin. (Father Alan warns me, courteously shaking his finger in Graham Greene's and Péguy's direction, instead of mine, that a mystique of sin is treacherous ground.)

I have been working on conservatism's moral apologetic for more than a year, and I have been making a poor fist of it. If I live, I hope to bring it off. Conservatives and Leftists will then find themselves co-existing in a most uncomfortable united front to revile it and me. But it is not really intended for them except insofar as they choose to mess with it. It is written for my son, now wearing the awkward uniform of the AFROTC. It might just as well be titled *Theory of Flight*, since it is intended, like the St. Benedict medal he wears around his neck, to go with him where I cannot—on that mortal trajectory between buoyancy and disaster which is also the trajectory of all of us, even when grounded, in this age.

The Bach you sent me seems to be almost the most beautiful music I have ever heard.[9] My wife and I spend hours listening to it.

You really must stop saluting me as "Mr. Chambers." I know, I know, the first-name business is always a hurdle for me, too. But 'tis a custom of the country.

I hope to see you soon.

Sincerely,
Whittaker

We met at my home in Stamford, Connecticut, and briefly (and unsuccessfully) at the Barclay Hotel in New York the next day with Willi Schlamm and Henry Regnery. A few days later Alger Hiss was released from prison and announced his determination to establish his innocence and the corruption of the agencies that found him guilty.

Nov. 28, 1954

Dear Bill,

I did not wait deliberately for Alger to answer your letter for me. But, in effect, he has done so. A few words from him have said more convincingly than thousands from me could do what

---

9 The *Clavierübung*, performed by Ralph Kirkpatrick on the harpsichord.

my path must be, and also, why those paths among the green hills into which you generously invited me, the more "orthodox" paths, to catch up your phrase, tempt me, but cannot be mine.

Alger came out more fiercely than even I had expected. I had supposed that, at first, probation itself would impose some deceptive restraint of tone. But he is a lawyer, and knows just about how far he can go and get away with it. As a tactician, he is trying for the advantage of surprise and the initiative. Do you think he has failed? He has not. He won, first, when, after his egregious statement to the press, no government authority stepped forward and instantly marched him back where he came from. He won, second, by his remark about fantastic stories in the press, etc. With that, every legal staff of every publication and network, which has ever referred unkindly to him, registered a cautionary impulse: "Better be careful. This may cost us money." After all, that is what legal staffs are paid for. He won, third, when the Attorney General was not snowed under by messages demanding that Alger be remitted for his statement, and when Congress was not snowed under by messages urging pressure on the Attorney General. On the contrary, every effort will be made "not to make a martyr out of Hiss," to see that he has "fair play and full justice." This is another rendering of "do nothing to disturb our delicate negotiations with the Soviet government (the Chinese Communists), etc., etc." These terms are interchangeable in a general situation that is all of a piece. Do I always sound forlorn? That is because I know, just as clearly as Alger knows it, that my side is the side of the disunited, the indecisive, the cowardly. And all from the most understandable motives. For, you see, after six years, my side still does not really know what this is all about or how Communism works.

Alger Hiss is one of the greatest assets that the Communist Party could possess. What is vindication for him? It is the moment when one of the most respectable old ladies (gentlemen) in Hartford (Conn.) says to another of the most respectable old ladies (gentlemen): "Really, I don't see how Alger Hiss could brazen it out that way unless he really were innocent." Multiply Hartford by every other American community. For the CP, that is victory. That is all that it needs. At that moment, confusion is rooted, morale split or sapped, truth poisoned. In miniature, it is of the same order as the voluntary sell-out of Indochina, or of Chiang Kai-shek, or the legal assassination of Mikhailovitch. It is worth more than victorious battles because it maims morale, which, as soldiers know, but most civilians do not think about, is the master objective in war. And all that Alger has to do for this victory is to persist in his denials.

As we drove into your beautiful grounds, I started to tell you how this will work out. I let it drop when you objected that Alger probably cannot sue me. I knew that it would soon be enacted past any power of mine to make credible. So why labor it? It has begun, though a tip-off in Alger's statement seems to suggest that suits against others will be a more effective strategy than suits against me. Anyway, my task now is simply to be equal to my necessity. I urge you to study on this spectacle because I believe that, in little, you will here see unfold the pattern of larger things.

You were most hospitable, kind and patient with me up there. I realized only in retrospect how trying I must have been. For I was speaking always from the fastness of my cold and remote foreknowledge, and that must have seemed gratuitously ungracious and ungrateful.

Sincerely,
Whittaker

Dec. 10, 1954

Dear Willi,[10]

I got back from Ohio last night, after several days spent in trying to order my son's affairs, to find a heap of letters from

10 WC sent me a copy of this letter.

had been St. Mihiel. I didn't start out to write this. But Luchow's made me think of it, as the tisane reminded Proust of the walk he and his grandmother used to take *au côté de chez Swann,* with the spire of the church, like the sorrier wedge of wall in sorrier times, the stake of the focus.

If you have patience, I think I should try to make clear to you why I plan to go south. It isn't because I want to go: I'd rather stay put. It isn't because I want to see anything in particular—I completely lack the tourist flair. I want to try to write a book. I wrote a good deal of it under the title: *The Losing Side.* Then I changed titles. Brent Bozell once questioned me about what I was writing (I dislike talking about such things), asked me what I was calling it, expressed distaste at the title change and asked why I had shifted from *The Losing Side* to *Cold Friday* (the name of one of the fields on this farm in the survey map). I answered: "In history, the losing side is always a minority. But today the whole world has reached Cold Friday." I am sure BB was unconvinced. But *Cold Friday* it is. I need more than peace to write it in. I need to be cut off from all I have been in too long. I feel that a severance is due. To a large extent, the severance will simply mark a grave. Practically all that held me here has died or petered out. The children are gone; the farm has lost its logic. I do not even have the capital to farm it halfheartedly, and I cannot, as in the past, make good the capital by my own labor power. This inability to work the place is perhaps the greatest burr in my mind at that angle. It torments me since, among other disabilities, I have no talent for being a country gentleman. It doesn't interest me; worse, it plagues me. So I want to cut off. I want warmth, the kind of seclusion that comes from being stranger among strangers. I want quiet and, above all, the backward glance. I have in mind a short book, the last book. Whether I outlive it long or not is completely unimportant: pointless. The advance copy I submitted to Random House carried a legend which tells more about the book and its mood and my southward thoughts than I need labor. It is the first line of *Prometheus Bound* and goes like this: "Power (to his companion, Force, and to their prisoner, Prometheus): We have come to the last path of the world, in the Scythian country, in the untrodden solitude." It is my translation into English of the noble French translation of Leconte Delisle. I know that "solitude" means "wilderness." I prefer "solitude." That is what I am up to; and where better to be up to it than in view of Ixtacihuatl, or, as Esther and I have come to call this last fool's errand: "Titzihuihuatl." I have shifted practical gears several times. Sometimes a car has seemed in all ways simpler, freer, etc. But there are possible mechanical and accident difficulties. So, again, I am back to Air France. No car makes Raoul [4] seem more useful. But Mrs. A is probably indispensable for finding quarters, preferably *lejos de* [far from] *la capital*. I would say a day or three in the capital to get rested, oriented, found. Then to find more or less permanent quarters. Another shift: I have begun to think about Cuerna [Cuernavaca], in part because Esther suffers from heat, in part because everything is there, I think, and still it is not *tan lejos de* [so far from] *la cap*. Still, there by no means rules out Oax [Oaxaca]. Some days in the capital means a hotel, perhaps the Luma. If we keep to our plans, we plan soon to go to N.Y. for a few days. Then we can talk with you. But I thought this background would give us something to talk about. I suppose what I want, on one practical side, is three or four rooms (furnished), ground floor, on a patio with a banana palm and a zonzontle in a cage on the wall. I daresay a Bryn Mawr sophomore would not permit herself such romanticism. But old men can.

Later, too, I hope we can talk more comfortably about *NR*'s affairs than a telephone permits, and about much else.

My best to Willi.

As always,
Whittaker

[4] The proposed driver.

Esther, of course, remains extremely balky about the whole venture because the doctor is so stiff about my going anywhere, even to Westminster. Like the Prex, I feel that my decision should be based on how I feel, rather than what the doctor advises. This is not because I suppose the doctor to be mistaken —quite the contrary. But I think there are cures that doctors know not of because they simply cannot know the congeries of ailment; couldn't know if I tried to spell it all out. Only I know this, and I am willing to pay for a slip in treatment by preferring to be, if necessary, dead as a lion rather than as a sheep.

One night recently, Esther asked me: "Do you know who Bubnov is? Well, he's just been released in Russia after twenty years in prison." Know who Bubnov is?—Old Bolshevik, former member of the Revolutionary Military Committee during the insurrection, Commissar of Education. Suddenly, I thought: "I suppose that there is scarcely anybody left who remembers who Bubnov was." He had been jailed and conveniently (and, it appears, quite literally) forgotten. Then there came a story of Bubnov, jailed when the SU was a peasant country, walking and wondering around modern Russia. I thought: "It must be like beginning life over again." Something of that effect, not so dramatic, of course, is what I have in mind for my own therapy. Only not, *D.v.*, a modern country—a good, backward, goat-trampled, mud-rutted, stick-in-the-mud place—forgotten, like Bubnov, by everybody.

My German friend (who was also Nicholas Roosevelt's language tutor) made me memorize, as a youth, these lines:

Heraus in eure Schatten, rege Wipfel
Des alten, heil'gen, dichtbelaubten Haines,
Wie in der Göttin stilles Heiligtum,
Tret ich noch jetzt mit schauderndem Gefühl,
Als wenn ich sie zum erstenmal beträte....

Denn, ach! mich trennt das Meer von den Geliebten,
Und an dem Ufer steh ich lange Tage,
Das Land der Griechen mit der Seele suchend....[5]

I am sure Willi will be glad to translate, correct and tell you it is the *Iphigenie auf Tauris*. It boils out of memory with Luchow's and the southward journey because now I understand (we get these glimpses so preposterously late) what the *Italienische Reise* meant to Goethe, and why he took off so incontinently.

May 8??, 1956

Memo

TO: Den Feldgrauen Eminenzen bei 37 Str., den Herren Buckley u. Schlamm.
FROM: Dem Good Soldier Schweik von und zu der Wolfschanze bei Westminster.[6]

As Comrade Noske once said to comrade Ebert: *"Sei nur ruhig, es wird alles wieder gut werden."* [7] On the other hand, as Comrade Noske once said to General Maercker: *"Mein General, ich habe die Schweinerei jetzt auch satt."* [8]
I am bringing *die Schweinerei* [9] along as fast as I can. That is

---

[5] Beneath your leafy gloom, ye waving boughs
Of this old, shady, consecrated grove,
As in the goddess' silent sanctuary,
With the same shuddering feeling forward I step,
As when I trod it first....

For the sea
Doth sever me, alas! from those I love,
And day by day upon the shore I stand,
The land of Hellas seeking with my soul....

[6] To the Fieldgray Eminences at 37th Street, the Messrs. Buckley and Schlamm From the Good Soldier Schweik and the Foxholes near Westminster.

[7] Be quiet; everything will be all right again.

[8] My general, I am now fed up with this mess.

[9] Chambers volunteered to write for *National Review* a defense of it against the assault in *Commentary* (by Dwight Macdonald) that had appeared in the April, 1956, issue. He never completed it, though he went through many drafts, none of which he permitted us to see.

all I have strength for. You can countermand it, which would in no slightest way offend me. But, if you still suppose that you want it, I can only do it at my own speed; slow, very slow. But, then, the problem is somewhat bigger than I first thought, or than, it is just possible, you may have thought about since you have not worked at it directly. My attempt at solution may appal you; and, in that case, you are free, of course, to reject it, again without any offense on my part. But the *Genosse Feldwebel* [Comrade Sergeant] asks me to impress on you, that, on his side, this is a voluntary offering; and that on no other terms will he submit it. It's not for sale; it's a labor of fidelity to Fortress *NR.*

I have been toying with two titles: "The Secret in the Daisy" or "The Air-Conditioned Auschwitz." One never should do this in advance of performance. But then I must have some fun. I can't be forever "extrapolating" (what wonderful Volapük!) the liberals. As Comrade Clemenceau once said to some general officers, visiting in Paris: *"L'heure du lourd règlement des comptes est venue."* [10]

For the rest, I can only assure you (since I began with this pair, I might as well end with them) in the words that General Maercker once pronounced to Comrade Noske: *"Für Sie, Herr Minister, lasse ich mich in Stücke hauen, und meine Landesjäger auch."* [11]

Don't be too puzzled. This is just Schweik, horsing around with history for relaxation—the humor in which my children know me best, but most other people never see.

Whittaker

It occurs to me that Bill may be in no spirit for such frolics. So I am sending this to you.

---

[10] "The hour is at hand for the judgment."
[11] "For you, sir minister, I would let myself be beaten to pieces, and the county cop, too."

Since Chambers didn't complete his answer to National
Review's *critics, I wrote a long essay (published in the August 1,
1956, issue) and sent the manuscript to Chambers.*

July 28, 1956

Dear Bill,

Nothing in that to be "ashamed" of. I think you outshot
them with their chosen weapons. I also reverse myself: I think
you have scored a tactical gain, at least with respect to the
worried or wavering in your own ranks. I doubt, though, that
you will ever be forgiven for saying that DMcD *"reads* French":
some slices never heal.

Willi sent me one of those memos, inviting me to contribute
to some round table on Russia. Doesn't he know that it takes
all I can do to write a few pages of a book each day?

Mr. Nixon's plight marches on. I find Mr. Stassen's ad-
venture [12] conceivable only under one enabling circumstance.
I trust *NR* will be discussing that circumstance. The Suez
seizure is, obviously, one of the most serious matters to date.
But a point is reached when nothing is left the individual man
but to enjoy the game qua game, cheering the good plays, hoot-
ing the stinkos, laughing at the errors. But with complete
detachment, if not, indeed, levity. In that sporting spirit, I find
this episode hugely funny. I thought so from the start, but
discovery of the fact that, at this historical moment, Mr. Dulles
was in Peru (what on earth could have taken him there—hints
from the Incas on how to lose an empire?) and that, on winging
back to Wash., his winged words were that Nasser's action
"is a blow to international confidence"—well, I just stood up
and cheered. It isn't every day that an earthquake is described
as a slight drift of sand, or that those for whom the executioner
waits can sum up in one perfect phrase the reason why they
are waiting and the executioner is coming, or vice versa. And

[12] Stassen, seeking to oust Nixon, had called for an open vote at the Republican convention on the Vice Presidential candidate.

the immense excitement of the British Labor Party—the petrol, you know. It makes it all much easier to understand why Lenin said of the British Laborites of his day that he would like to support R. MacDonald and Arthur Henderson in the same way that a rope supports a hanged man. I'm afraid that I have got quite beyond good and evil on this one and, as I said, just enjoy the play. *Life* has a very good picture this week of the Brioni conference, Nehru, Nasser, Tito—no doubt, Suez was discussed then; the expression on Nehru's face is unusual. There's no mystery about him, of course; he's simply a left-wing socialist. Everything else follows logically enough from that.*

As always,
Whittaker

* But then, who isn't a Left-wing Socialist. Yet this obvious fact, which explains all we need to know about current history, is one of the few mysteries still cherished in life.

Chambers' son, John, spent part of the summer in New York working as an editorial assistant for National Review.

Sept. 19, 1956

Dear Bill,

I do not know what good, if any, John was able to do you or *NR*. The good you did him cannot be measured. I have watched him pretty closely for twenty years. I have never before seen him so stimulated, nor have I had about him before a sense that doors were being flung open to his mind, and that he himself wanted to step out and have a look and even a stroll. College did much more for John than he supposes, but it did not do what his fortnight with you accomplished. Of course, your kindness went beyond anything I had in mind. I really meant for you to set him to replacing typewriter ribbons, sharpening pencils, with just a peep at people and processes.

You threw him into the middle of things; and, while it must have required much patience on your side, it gave John the kind of shot in the arm that he exactly needed. It touched me in a direct way that I can scarcely risk writing about. John's parents live for John, and for little else. In 1952, I sat and reckoned—so many years I must live to get John to his majority. It seemed an impossibly long course. Now each day is subtracted from the year that is left. You see, it is this you have so richly contributed to. I cannot say it; grateful seems an empty word.

John is back in his pen, Kenyon. One day, it is to be hoped, he will try to write you his own thanks. Perhaps he will succeed better than I, at that. Some day, I shall ask you, when we meet, for your impressions of John. I shall want them raw and cold-blooded: no others are any use to me.

I should probably stop short here. I have been splashing about in my private pool of ice water. No doubt, this reflects a passing physical condition. But what goes on just beyond the pool scarcely helps. In the Suez matter, it is not just that what the West did or did not do, it did so bountifully badly. The great hook is that there was almost nothing that the West could do; every move it might make was damaging in some other direction. Real checkmate. With that goes, as usual, the West's blithe unawareness that this is more than a scare-head; is a grand climacteric in the shocking series. But there is no point in waving one's arms, particularly when one is only one, and can, in any case, do nothing about it. If I thought that Dulles knew what he was doing, I should incline to think that his course was slightly the better of two worthless choices, both with a curse on them. But I do not know this; I seem to catch the note of expediency; I miss the note of insight.

Domestic politics, American plan, are dampening too. The Americans are, and always have been, the most mysterious to me of all peoples. I never know what they are about to do or why they do it. Everything reduces itself at last to pendulum swings, usually overdue, largely impulsive. Hence I never trust my judgment about American politics. Still, Maine jumps with my worst presentiment. I had thought that the nation meant to re-elect the President with a big opposition in Congress. I have begun to wonder if they do not mean to turn him out. This time, I feel as if I understood why; I seem to feel a stirring in the roots of the folk. Let's hope I am wrong as usual. Or I suppose you don't hope that, though I have never understood, either, what you hope in exchange. Clearly, the Democrats have forgotten nothing, learned nothing. But then, why should they? They are honest revolutionists so far as they go. If the nation votes them back in, it will be voting for the permanent revolution. American plan. I doubt that they know that revolution has its inertia, too, which keeps it moving always farther in a given path. Perhaps they do, and have discounted it, as our financial friends say. Perhaps they sense that there is a point where their revolution meets the Russian revolution, and that is the dim logic behind their impulse to peace at any price. Perhaps Willi would know. No, Willi is a European: I know what he will do and say next. Willi may stick Indian feathers in his hair and cheer on his Green Mountain boys. His Austrian eye (the left one) still keeps track of the score. He does not really fool himself about Knowland, and can't fool me. That brings us out on a line, however crooked. Incidentally, I thought Ralph's [de Toledano] piece very good, and that *NR* did itself a service to publish it. Only the last line made no point since it proves nothing and leads to nothing. Nobody in the West has any solutions to offer because there are, in fact, no solutions—that is, none that would make you and me happy.

But thank you again about John. I have come to think that his generation is less unfortunate than I once did. In America, they have no past *; only a present. Elsewhere, they understand how the present derives inevitably from the past, and, if that does not make the present more bearable, at least it makes it more intelligible. The mind, that is, still keeps its power to reflect, and, in reflection, is freedom, even in disaster. Here there was never any mind to reflect. Here what mind there was has always existed in an inner emigration, when it did not emigrate in fact. One is usually as undernourishing as the other.

As always,
Whittaker

* To put off.

Sept. 24??, 1956

Dear Bill,

Thanks, thanks for the timely and warning enclosure.[13] I don't believe that gentleman will find the Vice President at home (isn't he off talking to farmers?). But, no doubt, Washington is full of talkative tongues, and, I gather, that talk is chiefly wanted. I must also assume that he will put in an appearance here, unannounced, lest the telephone say: no. I have no intention of seeing this bird, so we must live a bit, I guess, with drawn venetians and unhearing ears. Too bad horseplay is in such poor odor. In the early days of the Hiss Case, when my office telephone never slept, though I seldom answered it, Jim Agee, who had happened in and got tired of the ringing, picked up the receiver and said crisply: "Alger Hiss's residence." I think the caller fainted, for the conversation ended. But, no, that would be out of tone. Besides, it seems beyond question that our telephone is bugged. I think I know who these buggers are; and, if I am right, they have in mind, among the usual odd lot of motives, my protection (there was a curious something a couple of months back that I may one day tell you about). These folk (again, assuming that I am right) often amuse me: they seem so innocent of any awareness that I am a skilled technician: I know so many angles of the trade that my attitude to them is much like that expressed once to me by a Bureau agent. Catching himself after making some massive confidence (I haven't the slightest recollection what it was), he blurted out: "I keep thinking you're one of *us*." To me "They" all act like

13 That a European journalist was determined to see WC and Nixon.

Communist activists; of course, for somewhat different ends. There is a fine scene about this in *Man's Fate*. Katov or Kyo, one of the revolutionists, is being interrogated by the Shanghai police chief, when the revolutionist suddenly realizes that the police chief realizes that they know the same kind of things; that their special knowledge puts them apart from other men, and almost uniquely en rapport. Yet what a bore it is. Incidentally, it is not, I think, the Bureau's tap. That was true in 1948. But it proved a bore to them, too—those long chats with the veterinary about ketosis and bumblefoot.

I have just finished reading *NR*. I found it one of the uncommonly good issues, and this could not have been good temper on my part. For taking John to Kenyon seems to have done me in for some time to come; and there was something else that I shall come to. But Derso's cartoon about Suez was so good that, without looking at the signature, I looked to see whether it was *Punch* or another. Then Lord Beaverbrook has come up with the irreducible summation: "My God, what a waste of electricity." No one will ever say it more tersely; but, after that, no one needs to. I went on to read about the Cornell *Daily Sun*'s opinion in re Alger, and Adlai's weaseling (which I had heard him do on the air); and that, with much else now going round, which I shall not labor here, made me sick at heart. It is a battle that cannot be won; they are many. I am one. They want Hiss, and whenever anything is wanted so badly, experience tells me, those who want it get it. By hook or by crook, they will get back their hero. It is cold comfort to know that the dish will poison them. It will poison everybody else first. But, of course, this is only a facet of my gnawing concern. I cannot overcome my intimations that the country is going to vote out the Administration. This means, in the long view, that the nation is still revolutionary; that they will be voting for a quicker revolution and against the slower-moving ersatz. Of course, revolution here, like near-beer, is a fraction of a percent. It is revolution, nonetheless. What they do about Alger is, by contrast, incidental. If they vote back the Democrats, they will have scrawled across my effort: Canceled. My business friends say: "You don't imagine, do you, that *either* party is going to upset the profit system?" Happy little legitimists. No one seems to have noticed that the Administration's whole viewpoint comes down to Marie Antoinette's: "Give them cake."

Oct. 8???, 1956

Dear Bill,

It was miserable watching you go off in the fog, condemned to the long drive through that, and, afterwards, the slow night train to N.Y. I lay awake a good while thinking of this. When I woke again, I was just conscious that day was breaking. But then my mind, still half asleep, was filled with an image. It was the mountainsides of a valley covered with cherry and plum trees in bloom. I seemed to be circling above them. I knew (as one does vaguely in such cases) that this was the valley of the Vardar, and that those trees had been blooming, spring after spring, immemorially. Then, consciousness growing stronger, I realized that this image was due to the *Life* piece, which my mind had been busy with, no doubt, even while I was asleep. This was Tito's country, and the image was the everlasting truth behind all the changes and confusions of politics—the blooming trees. Of course, Tito is a Croat and the Vardar is Serb; but that does not change the meaning. Fully awake, at last, my mind switched instantly to you and your journey and the hope that it had not been too dismal. Such a visit as yours means more to us here than I can attempt to tell you. There are not many, as you heard said last night, whom we look forward to seeing. But to have one of those come gives us a new hold of life.

It seemed to me that just when you had to go, the talk had really begun. There was more to say about Simone Weil and her passion for truth. Much more, I think, about *The Outsider*. No doubt, I could not begin to say anything sensible until I have read the book again. It is in many ways a thin book, and, while I think the effort should be made, it is difficult not to keep in mind that the author is only a few years older than my son. There is also the somewhat unpleasant statement that he means to write about a new religion, but first is doing a book about Jack the Ripper. But perhaps this is less Colin Wilson than his publisher's blurbs. I think, though, that I can make a point about the book, or, rather, why it hit me, which I did not make last night. The age is impaled on its most maiming experience, namely, that a man can be simply or savagely—above all, pointlessly—wiped out, regardless of what he is, means, hopes, dreams or might become. This reality cuts across our minds like a wound whose edges crave to heal, but cannot. Thus, one of the great sins, perhaps *the* great sin, is to say: It will heal; it has healed; there is no wound; there is something more important than this wound. There is nothing more important than this wound. If we cannot learn to get beyond it, to find meaning which includes it, the age can solve nothing for itself. All the politics in the world, in history, is as subsidiary as are the dirty doings of Tito beside the im- memorially blooming Vardar trees. It is this central wound which I take Colin Wilson to refer to (not fully grasping his own meaning) when he babbles about new religion. The socialists and that ilk tell us that there is no wound, or, if there is, the way around it is unsegregated men's rooms for every- body, with hot and cold running water and a TV in every com- partment. This is *their* sin, which they wear in the shallowness of their faces and their self-strangling complacency. The Right has its own deformation of this sin; its own shallowness; its own complacency. But it is forbidden us to turn away from the wound. You perhaps do not remember the mass graves of the First World War in Poland. But you do remember the Katyn Forest. It is not just those bodies that lie heaped there. It is that we lie, smothering alive, under the heaps. We cannot know this and not ask, in our living voices, an ageless question. Who has not heard it? It is Odoacer's question. Trapped in Theodoric's court, and cut down by Theodoric's sword, Odoacer cried: "Where is God?" One of Tito's purge victims, a lay assistant in an Orthodox church, hanged himself before he could be shot. He left this note for his wife: "I have gone to remind God of a world He has forgotten." This is our reality. And all Frank Meyer's theology [14] (and, as you know, I rate him high) cannot dispose of the question, no matter how effectively he plays with it. I cannot dispose of it either, of course. But neither can I forget it since I cannot forget the death pits of Poland, though those were grassed over thirty years ago, to be followed by that mountain of shoes, men's, women's, children's—children's— which an eyewitness described to me as he saw it before the Nazi crematorium at Polish Maidenek. This is what Willi forgets in his jaunty thrusts at Sartre, and this is what, I fear, Frank may forget in packaging Colin Wilson. No! The wound is also in the package; or, if it isn't, there is nothing in it.

After an outburst like this, there is really only one thing to do; to stop short, to stop, in Randall Jarrell's winged phrase, "all over at once, like a locomotive." But can a locomotive stop short on the downgrade? I suppose I shall go on dogging this point past bearing. For, indeed, it is the only crucial point of our time, and all else, wars, peace, social and political systems, dwindle beside it.

The man who described to me the shoes at Maidenek was a Communist, a most unpleasant one too. He loathed me too, and I did not like him. But this we did have in common: we both stood upon that common dark and bloody ground; we both saw the same question, though his answer to it could no longer be mine. It had been once.

Thank you for coming. Both Esther and I shall keep referring to points about your visit for some time to come, as we sit by our fireplace.

As always,
Whittaker

[14] Frank Meyer, formerly a Communist, now an editor of *National Review*.

Afterthoughts—after 24 hours, that is.

Bert Brecht says it much more thriftily than I manage above: "Terrible is the temptation to be good." His "good" means, need I say, to live as if no wound existed, or (because the wound has always existed), to live as if in our age it had not grown too mortal to be lived with. Yes, terrible is the temptation to be good. Will Frank forgive my presumption if I commend to him that line? He will know that, as who says A must also say B, that line instantly invokes another: Terrible is the temptation to pity. Terrible because, as the first line invites stultification of vision, the second line invites paralysis of action. He will instantly know, too, then, where that leads, that who says B must also say C. This time he may be mistaken. At that point, he will see, the man who has said these things stands on the Tarpeian Rock.[15] That is where the outsider stands. C. Wilson is saying that the man who throws himself off the Rock solves nothing—and there are, as Frank and I know, many ways to throw yourself off the Rock. (Emmet Hughes appears to have jumped.) It is the man who, on the Rock, even while he dizzies and all whirls below, does not throw himself off, begins to mount upward on his knees—it is that man, and certain circumstances of his necessity, that Wilson is concerned with. That is why, if they understood what Wilson is talking about, the liberals must hate him, because it is precisely that man they most hate: what he is and climbs toward denies them as a breed. Conservatives, if they do not hate him, also fear him and deny him (as the good and intelligent Max Eastman has had to deny me). For to them, too, he brings not peace, but a sword. I beg Frank: do not let the liberals have C. Wilson by default. The saints would know what he is saying and must we damn him because he is born, like us, into a time which the saints have fled? I must stop it, with this word: there is something journalistic and sophomoric in the term: *The Outsider.* But this young man is looking for a popu-

15 From which the Romans hurled criminals to their death.

lar focus; and I do not think we can refuse him the means he has found to work with, even though we may dislike it.

The enclosure is for Eudocio Ravines.[16] Will you send it to him; it is not necessary to name its source. It is insultingly little. In fact, I have not got that little to give. But even so little, to a man circumstanced as he is, means the difference at moments between hope and no hope; means sometimes Golconda, the power to buy the cup of coffee he otherwise could not buy, to sit for a while in the restaurant he must otherwise look in at but not enter. Believe me, he will know. And he will know that someone else knows, and that is often more important than the pennies.

Oct. 9???, 1956

Dear Bill,

Of the three pieces,[17] Willi's seems to me to get there firstest with the mostest, though I suspect that many readers will be unable to remember whether Honky Hegel plays for the Yankees or the Dodgers. But much must be said for Burnham's intention: to get it coolly set forth. His great premise seems to me not so much wrong, as wrongly accented; and I have the feeling that he takes it to the point he does chiefly as a temperamental reaction from what he calls "rhetoric." But we are not indicting theses; we are trying to pierce ears sealed tight with the wax of complacency. The wax invokes the rhetoric, as deafness raises other people's voices. In quiet conversation, I believe that he and I would not find ourselves far apart on the objective facts, insofar as they are facts. I think so; I am not sure.

I see I dreed my weird too late in Frank Meyer's case. I'll say no more about C. Wilson; he is too slight a cause for so much hollering. I wonder if Frank has ever come across a book by

16 I had mentioned seeing the ex-Communist writer, Eudocio Ravines, in Paris. He was writing free-lance columns for Latin American newspapers at one dollar per column. The enclosure was a twenty-dollar bill.

17 Analyzing the meaning of the "change" in Soviet policy ushered in by the 20th Congress.

Father Henri de Lubac, called *The Drama of Atheist Humanism*. It is hard to come by in English, but the French original may sometimes be had. It is one of my "indispensable books." In it Frank will find two passages which seem to me worth some reflection. In the first, Fr. de Lubac is citing a letter (1907) of Jacques Rivière to Paul Claudel, which I must paraphrase, rather than take time to translate: "I see that Christianity is dying (*se meurt*). . . . We no longer know what those spires are doing above our towns since they are no longer the prayer of any of us. We do not know the meaning of those great buildings, surrounded today by railroad stations and hospitals, and from which the people themselves have chased the monks. We do not know what those stucco crosses stand for on the graves, encrusted, moreover, with a revolting art." "And," says Fr. de Lubac, "doubtless Claudel's reply to that cry of anguish is a good one: 'Truth has nothing to do with the number of people it convinces.' " Then Fr. de Lubac notes how many are still drawn by the Faith. And yet "among the best, some of those who are most discerning and most spiritual find themselves caught by a contrary sentiment; we see them captivated by the Gospel whose teaching still appears to them full of force and novelty: drawn to the Church in which they sense a reality more than human, capable of bringing, together with a remedy for our ills, the solution to the problem of our destiny. But, on the threshold, see what stops them: the spectacle that we present to them, we, the Christians of today . . . that spectacle repels them. . . . It is not that they violently condemn us; it is rather that they can no longer take us seriously. Does History condemn Romulus Augustulus because he did not renew the work of Caesar and of Augustus? History notes only that, in that last heir to the Empire, the sap had dried up." Fr. de Lubac does not, of course, stop there; that is, rather a beginning. I mention this moving book because its author does not move his eyes from the wound which I mentioned in an earlier letter, the wound where the spear, century by century, pierces the side. There is only one fully logical conservative position

in the West—that of the Catholic Church. It has nothing to do
with Frank Chodorov.[18] But I think it has a good deal to do
with Frank Meyer. Otherwise there are only schism and heresy.
Moreover, the Church is the only true counterrevolutionary
force, not because it is against the political revolution in this
world, but because it contains the revolution wherever the
revolution manifests that wound. If this is too much of a
paradox, perhaps we must invoke Honky Hegel. But we must
also remember the priest-workers. For what happened to them
is more meaningful than Yalta. It, too, says: Terrible is the
temptation to pity. This age is of a grandeur that it sins against
persistently by not letting itself know. Each of us, Frank too,
must beware of letting ourselves be less than what is.

As always,
Whittaker

I cannot refrain from offering an incident, offering it in all
humility as of a man before minds that he respects *au fond*.
The fate of the Russian imperial family was sealed when Lloyd
George, moved by Labor and related sentiment, withdrew the
British offer of asylum. So the Romanovs were moved, largely
for safekeeping, to Tobolsk. The Bolsheviks moved them back
to Ekaterinaburg and kept them, closely guarded, in a dwelling
called the House of Special Purpose. We do not know how
clearly the Tsar foresaw what was to happen. But we know
that the Tsarina did. For, shortly before it happened, she wrote
a friend: "The Bridegroom cometh." Among the terrible lines
of this age (I can think at once of several others) this one
touches the place above our hearts with an icy finger. When
the family were called to the cellar of the House of Special
Purpose, the Tsar was carrying the Tsarevitch, who was too ill
to walk. Yurovsky was armed with two revolvers, one in each
hand. He seems to have fired first; the Tsarevitch was only
wounded and had to be dispatched with a second shot. The
other bullet marks are curiously low on the cellar wall, so that

18 A writer of the individualist school of conservatism.

it is inferred that, at Yurovsky's shots, the Tsarina and her daughters fell to their knees. Some of the guards had been German prisoners. This line was found scratched on a wall of one of the rooms: *Belsazar ward in selbiger Nacht/Von seinen Knechten umgebracht.*[19] * It is, of course, a line of Heine's. Automobile engines had been kept running (a common practice) to drown the sound of the shots in the cellar. But, on the farther side of the house, two guards heard the shots. One said to the other: *"Panyol?"* (You understand?) The other answered: *"Panyol."* (I understand.) In an age where such things happen in multiples, books like C. Wilson's will be written, and it is exceedingly unlikely that by a click of the typewriter, it will be possible "to end this Existentialism business"—not by *ukase*.

* Curiously, this was, I think, the first German poem I memorized: *Die Mitternacht zog näher schon,/In stummer Ruh' lag Babylon.*[20]

Oct. 19, 1956

Dear Bill,

To your gladdening letter, I wrote a close-set, three-and-a-half-page reply, which I have just had the pleasure of setting a match to (together with that part of your prose which you asked me to make nothing). I found what I had written prolix. More damnable, I find it impossible to treat in detail the personality question you ask counsel about, without being cruel. It is no good to say piously: let me not judge. Judgment is implicit, and this particular judgment risks being mistaken. ... If a faction is forming, that is something else. You will then know better than I can what is, or is not, to be done. You know, we are very seldom our brother's keeper (the very word smacks of the elephant house at the zoo); most of the rigors of parenthood turn on the point of not being even our children's keeper.

[19] Belsazar was on this very night by his own servant brought down.
[20] The dark of night drew on still nearer; in dumb rest lay Babylon.

I was greatly heartened by the enclosures of the one writer
you sent me, and interested by the other—[Dwight] Macdonald,[21]
is his name? "Coy"? He means murder. I should have thought
that, as reviewer, he first of all would have been struck by the
discrepancy between the target (as assessed by DMcD) and the
size of the depth charge. On and on it goes, four, five, how
many columns? When a review so outranges a subject damned
at sight, it draws suspicion on itself. How familiar it is! The
full legal brief: pretrial testimony, certifications of poor character, bad school records, etc. In time, the world will not remember whether it was C.W. who lived in a dive in New Orleans
or W.C. who slept in a bag on Hampstead Heath. But it doesn't
matter because, of course, all that has nothing to do with the
heart of the matter, which is that Colin Wilson has committed
the unpardonable sin: he has raised the religious issue. Just
when DMcD and his ilk thought they had it roped, or, at least,
laced into their own particular straitjacket. Along comes this
uncouth child and says: But man is a volcano; Empedocles
gave himself an unnecessary walk up Etna; he could just as well
have jumped into the crater of himself. All these liberal folk
would like to suppose that the world can be made reasonable
(how else are they to find a cranny safe for themselves?). It is
too shocking. The talk about style is rot. I have a fair ear for
prose style in more than one language. Allowing for the occasional lapses of a youth doing his first book,* I found nothing
especially offensive about Wilson's style; it seems to me, in fact,
a rather adequate instrument. Dwight writhes when Wilson
says: "With that, T. S. Eliot is over his stile." I took Wilson to
be echoing the nursery tale about the old woman and the pig
and dog and stick or whatever it was: "And so I shall get over
the stile and home tonight." I thought it was rather neat. As to
Dwight's pun about styles and stiles, I find it dreary. Wilson
looks at the Outsider from a number of angles, duly investigating each. How odd that among his mustered excerpts from

---

[21] Reviewing, in the *New Yorker*, Colin Wilson's *The Outsider*.

these definitions, McD omits the absolutely basic one, which occurs at the very beginning of the book (page 13, I think): "He is an Outsider because he stands for Truth." The whole argument swings on that line. McD missed it, I prefer to believe, since, otherwise, it is necessary to suppose that he dismissed it.

My day was topped off pleasurably, nevertheless, by a late find. I seldom look carefully through the heap of mail the first time round. On the second go, I was startled to find a postcard with Russian type and Soviet stamp. It was from C. Marshall Taylor. Marshall Taylor is a Quaker with a wry sense of humor, and wonderful knack for puncturing the whimsies dearest to Friends, but of such vetusty in the faith (and so well-heeled, to boot), that he is suffered and even vested with office. His card was a photograph of the Livadiya Palace at Yalta, addressed clearly enough to Mr. & Mrs. W. C., with some kind wishes from one who is there. Must have startled the postal (and other) systems of two great powers. One hesitates to think of the ultraviolet rays that poor pasteboard has endured at Lubianka House and wherever we do such things. So unrewarding, too, which is perhaps suspicious in itself. There let us leave off, laughing.

As always,
Whittaker

* Or, for that matter, anybody else writing at length. Who can keep from wincing sometimes at the after paper?

Just to make it perfect, Marshall Taylor's card bears a credit line, saying that it was made in a factory belonging to the Red Army. To make it more ominous, it says it in Russian.

Nov. 6, 1956

Dear Bill,

Five minutes (it's all I can spare) for the fortnightly howl. I don't see how *NR*'s intellectual franchise can long survive two such reviews in one issue as the one on Orwell and the one on [Ludwig] von Mises. To take second things first, I can see that a certain diplomatic handling was in order in the case of von Mises. Even so, it was *NR*'s job, or its reviewer's, to point out just how serious this book is, how seriously shocking. I am speaking from the condensed version in *U.S. News*. Von Mises' point is that the anticapitalist mentality is the product of envy. Hitler explained it differently. He said the Devil in history is the Jew. Envy is von Mises' Jew. Now, this book is not going to harm any one above the mental age of twelve. But its power to harm minds under that age is great indeed. For, as we know, it is always more painful to think than to use stencils. It is extremely difficult for conservatives to think (and for this there are historical reasons of high cogency). Since this book appeared, I have seen revolution explained by envy in a number of places (this week's *Sat. Eve. Post* editorial, for one). Ah yes, of course. Who understands history and its forces? But envy—who does not suspect that everyone else is envious? *There* is something we can deal with—the veritable Jew. Only, it isn't true. Whatever the motives or the reasoning, the book's effect is profoundly and dreadfully false. It misleads in an area where the greatest intelligence is required, and clarity. It is, of all mischievous things, the worst—the easy error, the plausible fallacy. This, I think, *NR* owed it to conservatism to point out at some length. For this is what a know-nothing conservatism can breed at its know-nothingest. The class struggle is rancid with envy. No, that is wrong, too—the masses are rancid with envy. But it is not the fruit of what von Mises supposes. It is the fruit of a materialism which, to prosper, must deepen and widen mass appetites. Envy begins where the Cadillac dangles always just out of reach at the end of the stick. Since the revolutionist cares little or nothing for such materialism, he stands almost wholly outside von Mises' equation. Revolutionists, when they apply their talents to capitalist activity, often do rather well. Their chief handicap is to get off the ground in the first place; to overcome, in other words, their aversion to a way of doing and being that fills them, not with envy, but with an annihilating boredom or sense of futility. Still, there is always the shocking case of Parvus-Helphand, who, as a revolutionary fugitive from Tsarist Russia, made a fortune in munitions during the Balkan Wars, became a Reichstag member and negotiated some of Lenin's more sensitive dealings—finance of the Bolsheviks by the German General Staff is suspected.

(Here you telephoned.) So I shall skip Orwell altogether. As you noticed, I skipped nimbly away, too, when you mentioned Suez. I hope you are right and that a bomb has not been planted at the heart of history whose ticking will mark the pulse beat of the Arab East, from Casablanca to Jakarta, and for how long, knows only Allah. What is it Hagen cries at the end: *"Zurück vom Ringe!"*—Get away from the ring! But even the best of baritones usually has trouble making himself heard over the fate motif, as the risen Rhine sweeps on to Valhalla burning, and the Curse is fulfilled. I suppose you know that Wagner wrote the *Ring* as an allegory of capitalism. People have got so used to the upholstered mortuary of Bayreuth that they have forgotten the future composer of *Parsifal,* leading the revolt of the Leipzig garrison side by side with—I know it's too much, but it's true—Bakunin. The fuses that lead from Leipzig to Budapest are exceeding long, exceeding complex; and the little flame seemed to have died in the tube long after it was still traveling toward the charge. My wife (listening to the reports about Budapest on Sunday [22]) suddenly: "Why don't they stop those horrible commercials? Why don't the (radio) stations simply pray? Why doesn't everybody simply pray to God for the Hungarians? Oh, poor people, poor, poor people!" Then she rocked back and forth not to give way to her grief. I was going to say: It is the voice of the West. But, no: it is the voice of counterrevolution. What does the West know of revolution or counterrevolution, hope or despair, life or death—the dying West? What does it know of Hungarians or of extermination? What does it care? I am obliged to believe, on the evidence of

[22] The day the Russian tanks moved on Budapest.

the last 48 hours, that it does not care at all. "What is the matter you read, milord?" "Words, words, words."

This has been one of the most beautiful of days. Four years ago, this day, I left the polling booth and managed a heart attack on Main Street. Some time past midnight, I came out of drugs and the little nurse, who had been sitting in a corner, hurried over to see what I wanted. I asked: "Who has won the election?" She left for a few minutes and returned to say: "General Eisenhower." I could not believe it and made her go over the key states. They were all for Eisenhower. Then I fell asleep. But our beginnings never know our ends.

Get over the flu. Come see us: we look forward to it.

As always,
Whittaker

I got up around 4:30 A.M., my custom of a morning. A landslide indeed. About the best Christmas present, there is always, as has often been noted, some sense of disappointment; the desired has passed into the merely actual. I am content. Now I wish no further part of these wars. Man, the politician, has ever been among the least edifying of manifestations. In the end, man, the sufferer, alone holds attention.

Dec. 2?, 1956

Dear Bill,

Was that ———, the clip you sent me? The style speaks strongly for it.

It lacks a few months of nineteen years since I broke with the Communist Party. Babies that were born that day are now making for men and women. Meanwhile, I have done certain other things, more difficultly done in 1948, and its Communist-flooded mood, than is remembered by the large optimism of the West before Communism's current crisis. By my acts then I hoped to give the West a slightly better chance against Communism. I have tried since not to know how complete the failure was. ——— reminds me by reducing the effort to its ultimate term, its absurdity.

Incidentally, I strongly doubt that I ever wrote anything about ——— at *Time*. First, because I never wrote Press or People, where such an item would be looked for. (But I did edit Press for a stretch; People very intermittently.) Second, because I knew scarcely anything about ——— while I was at *Time*. I knew his name and must occasionally have seen his column and formed an impression. But this would be much the way that I now know Elvis Presley's name, have heard a few bars of him, and formed an impression—not a violent one because he lies wholly outside my range of interest. So it was with ——— of whom I first became acutely conscious only after his blows in the Hiss Case. Sample: "Was that Whittaker Chambers seen leaving a Park Avenue psychiatrist's office?" I suspect that ——— has been sold a story about me by the Left, one with about as much substance as my visit to the psychiatrist. I am wholly vulnerable to such stabs. I can do nothing to defend myself. No one can defend me. It seems better simply not to know about them.

Since November 6, 1952, I have ceased to understand why I must go on living, just as I have no rational defense (to myself) why I permit this to happen.

As always,
Whittaker

Later: we seem to have sold this farm—that is, the house, outbuildings and about 30 acres around and behind them. It turns on the buyer's raising a $20,000-dollar mortage in a tight market. He is pinched since he has just bought a $70,000-dollar building in Baltimore and does not wish to dip into his 8%'s. If this proves out, we shall go to live on John's farm. This has always been my favorite, a smaller house of beautifully toned brick, shaped and fired from the clay bank on our reach of the Big Pipe Creek. Ten or so feet behind the house is a small pond. On all sides, wooded hills, some with pine. One vacation, John

took a classmate over to see his property. Afterwards, I asked
Eddington what he thought of the place. "It's like, it's like,"
he said, fumbling for the just phrase, "it's like you imagine
heaven." That's exactly what I thought—simple but celestial.
Still, I have heard one local man say it would make a good pig
farm: and he sketched out where he would run the hogs—
where the little brook goes down beside the house and we have
started making our flower gardens.

Jan. 3, 1957

Dear Bill,

For two or three days, I have sat, looking, from time to time,
at the envelope of your letter. But I have not taken it out to
read over nor done anything about its enclosure. This is what
it is to be struck silent. I have been wondering how to tell you
what I felt when I first opened it, and some thoughts I have
had since, some of them rather sordidly practical. Now I see
that that is exactly what I should not try to tell you, at least to
write you: perhaps one day I shall be able to talk about it.
Such generosity as Johnson's is like lightning: where it strikes,
you raise a little altar, but you don't tell anybody about it
because it has initiated a mystery. All we know about what
really happened at Eleusis is that, at the climax of the rites,
"something was said, something was shown." We believe that
what was shown was a full ear of ripe barley. I suppose you
have to be half-buried in the earth, as I have always been, to
have that jolt you to the toes, even as the initiates of Eleusis.
Otherwise, like what I write here, it remains gibberish as some
things deeply felt and known always defeat language because,
in fact, they are not meant to be communicated. Beyond that:
three men in the West have grasped that the great battles are
not invariably fought by plumed legions on the rounds of
flame-lit clouds. In this most practical-minded of lands, in this
most economic of worlds, and especially if your hands are rather
roped behind your back, the battles are likely to be fought in

simple addition and subtraction. This is what the three grasped. One offered me money help which he could not afford to offer, and which I declined. Another helped in a tremendous way which I shall some day tell you about. You are the third, through your friend. What troubles me most is that I do not know whether he can afford this, either. I have never known of anyone who could afford $1000, let alone three. Afford, of course, has to do with relative scales, so that $1000 is, in general, as tightening to a man in that bracket, as $10 would be to a man in another bracket. I feel that it is rude and pawing for me to get into this matter at all. In the past, I have rigorously kept away from thoughts about your friend's circumstances, in part because I so much dislike the speculations of others in this connection. Forgive me for what I must say, and try to understand. But it would be wrong, it would be dishonest, for me to accept his generosity as you convey it. That is not the nature of the need. Yet there is a need: at the moment it is somewhat harassing. I should like to accept his kindness in these terms: the $3000 is to be a call loan, which he may have in full, tomorrow if necessary: later in the year (for reasons I shall come to) if that will not unduly straiten him. It is to bear the usual 5% interest (unless they have upped the rate again while I dozed). At this moment in my affairs, this loan will be a lifesaver to me. If it were not so, I should make his $3000 earn more than 5% for you. For believe me, von Mises is a goose, and I strongly suspect that many a revolutionist knows more than the professor about making money work for him. I am bound, too, to explain this wizardry to you: and the fact that you know more about such affairs than I ever shall, will only make it funnier. Meanwhile, it turns on your friend's generosity. I have not yet told Esther about this matter, but I shall: and, should anything abruptly happen to me, she will take care of it; and it will be secured in tangible ways. The great mercy is to know that, should I be out of sight, you will stand by to help in the pinches. But only in the pinches. This in no way lessens your generosity or my gratitude.

Now for some sordid bits. At the end of my last letter, I told you I thought we had sold this house and 35 acres. Well, we did, or, rather, my agent did, in the course of a great champagne supper of the Green Spring Valley set. It took two jeroboams and two preposterously funny, hour-long telephone conversations with Esther and me. We are due to move to the other house March 1. Settlement is July 1 or sooner, depending on the leniency of the bank. This seems to me very tidy and terribly funny. For Esther and for the children, it is a wrench to leave this house. For me, no wrench at all. I feel like a combat soldier who has slipped full gear and is preparing to rest in the shade of the trees.

I have every intention of mortgaging the other house to the hilt and of letting that money work for me too. If materialism is what the world really respects, I should like to prove that I can play the game, in my modest way, along with the best. Precisely because I do not respect materialism, but would like to show that there is no fortress that the Bolsheviki cannot take. Run hounds, and all after. Capitalism can be fun. If I fail, at least I shall have fought. And you must visit us, some time, at the country farm. But first here if you get a chance.

As always,
Whittaker

I gather that what really swung the house deal was the pumpkin patch—the bubbly idea of owning Whittaker Chambers' calabash-bed. Wonderfully queer world! But this, too, is strictly not for conversation.

In the morrow's dawn:

I not only mean to mortgage the other house; Esther and I have talked, halfheartedly, of renting it soonest, preferably to some slick trade writer or other "brain worker" who is seeking some months of seclusion to complete a project. We would then take off for Mexico as per last year's plan. This idea has merits.

Yet it falters always on a question: why should we, who manifestly stand, though without knowing at just what removes, from a final frontier—why should we disarrange ourselves, take the physical trouble, to cross, so late in the afternoon, a merely political frontier? We haven't even really bothered to answer the question. Instead, we have drifted with the days, and, of late, have begun to look forward to contriving our new gardens at the new place. Spring is always our undoing.

Meanwhile, two matters are developing which promise to jangle the rites of spring. One is Alger's book.[23] The other is a play about the Hiss Case by Mr. Sol Stein.[24] The book, I gather, is to make noise and little else. The play I consider untimely, especially since its effect (or one of its effects) must be to add to the racket, and thereby play the game of the book and its author and partisans. I would treat the book with silence as the simplest means of letting it pass promptly into the larger silence which I am told it is headed for. The play puts me on a spot which, in prospect, looks more difficult. I wish no ill to Mr. Stein. But I do not think him a good playwright, and there are higher considerations in the Hiss Case, as a public property, which make it undesirable for me to give his play my blessing, or to have any open opinion about it, for or against. (I have not seen the script and do not wish to.) Nevertheless, Stein is actively, in several ways, seeking my public blessing. It seems all rather wearisome, piddling and unnecessary. So, again, we have begun to wonder if the simplest way is not just to remove ourselves physically from the scene while the press is making copy and the factitious hubbub swirls. This means Mexico. Since I expect the book to wither on the vine, and the play to fail rather promptly, we should be back in time for some late spring planting. Meanwhile, I have kept up my crash project for learning Spanish, out of a growing interest.

---

[23] Alger Hiss, *In the Court of Public Opinion*, published in 1957.

[24] Mr. Stein's play, sympathetic to WC, opened in New York on December 11, 1957, and folded after one week. It was called *A Shadow of My Enemy*.

Crash project with me means, as usual, memorizing pages of prose and verse. I have got trippingly by memory some phrases that may prove indispensable. As conversational gambits, for example, consider: *"Debajito de ese tamarindo, Montero mató al mayor de los muchachos de un balazo entre los ojos,"* [25] or *"En la playa, los caballos se sobresaltaron y retrocedieron, viendo pasar en la corriente dos serpientes."* [26] What more fitting to follow up an introduction to any matron than: *"Conmigo no hay cuidado, señora. Aunque no lo acuerde, Usted me curó cuando me hirieron los hombres de Vicente Salazar"?* [27] While I think I might empty any bar in Mexico by remarking casually: *"Acuérdese de que por aqui hay muchos caimanes."* [28] This reminds me that Random House has published a highly amusing book * by Truman Capote about the adventures of the Porgy and Bess troupe in Russia. *NR* could have great fun with it simply by letting Capote do the talking, and with scarcely any, or no, editorial asides. Reminds me because one of the female members of the company is preparing herself with the help of an English-Russian phrase book issued by the U.S. Army during World War II. So, among others, she has memorized the Russian for: "I have been wounded in the privates." "I don't," says a colored member of the cast, "see why you would want to memorize that, dear."

* *The Muses Are Heard* [1956]. I cannot refrain from citing the heroic moment when the possibility of concealed Russian microphones is borne in upon Mrs. Gershwin. "But, darling, how are we going to gossip?" she asks. "Unless we stand in the bathroom and just keep flushing?"

25 Just behind that tamarind, Montero killed the oldest of the boys with a bullet between the eyes.
26 On the beach, the horses leaped and drew back, on seeing the snakes glide by in the stream.
27 With me you have nothing to fear, lady. Although you don't remember it, it was you who cured me after the soldiers of Vicente Salazar wounded me.
28 Bear in mind there are lots of alligators here.

The papers carried the news that Whittaker Chambers' house had been ravaged by fire. I received a telegram from him, reporting merely that the family was well....

Jan. 23, 1957

Dear Bill,

Sat. last, I wrote out a telegram for a friend to send you out there in the big world. I hope she remembered. This will be skimpy (well?) as a letter, and largely indecipherable: my typewriter is a minor casualty, and pens and inks have disappeared somewhere in the heaps.

In the old house, the attic is a total loss: the chimneys are holding up the roof. Floor 2 is fire-gutted. The rest of the house stands, but gallons of water have made it a wet and warping tomb. My purchaser had, with enterprising foresight, put $45,000 worth of replacement insurance on the place (he had known somebody who bought a house in Baltimore only to have it burn down before she could take over). So my man is pooling his cut of the $45 thousand with our piddling $55 hundred, and will proceed to rebuild at once and go through with the purchase. My chief loss is in another direction. I am afraid that our bank will not now give me the $10 thousand mortgage that I hoped to put on this place, and that will be not only a considerable loss to me in unearned increment, but most frustrating, to boot. I think I am obliged to tell you, if you are interested in a quick turnover, to have a thought to Phila. & Reading Coal Co. It stands at 27 and a fraction, or did yesterday. I have reason to believe that, within the next 12 days, it will make interesting gains. If you will look into its career, you will see that, on a somewhat seasick market, Phila. & R. has graphed a general upward line *against* the general drift. This is in no sense advice, or even a tip. But you might be interested to look. On the other hand, you may know of much more interesting things to look at. Yet I guess I must say, too, that if you want a quick in and out, I think you can, in a fortnight or so, pick up several thousand dollars in Phila. & Reading without leaving your chair at *NR*. Since I think so, I owe it to you to say so. Only, check into the last twelve months' history of this stock. I know, I know—we old revolutionists are peculiar birds. Or, as Arthur K[oestler] has it, "Such peculiar birds as you are found only in the trees of the revolution." People expect us to be saints or monsters. We are only men.

To return to our disaster, many neighborly hands rescued about all of our household effects, and then moved them over here, where, in a confusion, like that of the Collyer (Collier?) brothers, we are trying to sort out our living without getting trapped in collapsing tunnels of stacked books. In about a month, I should think, all going well, we might make a clearing and some order. For the rest, I find it extremely beautiful here in a modest way that suits my disposition much better than the old place. For one thing, we hear the wind in the woods here as we never heard it over yonder; and, from all the rear windows, we look across the little pond to Cold Friday on the opposite woods where, at night, Orion and Taurus blaze tremendously—as I noticed the first night we spent here. So we have reached the House of Special Purpose in a way quite different from any we would have chosen. What I once wrote you about that historic House was, in fact, part of Chapter V of a book called *Cold Friday*—after the name of the hill field that stands above this house.

In the main, I find myself in agreement with Willi on the crisis.[29] But the striking point, both of his piece and Burnham's, is, of course, that neither has an answer good enough. Burnham's answer seems to me questionable and too schematic. Willi would replace Burnham's planned effort (which is certainly self-justified as something tangible by contrast with all the mere talk) with an accent on our immortal will to win. Moreover, this will does not exist. Perhaps I should forgo my opinion, since I have not, so far, been able to formulate my own with

---

[29] How American foreign policy should proceed toward the Soviet Union and Eastern Europe in the wake of Budapest.

force and cogency. Yet, I cannot refrain from saying that both
B. and W., it seems to me, miss the meaning of the crisis because
they tend to see it on its own terms, and not as a late stage in a
total crisis that has spanned our lifetime. That slight shift in
vantage point shifts many interrelationships. We are, I am
trying to say in my own writing in this matter, at the point for
which Marx forecast two alternatives: (1) "The revolutionary
reconstitution of society as a whole"; or (2) the "common ruin
of the contending" forces. This revolutionary reconstitution
is not done, in our part of the world, with gunfire: it is in full
legislative play all around us. It is to this set of "objective
factors" that the theses of the 20th Congress addressed themselves. The current crisis, while changing many relationships,
has not changed the basic forces at work. They work on, ignoring
any one man's purposes or preferences—Molotov's or the President's—and, objectively viewed, the President gives promise of
being a promoter of revolutionary change, which he appears
not to grasp too clearly, but which, in my opinion, he understands much more clearly than most people suppose. Only, he
calls it a spade, instead of a damned old shovel, and then it
ceases for millions to whom words and names are more important than realities, to be revolution, and becomes change.
Who is against change? The road to Paris, we used to hear, runs
through Peking. In fact, the road to Washington (a trunk line
of history) runs through Soho (Marx's old digs). Of course, we
don't admit this. The President believes, quite as fervently as
John Chamberlain, that Marx was a nasty old blunderbat.
Mischievous? Yes. Mistaken about much? Yes. Stupid? No. In
fact, piercing insights. He even foresaw (quite a feat in 1848)
that the U.S. might achieve the revolution without violence—
as the 20th Congress reminded us, resurrecting this long un-
welcome aperçu—and thereby giving us the clue to much
thinking that underlies the thesis. Frank Meyer understands
these things well. But then he was never a Communist of the
Right, that bog where armies whole have sunk. Willi is right
about the decisive role of the anti-Communist will. But I

think he does not grasp who the anti-Communists are—not he and I: we are history's rejects. Objectively, he and I and our like are reactionaries. We are in opposition (though no longer in revolt) against both worlds. For both are materialist. The real anti-Communists are in the satellites. They are materialists, too. But it may be that circumstances will evolve in them a new blend that goes beyond the materialist limit. It is in this sense, and scarcely in any other, that I tend to agree with Burnham that the historical crux lies in Poland, etc.[30] Here, and, in time, farther east, something restorative may develop. Look as I will, I can find no signs of anything like that in the West, and it is this spiritual (and intellectual) deadness that invests the current crisis with that numbing sense of: so what? The Hungarians, looking westward with hope, made a tragic historical misjudgment. Does anyone suppose it possible that this lesson will be lost on all the other satellite peoples—or, indeed, on all Europe? Comrade, look not on the West / I will have the heart out of your breast. At the moment, the Poles are making history. The West is making politics. The difference is between a creative act and pettifoggery. Unhappily, the Polish historical record is erratic, a small nation, too, living on an indefensible plain. Czeslaw Milosz's book [*The Captive Mind*] now makes better reading than ever. And the news photographs from Poland (see a recent Sunday *Times* magazine) tell much. "What do they remind you of?" I asked my wife. "Yes," was all she answered. Both of us were thinking of the days when the West European delegates were welcomed to the revolutionary capital with the slogan: "Enter here. Here dwell the gods." Hopelessly bombastic. Yet this bombast included a truth truer than much more calmly pitched notices. What is opening on the Polish plain is a new phase of history, a new thrust of the spirit. Neither Willi

30 Burnham had proposed (*NR*, January 19, 1957) that allied forces withdraw to westernmost Europe, in return for complementary moves by Russian troops: intending either a psychological embarrassment for the Communists (if they refused to cooperate), or the (eventual) manumission of the satellite nations (if they did cooperate).

nor I would enjoy it (we have been through all that). Yet we must see it for what it is. Here the prudent, practical thinking of the CCF [Committee for Cultural Freedom] is not good enough, misses the point entirely, by trying to convert it to merely useful ends. I think Burnham misses Emerson's meaning:

> *The litanies of nations came,*
> *Like the volcano's tongue of flame*
> *Up from the burning core below;*
> *The canticles of love and woe.*

Willi, the revolutionist, is closer to what can be felt but eludes thumbtacks and taxidermy. The Fire Bird is glimpsed living, or not at all. In other words, realists have a way of missing truth, which is not invariably realistic.

Much, much, too much of this.

Our very best to you and your family,

Whittaker

Feb. 9, 10??, 1957

Dear Bill,

Scarcely had I hung up after our last telephone conversation than I went down with a cold; the more annoying because I take rather extravagant precautions against such things. So I have been slow in answering. About P & R [Philadelphia and Reading] and p & c [puts and calls]—you are generous as usual. But I can't do anything. *Es muy sencillo. Al momento no tengo los fondos para invertir. La venta de la otra casa se efectua hacia el 1er de Julio. Había esperado que la banca nos daría una hipoteca en esta finca. Pero, de jure, Juan es el verdadero proprietario. Pues tambien es menor de edad, para dar una hipoteca, hay que la banca se hace el tutor de Juan. Eso toma cuatro semanas a lo menos y, huelga decir, muchos tramites enojantes. Juan alcanza su mayoría el 18 de Agosto proximo.*

Creo que esperemos.[31] I think I will shift gears too. This is my first venture into that much Spanish prose. No doubt, it is full of syntactical and other shockers. But for me it marks an advance—over sign language. Very exhausting, though. Since mine is a long-haul interest, I never follow the daily vicissitudes of *esas acciones* [those stocks]. Instead, I check once a month or so. But I have not yet made up my mind what I shall do next. I'll decide within a few days and then let you know.

I am deeply disappointed that John is not going abroad this summer. Or, rather, I think he is making a mistake. But then we never know in such cases. He really has to make his own decisions now, which, I see, are not necessarily the ones I should make. I went abroad on my own steam and against everybody's wishes and fears. But I was twenty-two; and when, at Bremen, I found myself in the Ratskeller with the two Yalies who had worked their passage, I asked one why he would not speak to me on shipboard. He said: "I didn't know you could speak English." He was immensely relieved, at last, to find another American who could guide him through the horrors of ordering supper and buying a railroad ticket. He was scared to death at finding himself in a strange land; and in his state of mind I see John's today. Of course, your fellow alumnus did not know that my German was much like my Spanish above; chiefly daring.

Thank you for the *Permanent Revolution,*[32] which, I gather, from a cryptic notice, is at the PO. Ordinary post gets here much quicker than any other. Plane mail usually loses a day between airports. Your special delivery lost two days because the post office forgot to give it to the carrier. The mailmen are the last conservatives; they are not up to 20th-century

[31] It's very simple. At this moment I have nothing to invest. The sale of the other house takes place about the first of July. I had hoped that the bank would give us a mortgage on this spread. However, *de jure,* John is the actual owner. And he is a minor, and in order to grant him a loan, the bank must become his trustee. That takes four weeks at least, and lengthy and boring transactions. John attains his majority on the eighteenth of next August. I think we'll wait until then. (The Spanish is homemade.)

[32] By Sigmund Neumann.

traffic. Besides, we are now located half a mile from the county road. Most people hereabouts regard this area as the Romans regarded the Teutowald; they remember what happened to the Legions. Darkly, they refer to this land as "the holler." It is the most beautiful place I have ever lived in; and I have been wondering, in my new, capitalist phase, how I might most profitably ruin it. Development, I mean. I have even played with the idea of turning the back of the old place into a cemetery, as one way of getting the most out of every foot of soil. Disgusting, isn't it? That's why I do it. It is my form of contempt. For I said to myself, from the dark nadir of Christmas, 1955: If that's the kind of a world it is; if that's what it respects, and the kind of games it likes to play, why shouldn't I play too? The answer seems, of course, very simple: Because I was not meant to. But there are other considerations.

We are still getting sorted out. I think if the paperhanger at last gets here to cover these raw walls, our morale would go up like the swallows. He has been coming for a couple of weeks. The delay, his wife confided yesterday to Esther, is a fear that he may have "cancer of the breast." Since none of the symptoms, described in great detail, sounded to me much like cancer, I ventured to hope that it was only milk fever.

I seem quite unable to get my *Life* piece about the [Budapest] crisis off the ground. I have begun to suspect that that is because what I am really writing is a book. What baffles me most is that everybody seems to see the crisis as an exclusive crisis of Communism. The whole blasted world is in crisis, has been ever since I was born; and, if it weren't, there would be no Soviet Union there to have a crisis in.

As always,
Whittaker

Later: This letter has a cold in the head too, and a low-grade fever. Since I typed it, this enclosure came. P & R had a bunch of the writing boys up to Pottsville. This Coal Age special is a by-product of that junket. It is so circumspect that somebody

must have talked quietly to Assistant Editor Raleigh. I have
ringed certain passages, which are prudent beyond belief. But
I think they will tell you something. There is also something
more, nowhere hinted here, that, should it come off, is most attractive. But there are great obstacles, so perhaps Mr. Y————'s
reticence [in his stock market letter] is much the best.
Union Underwear is Fruit of the Loom; and a coal company
that is poised on an underwear and a cowboy boot company is a great joke to many. Acme Boot buys the whole
Australian kangaroo-hide crop, and since this is of the breed
of fact that readers love to read about, I am trying to get a
friend to do a piece on Acme for the *Sat. Eve. Post.* But, to me,
much the most teasing fact in Coal Age's story is a mere passing
reference to Glen Alden Coal. I have been casually watching
Glen Alden for some time. When last I looked, around Christmas, it was quoted at $8 or thereabouts. It appears to be in
bad shape. So must not one of two things happen?—(1) its
restive shareholders or somebody must force a more energetic
management; (2) P & R must absorb it. Either is thought-
making. I asked you on the telephone if you had ever heard of
Parvus-Helphand.[33] He was (with Trotsky) the co-preacher
of permanent revolution. But that isn't why I mentioned him.
After 1905, Parvus had seen it all. So he decided to test
Prof. von Mises' theories. Finding himself in Constantinople
(he had escaped from Siberia), on the eve of the Balkan wars,
he thought it might be fun to try capitalism for a change. He
dealt in military supplies to such profit that he turned million-
aire, and became, unless memory fails me, a member of the
Berlin bourse. No, no, no analogies. Parvus belonged to that
race specially chosen by God to indite Psalms and bills of
change. Me—I'm just a *bednyak,* a poor peasant. But I like to
laugh; I should like to laugh a great deal, and to have a great
deal to laugh about—to myself and a few friends, a very few.
What a pity that you are dedicated to mental strife and feel
no yearning to move in on the Glen Alden Coal Co. or what

---

[33] "Parvus" was the pseudonym used by A. L. Helphand.

have you. Or if only I could make John Chambers see that, now the revolution is over (drowning in its own filth and blood), the time has come to laugh—for those who would not weep; to laugh and to work hard and study the hard, killer, crotaloid eyes of Mr. Y————,* from which at least as much is to be learned about the 20th century as from the eyes of Nikita Khrushchev.

* See enclosure [a stock market letter].

March 10, 1957

Dear Bill,

My silence has lasted too long. There have been two main reasons. First, I have been writing in such a way that, when I come up for air around noon, it takes the rest of the day to get my breath back. I have been tormented by my inability to get my reading of the current crisis off the ground. Slowly, the realization dawned that I was trying to cram into an article something that could not be done in less than a small book. I may have written you this. I do not know why it should take so long to realize anything that, in hindsight, seems so obvious. I can only point to my betters and recall how long it took Tolstoi to realize that *Resurrection* could only begin with that astonishing evocation of spring, in city and prison, which is probably the best thing in the book; at least one of the best things. Anyway, once over my silly stile, I began to run and in a way I seldom do—without pausing to trim or polish, but just to get on. Of course, I do not know to what purpose I am running—I never do. But I must try to show why most of the argument about the crisis has seemed to me almost wholly beside the point. Actually, there is more than one point. But one of them has to do with the absence in the West for forty years of a sense of destiny. Power, yes; a sense of destiny, no—and this has found expression in a failure of will, and, to a large degree, of rational hope. Hence, too, by default Communism has been the only force in the world, felt as a force of destiny—

its only real strength. This force is not only now corrupt; it is insanely preposterous. It is insane that Communism itself should have destroyed more Communists than all the other governments of the earth taken together; or that, by official record, the last three chiefs of the Soviet secret police should have been traitors to the revolution, intelligence agents of foreign powers all their active lives. And it is insane that the rest of the world could co-exist with, and largely connive at, such insanity. These are only the more fantastic instances. The relationship of the West and Communism shows, as a whole, the same insanity. In the absence of any other effective force, there has now emerged, on the Polish and on the Hungarian plains, another force, pathetic in its physical impotence and inequality, but heroic in its purpose which has challenged both the morally empty West and the corrupt Communist power in which, hitherto, destiny has inhered. This is the dialectic force of the revolution itself, creating, out of its own inner conflict, a new force of destiny to counteract and challenge the older force, which corruption has long made into a fiendish masquer-ade of fated force. That is why I began with my friend, Elena, like me in her fifties, who, I discovered in 1953, was serving a twenty-year term at Vorkuta. She got this message out to the West: that, as a slave, at last she felt free, since there was nothing left that she any longer needed to fear because there was nothing left that life could do to her.

My other reason for silence had to do with my sense of *NR*'s financial straits and what they must be doing to your days. Since I do not know details, and cannot, anyway, be of help, I thought it better not to break in irrelevantly. Perhaps I have broken in too much as it is. Brent Bozell and Frank Meyer were up last week. It was said, half-jestingly, I chose to believe, that I really "had no business counseling *NR*." I answered that I was not counseling, that, when I was asked questions, I simply answered them. But perhaps even the appearance of interference should be avoided. This only drove me harder on my main task: the effort to state the general position, which is what I am, temperamentally at least, better suited to than the wars of Willi, Frank and Burnham.[34] I said, at one point in the talk (when Frank was taxing me, apparently under the mistaken impression that I had been an Oppositionist), that I had always thought Trotsky, in general, wrong at the time, but that I loathed the inefficiency that could solve the problem only by killing off the Party's best brain. Brent picked that up with respect to Burnham. The other two times Brent has been here, he has been largely silent or worried (I gathered) by his Senator's affairs.[35] For the first time, I had a strong impression of how good a man and head he is—an impression that Esther echoed voluntarily.

You might glance at Niebuhr's piece (current *New Leader*) on the President's Sunday school confusions about the relationship of power and morality. It is a brief piece of no great resonance. But it makes simply a couple of timely points. And it has caused one learned Theban, a Republican of some potency, to call Niebuhr "a son of a bitch," proving, I think, that Niebuhr was well within the target area. But I am at odds with Senator Knowland's "no help to Poland." I guess this proves that tactically, I am close to the Burnham line. I may change my mind abruptly as the situation seems to change. For this is revolution, where, as someone has said, nothing can be surely forecast, where much depends on the locomotive that somebody forgot to hitch, the man with the message who failed to make the vital rendezvous, the X factors. As well, of course, as on grander lines clear to me (at times), though perhaps less incontinently so than to those who haunt the sovereign peaks. Perhaps for the consideration of all *NR*'s warring dialecticians, you should hang up Heraclitus' old hat: "No man can stand in the same river twice." Communism is no more free of the laws of dialectics than anything else is. The revolution is against the Revolution *; that, I think, is the crevice that Burn-

---

[34] Who were beginning to disagree on policy—a disagreement which resulted in the resignation of Schlamm a few months later.
[35] Bozell had been writing Senator McCarthy's speeches.

ham has been driving into, or groping toward. Does anybody doubt that there is a crevice? In March, 1917, a crowd of 80 thousand swept into the Duma buildings and forced that wobbly assembly to end the thousand-year autocracy. *"Ils viennent jusque dans vos bras,"* said a witty conservative minister, echoing a line of the *Marseillaise* that the crowd liked to sing. Let us not, in turn, be too witty. Crowds of 150, 250 thousand, crammed the squares and streets before the Polish public buildings during the October days. Such a crowd is not in the first instance a menace. It is a notice: it says that official power is impotent in a profound way and is seeking a new center in the mass. Good God, don't you have any *revolutionists* among you ex-Communists? But, here I am, counseling again.

If you get a chance, drop me a line.

As always,
Whittaker

* It is against the Revolution because it wishes to complete it—this is true. The point for the West is timing and tactics.

John is off to Europe again; end of June, Greek Line. Don't ask me why. Something he and his college shipmate have cooked up. I decline to counsel, beyond saying that the sailing date seems late and that I fear the Greeks.

This letter has lain here, unmailed, a couple of days. How hard it is to write about the West and destiny. I know, I know—only the supremely difficult is worth trying to do. I have been working between two quotations somewhat as in ploughing we guide ourselves by a tree on one side of a land, and by another tree, coming back. The first quotation is Dostoievski on destiny: "Science and reason have, from the beginning of time, played a secondary and subordinate part in the life of nations; and so it will be till the end of time. Nations are built up and moved by another force which sways and dominates them, the origin of which is unknown and inexplicable: that force is the force of an insatiable desire to go on to the end, though, at the same time, it denies that there is an end. It is the force of the persistent assertion of one's own existence, and a denial of death. It's the spirit of life, as the Scriptures call it, the 'river of living water,' the drying up of which is threatened in the Apocalypse." The other quotation is from Bukharin's last words to the court which condemned him to death. I do not understand how men, knowing that, in our own lifetime, another man spoke these words at such a moment, can read them and fail to be rent apart by their meanings. Yet these words are scarcely known. I would print them bold and hang them at the front of college classrooms, not to be explained as a text, but to be seen often and quietly reflected on. Bukharin, it must be remembered, is literally innocent. He is guilty only of the logic of his position, the fact that, in the given historical juncture, the position which he held in theory, might, if pushed into the realm of practice, work against the revolution. It is his uncommitted crime that he pleads guilty to. He said: "I shall now speak of myself, of the reasons for my repentance. . . . For when you ask yourself: 'If you must die, what are you dying for?'—an absolutely black vacuity suddenly rises before you with startling vividness. There was nothing to die for if one wanted to die unrepentant. . . . This, in the end, disarmed me completely and led me to bend my knees before the Party and the country. And when you ask yourself: 'Very well, suppose you do not die; suppose by some miracle you remain alive, again for what? Isolated from everybody, an enemy of the people, in an inhuman position, completely isolated from everything that constitutes the essence of life.' And at once the same reply arises. At such moments, Citizen Judges, everything personal, all personal incrustation, all rancor, pride and a number of other things, fall away, disappear. . . . I am about to finish. I am perhaps speaking for the last time in my life." Is there not a stillness in the room where you read this? That is the passing of the wings of tragedy. I was never a follower of Nikolai Bukharin;

I never admired him. About a month after he uttered those words, I broke with Communism. Some months ago, Mr. Allen Dulles said words to this effect: "There seems no reason to suppose that the Russian mind is not the equal of the American mind." That of the mind which, within 70 years, produced the greatest intellectual and spiritual conflagration of the age, only partially fixed in the names: Pushkin, Gogol, Turgeniev, Dostoievski, Tolstoi, Soloviev, Chekhov, Bakunin, Mendeleyev, Moussorgski. Perhaps Bukharin's last words should hang in Mr Dulles' office too—in the offices of both Mr. Dulleses. Thus they might muse, during the coffee break, on just what degree of handicap, power without purpose sustains in the presence of a sense of destiny.

Some hours later: Nothing could be much more preposterous than the leap from what stands above to what follows. *Es, como decimos nosotros los costarricenses, delicioso. Mi bolsista acaba de telefonearme para me urge de que compraria al punto otro "bloque" de nuestras acciones favoritas.*[36] This is, probably, such gibberish as was never spoken by man alive; tenses reeling while my speech sonar tells me that *bolsista* probably has the sense of "operator," and that the word I am groping for is more likely *corredor*. I should like to reel on, but I am afraid my Spanish is not equal to the simple facts I must discuss. This news is extremely welcome, not only on my own account, but on yours. There it is a great relief. My guess is that something, which I did not describe to you earlier, is at jelling point. If so, it is fairly tremendous, and in quite another direction from the gasifier. It may take me a day or so to confirm my surmise. That done, I shall know (insofar as one ever can) what kind of a rise to expect, and whether the smart move for you (and for the p & c part of me) is to sell fast before profit-taking gnaws off the point gains. If my *bolsista* or *corredor* has caught

[36] It is, as we Costa Ricans say, delicious. My broker has just phoned to urge me to buy at once another block of our favorite stock.

some whispers, those whispers must already have been caught, or soon will be, in that organ of black reaction, the *Wall Street Journal*. But the whispers will take a form deliberately contrived to draw attention away from the main operation, if I have correctly surmised which one, of several, it is. I am in the most extraordinary position with my man. He knows more than I will ever learn about the subject matter of his profession. But I know more about this particular deal. Thus, our conversations run to a rare surrealism; he earnestly plying me with an informed tip; I, acting the *zoquete cumplido* [complete blockhead] while trying, at the same time, to discover how much news has got about. Anyway, if all goes well, and you get out with advantage, it will be a great relief to me. It is no fun sweating out these things. One of my friends said recently: "I sweated out the Eisenhower heart attack market; and I sweated out the ileitis market; and now I am sweating out the 'hair-curling depression' market." Mr. Hoover's comments [37] did not help. "The trouble is," as some government wit observed, "Herbert Hoover is popularly believed to be an expert on depressions." I have sweated most of all to think that advice of mine, even if qualified, may have caused you to sweat. That is "counseling" with a vengeance. Now let us pray, while shouting: «*Cierra Espana!*» *Y accuerdese de que la contraseña es: Otorgar.*[38]

I'll let you know soonest what I learn. Come to think of it, suppose I should want to dump half of my p & c in a hurry. Can I simply telephone your brokerage house and order them to sell? Or must I first call you?

[37] The references are to Eisenhower's successive illnesses; to George Humphrey, Eisenhower's Secretary of the Treasury, who warned in January, 1957, of the possibility of a depression that would "curl your hair"; and to Herbert Hoover, who commented: "Mine has already been curled once, and I think I can detect the signs. I just suggest to you that, even in a partially free economy, unless we curb inflation on its way up, Old Man Economic Law will return with a full equipment of hair curlers."

[38] Santiago y Cierra España was the Spanish war cry during the Moorish occupation.

March 21, 1957

Dear Bill,

I liked Galbraith at sight.[39] This happens so seldom with me that I wondered why it happened. As I listened to him laugh, watched him study the titles of my books, watched his mind fasten on one or two points of no great importance in themselves, but somewhat as an ant, at touch, clamps on the rib of a leaf that may be littering its path, I liked him better. I decided that what I liked was a kind of energy, what kind scarcely mattered. One of our generals was once being ho-ho-hearty with the ranks, as I understand generals are sometimes, especially if newsmen are present. He asked a paratrooper: "Why do you like to do an insane thing like jumping out of airplanes?" The paratrooper answered: "I don't like to, sir. I just like to be around the kind of people who like to jump out of airplanes." I felt something like the paratrooper about Galbraith. But I felt ashamed, for your sake, that you should have found us, particularly me, in one of our more unbuttoned states. But what fun it was to see you. And what a trip it was to make. Come often though.

The big news seems to be the radio station.[40] Be he ever so oily, blessed be the night on which it was said: This Broker is conceived. At least, I hope that is how it will turn out. *De la commerce, de la commerce, et encore de la commerce.* Please feed me the facts; I promise gluttony. I will gobble prospectuses; I will, even, read annual reports. I find bizness of an appalling dullness, but so much more "viable" than anything else.

Your two statements of the opposed positions (Burnham's v. Willi's) make it all much clearer to me. The sad fact is that I haven't done all my homework on this great issue, in part because I couldn't quite grasp how great it was. I see (as I usually see in such cases) that both sides are right from the ground they stand on and an arm's length all around. This

<hr />

[39] Evan Galbraith, a classmate I drove out to Westminster for a brief visit.
[40] *National Review* had resolved to buy a radio station in order to help with the deficit.

makes me, in the mother tongue that Willi, I and the rest once spoke, a "conciliator" (*Versöhnler*), and that, should you not know, is only a shade less frightful than a "liquidator." Of course, there is a real satellite revolution. Of course, elements in the Polish government are promoting the revolution. I do not see how anyone (unless, perhaps, Fulton Lewis, Jr.) could fail to know that this is true. It doesn't need to be proved or otherwise tormented; it *is*. Here I am eye to eye with Burnham. Obviously, too, Willi is right in supposing that official Communism will try, is hourly trying, to stifle the revolution. If reports prove correct, this is having some success. It may prove a complete success, and that regardless of how clever or how apathetic the West is. Here I am eye to eye with Willi. I am not at one with him, if I understand him to be saying that the masses are always against the revolution. Crowds of 150 thousand do not demonstrate in order *not* to make a revolution. This brings us to what kind of revolution it is. Without being certain, I surmise that neither Burnham nor Willi has cared to say. Willi, I am sure, knows but would rather not know. I do not see how Burnham can fail to know. It is a socialist revolution. Where that takes us is what chiefly matters. I said to Frank when he was here with Brent: "What has opened on the plains of Hungary and Poland is the socialist phase of history." My recollection is that he answered: "Precisely." What is the argument about? What we do next? Less heat, more light. The level of discussion, the personal assaults, which I caught from Frank's talk, and which your letter particularizes, is shocking. It is not even the tone of mayhem in the Politburo. It is the tone of unenlightened kilkenny in a district cell.

Page one of this letter has lain for a week on my desk. For the sight of my earlier letter in cold type, in *NR*, stunned me into silence.[41] But it had two immediate effects which may be salutary: (1) I dumped what had been the last two pages of this letter; (2) I resolved to write no more in that vein. Of course, I

[41] I had asked permission, and received it, to publish excerpts from his letter of January 23. They appeared in *National Review* of March 30, 1957.

know that resolution will fade, and I shall drool off again into garrulity. I thought your sister's piece on Mendès-France [42] extremely good, one of the best things *NR* has done. I should like to read a piece by her on de Gaulle. More important, perhaps, would be a piece on Sartre and his current turn. This would present all kinds of difficulties, and may not, in any case, be your sister's dish. I mean she might feel that it was not. I cannot imagine a piece which, properly done, would be more *NR's* dish or more timely. It also occurred to me that your sister might be just what you need as managing editor, which (increasingly and presumptuously) I more and more feel is what *NR* needs. Someone to spare you the imperative detail work while keeping the spindles smoothly humming and the threads from knotting or breaking. There is something else that, it seems to me, is falling to *NR* almost by default. You and Brent must know just about what it is that the Senate Judiciary Committee has locked up in executive minutes. I mean in the area of the Josephine Adams testimony. It seems shocking that the press, which must know as much or a good deal more than I have heard about this matter, has nowhere had the enterprise to break this story. The answer is, of course, that it has no desire to. In *NR's* case, questions of discretion and protocol are involved. But surely it can be pointed out that this testimony exists, and pretty closely what it is, and that it is being sat on for reasons prevailingly political, to shield certain persons *de gran poder*. After that has been pointed out, if nothing happens, I should begin the editorial column each week, like this: "It is now four (5,6,7) weeks since this testimony was taken. Why is the Committee keeping it secret? Why is the press afraid to break it?" [43]

Chastened newly, I shall be terse and end here.

As ever,
Whittaker

[42] *National Review*, March 30, 1957, "The Eclipse of Mendès-France," by Priscilla L. Buckley, who became managing editor in 1959.
[43] Josephine Adams, it transpired, was used by FDR when he wanted to communicate directly with the Communist Party U.S.A.

Untersed already:

Of course, a piece on Sartre, if it was to have any ring, could not begin with the *grito* [cry] (or even the premise) that Sartre is just a damned old existentialist and hence. Rather, it must begin with some sense that Sartre is an existentialist because. . . . He may also be a large part fraud (of a high grade) as I suspect he is. But, then, I have never been able to get into *l'Être et le Néant,* and that always tends to make us resentful.

April 16, 1957

Dear Bill,

In prospect, this looks like one of those all over the lot letters, so that where to begin is defeat to begin with. I had better begin with the rising sun, which had risen pretty high when certain bustlings of my also risen wife compelled me, most unwillingly, to open my eyes and realize (what I had known slumbrously all along)—that this was the morning when we loaded lambs. That is, we load them to ship (gruesomely) for the "Easter market". It is also a dirty and exhausting job and requires three people: Esther to tend the tail-gate of the truck (i.e. stand and swing the gate a little as each victim is heaved in and to see that none of the blatting captives escapes); Mr. Pennington to catch, haul and weigh; I to pick the victims (I have a shrewd eye for weights) and sometimes to catch (which I have learned to do with little waste of energy by being quiet instead of aggressive) and generally to lend a hand. Every year, Mr. P. and I have the same conversation:—I: "The lambs are ready to cull"; Mr. P.: "Not more than three will make weight." The race is always to make that Easter market; and this year, it turned out, there were not three but 26. I doubt that sheep are any more innocent than anything else in nature, but, they are, if you have a turn that way, singularly appealing. "Little lamb, who made thee?" I kept thinking as we grabbed them up for the abattoir. Those who suppose that farming is an idyllic business should learn that it is blood, sweat, tears, accidents, sudden, and sometimes lingering, death. This will defeat only those who do not know that life is rooted in horror as every field of springing grain is dunged with filth and death. We have learned wonderfully how to upholster sacrifice and insulate ourselves against its reality. I am not sure that we are the better for it. Not that much is gained by an unrelieved concentration on this side of things. Yet those who have lived in these terms cannot help but feel, without feeling (I think) any particular need to justify or explain their feeling, that those who have not lived into this reality have, in some telling way, not lived. No judgment is involved except in extremely raw and simple terms—what the peasant knows, what he feels to be a difference which he does not analyze, when he looks at you. What those Poles and Hungarians (this is what I have been zeroing toward) feel when they look at us. Are they better than we, man for man? On what grounds? But they are different. Yes, they are different. They are, some 800 million souls from the Elbe to the China Sea, different from us; and they stand looking at us from the fastness of that difference which is rooted in a simpler experience of sweat, blood, filth, death. Why should this seem a strength since no specific merit seems indicated? Yet, there is little doubt that they feel it to be a strength; and so do we, uneasily. Something like this is what I have long been trying to make concrete. It is more elusive than doomed lambs; and cannot be caught in pens so primitive that we tie them together with baling twine, but so baffling to the victims that for them they mean certain death.

Coming from this scene and these thoughts (if they can be called thought), we passed the mail box and found your letter. It was a spacious refuge. Especially, I liked your father's bringing informal order into the grounds around him. The South has lured me all my life; and yet, once in it, I always feel something broodingly sinister. I am not sure that that is not a secret of the lure, which those who truly feel it, know though they see no reason to confess it. That vegetation, crepe myrtle and bull-bay magnolia, is surely no better than ours, plant for plant. Yet we feel some special attraction. This farm is on an outermost line where such things can, with a little care, be made to grow. So one of the first things we did on coming here was to set bull-bay and crepe myrtle. One of the hardest wrenches, in leaving the old place, was to leave the magnolia which we had coaxed from a shrub to a tree twice our height—one of the finest hereabouts. When there were rumors, during the Hiss Case, that I was fleeing to Canada, Margaret Reese laughed and said: "I knew they couldn't be true because I knew Whittaker would never leave that magnolia." Enough of this.

I find the dropping Hooper rating worrisome.[1] Your gloss of the phonograph recording also has a worrisome sound.[1] Close attention, possibly quick action, seems to be in order. I cannot supply even a hit-or-miss guess about the problem without knowing more detail. Here something else enters, fortuitously. Bear with some background. I have deliberately kept from adverting to Alger and his book.[2] I have made no effort to find out what is in the book. But for some time the press has been at me to review it; NBC has asked me to be interviewed about it. To all I have said no. Alger's tactic is to make noise and to let the press, in pursuit of copy, increase the din by forcing me to participate. So I mustn't— not so long as I can avoid it. I cannot comment while the book is spot news without playing Alger's game. Therefore, I plan to vanish, or try to, while the story is fresh—a matter of four or five days, I should think. Afterwards, I can re-emerge and say whatever seems to need saying (if anything). But I trust that, by then, the news will be a little stale. Just how I shall flit doesn't matter. I don't know quite when, either, since I still don't know quite when Alger is publishing. If you are still of a mind, or in a position, to have us in for a day or so, perhaps this is the moment. Esther will be with me, of course. And, of course, too, strict secrecy is necessary in advance. No one in your office should know; no one anywhere. If this is inconvenient for any reason, please do not hesitate to say so. If it is possible, we shall have a better opportunity than letters to discuss a number of things, including the radio matter.[3] Best procedure from my side would seem to be to

---

[1] I don't recall to what this referred. Ed.

[2] Alger Hiss's book, *In the Court of Public Opinion,* had just been published.

[3] The reference was to my plan to purchase a profitable radio station in an effort to meet *National Review's* deficit.

telephone you from somewhere not too far from your home. I seem not to have your home telephone number. Will you send it? Esther is dreadfully afraid that I shall not be up to such a trip. I think I shall be. In the last month, I seem to feel better than for a long time. It is true that I have no reserves of strength and tire unbelievably fast. Still, I think we shall make it. I should make it clear: I have alternative plans, one including a visit with you, one without. If you cannot have us, it will not wrench my plans at all. If you can, it will put a pleasure at the end of necessity. So perhaps you will be able to tell me again, in the same setting, what was my conversation stopper about Conservatism. For I have forgotten.[4] I am, of course, extremely interested in the point and a half drop in Canada Southern.[5] Why should it drop? We can discuss that, too. About your question in Spanish: *Un millon de gracias. Pero eso si que es imposible. Solo debes entender como (y cuanto) soy grato.* [A million thanks. But that's impossible. You should know only how grateful I am.][6]

Your letter to the duck men is amusing, and I hope that it will close out the nuisance, which is too much like some that I find myself gratuitously meshed in for me to take it for its fun. John Cort. He once interviewed me for a piece he was doing for *The Sign* about *Time* Inc. If he had been just a little more sensitive, a little more human, a little less blue-printed about life, he might have had an important story. For it was not long before the Hiss business broke. John's brother, Dave Cort, was a classmate of mine; and was on *Life* while I was at *Time*. So we have known each other, in a way, for about 30 years. I always liked Dave; and he gave me a feeling that he liked me. I felt that we were always about to begin the conversation that would make us friends. Neither of us ever began it. Instead, we always studied each other through that cellophane wall. I don't know what's become of Dave.[7] This leads,

[4] So have I. Ed.

[5] Canada Southern, Inc., an oil exploration company founded by my father, in which WC had made a minor investment.

[6] Letters to Chambers from WFB are not extant. Ed.

[7] David Cort wrote a scandalously hostile obituary of WC for Columbia's Class of 1924 Newsletter in 1961. It elicited outraged letters from several Columbia University figures, including Lionel Trilling and Herbert Solow.

naturally, to Willi. The mail that brought your letter brought the current *NR* with Willi's piece[8] on Cardinal Wyszynscki (I suppose I've spelled it wrong).[9] It raises the perennial question: Why should a man who can write so excellent a piece, so clear, readable, informative in a quarter where information is scarce—why should he not give himself to this kind of thing? Why should he want to stamp around a field where those who are at home in it find it difficult to take him seriously?[10] Of course, Willi and I are as wide apart about the Cardinal as about many other things. I have been a Wyszinscki man ab initio. I have argued that his course was right because no other course was possible. I am afraid that I have deeply disappointed (perhaps even estranged) certain Catholic friends by my unbudgeability on this point. I point, in a way that Frank Meyer likes to call "existential", at contrasting Poland and Hungary, and the contrasting attitudes of their Cardinal's. No one who has not suffered so much may judge Cardinal Mindszenty, even if he were stupid enough to incline to. But contrasting policy results can be appreciated; I hold that the contrast favors the results in Poland. Early in the crisis, I took part in a private group discussion on these contrasting policies; a discussion that under its formal courtesy constantly threatened to flare, in part, I believe, because one faction was astonished to find me pro-Wyszynscki, and took it as a defection. It is nothing of the kind. With the knife at your throat (the situation of the Poles and of their Cardinal), there are only two choices: to maneuver, *knowing fully the chances of failure,* but remembering that Hope is one of the Virtues; or to hold your neck still to the knife in the name of martyrdom. But just here is the crux. Cardinal Mindszenty is not a martyr; he is a man who has suffered horrifyingly. He would be a martyr only if he walked out of the American Legation and said: "I have come to be with the Hungarians in their death." No doubt, there are strong reasons in religion, as well as in common sense, why Cardinal Mindszenty should not do this. So we are not talking about the Church Triumphant. We are talking about the

---

[8] "That Polish Cardinal," *National Review,* April 20, 1957.
[9] Wyszynski.
[10] Willi Schlamm also wrote a fortnightly column for NR on the arts.

Church in this world, the world of Warsaw and of Budapest whose streets are of a drabness that squeezes the blood from the heart. In that sad light, the figure of the Polish Cardinal is a figure of hope. We are back where I began this letter, in the capturing pens, in sweat, blood, filth, death. I say: we know nothing about these things. I say that what makes us all sick with a sickness we cannot diagnose, is that, in the current crisis, the West has gained the world (or thinks it has), but has lost its own soul. I say: that the Poles and the Hungarians have lost the world (or whatever makes it bearable—they live in Hell), but they have gained their own souls. The equations of Power (in terms of technological and supersonic and electronic might) are all in favor of the West. Was there ever a time when they weren't? What price, Power without purpose? Dulles mouthing moralities while on the streets of Budapest children patrolled the shattered house-fronts, with slung rifle and tormented faces. I say those children, whatever their politics, will have grown to men while Dulles and his tribe lie howling. Let us not forget: "What all mankind lay groaning in the dust, one Greek man arose and paced far out upon the flaming walls of the world—*processit longé flamantia moenia mundi.*"[11] It is on that horizon that Cardinal Wyszynscki can alone be seen or his meaning known. That is why I keep beside him. That is why Gomulka keeps beside him and he beside Gomulka. In each other they recognize men; they are scarce enough. How lonely these two men must be. Was ever such loneliness endured, and not made less by the knowledge, clear to both, that, under necessity, Gomulka may destroy the Cardinal before he is destroyed himself. But these men at least acted: "they stayed and earth's foundations stay"—at least for the moment of their act. I think we must see this clearly.

But let Galbraith[12] rescue us from ending on such an outburst. Of course, he was a wrestler. So was I. I should have recognized several signs at sight. Wrestlers (I mean amateurs, of course) are a special breed. They lack almost wholly the unpleasant killer

[11] Lucretius, *De Rerum Natura*, Book I.
[12] Evan Galbraith, see above, page 166. (in old edition)

strain that boxers seem to have to have. Yet they are combat men. And curiously chivalrous. The sport is so violent—each man knows every minute that, even inadvertently, he is capable of seriously injuring his opponent—that an odd dialectics results; so wrestlers are, as a group, probably the most courteous of sportsmen. They have the soldier's feeling of shared danger for the enemy. I can remember only two in my experience who lacked it: one who was so good that he had got conceited; the other who was not good enough to know how dangerous he was.* I remember them because both managed to injure me. I almost never confess it, but at college I must have spent almost half my time in the gymnasium or trotting in a sweat-suit around Grant's Tomb. How very funny to think of; and how very far away. Time, I think, to shower.

As always,
Whittaker

* Incongruously, but rather suitably, his name was: Faust Marseglia.

While John Chambers was home for spring vac, a Freedom Conference was impounded at Kenyon. Peter Viereck and Russell Kirk descended, like sheep on the fold, where some earnest students had given up their recess to lie, like wolves, in wait for them. A letter from John came in the same mail with yours. An excerpt: "Those who stayed for the Freedom Conference gave me the lowdown. It rained all week and everybody drank too much. I questioned Detlev (one of John's cronies and Kenyon's more promising geniuses: Christ Church next year: Edit) about Peter Viereck. I guess you were right. 'Oh, he's just crazy,' was the natural reply. Russell Kirk was so nice to everyone that all those who stayed just to insult him were disappointed and couldn't even argue with him." I think that is quite a tribute to Kirk.

"I guess you were right" refers to a conversation John and I chanced to have about Viereck. I explained that, in German, Viereck means a Square (Vier-Four; Eck-Corner). Oddly, Viereck's father was a friend of my father's. So, early in life, I was repeatedly tempted to try to read an autographed book of the elder Viereck's verse. It was called: *The House Of The Vampire*, and had on the cover a draped skeletal figure (prevailingly female), draining a glass of champagne (I suppose). But the contents of the book did not live up to the cover; and I never got through.

April 22, 1957

Dear Bill,

The wonder to me is that you did not throw the telephone at me. I mean when I reacted with blank astonishment to the news of what your friend had done for me in the matter of calls. I can only plead: how can anyone feel anything but blank and somewhat limp? So far as I know, nobody has ever done such a thing for me in my life. The more I think of it, the more I am staggered. Bear with me while I hold on to something: I will get myself in hand in a moment. First step is to laugh a while at myself—a long while; for this will be funny forever. Happily, it is good clean fun. But how could he take such a risk? I believe *I* knew; you had only my unsupported judgment to go on, and at the very moment that I was self-disclosed naïve. Now I will bow my head—not in any silly, idle shame, but because, as I hope you will understand, am sure you, just you, will understand, there are things that cannot be said. And all the while I was worrying because (as I supposed) a word from me had led you into buying calls for yourself at the very moment when P & R started to slide down. I am going to have to live with a little interior earthquake today and for a good many days to come. I am going to have to re-examine a number of conclusions, and even premises. You have upset history. We are told that while there are seven just men in a city, it cannot be destroyed. You mean that, in the West, there are.... I shall have a great deal to think about as I drive northward. I think I had better be very silent, beginning here.[44]

As always,
Whittaker

I wrote the above directly after our Monday morning telephone conversation. In it, a pretty strong riptide is running. But I send it along for what a spontaneous burst is worth. Since then, a day and a night have passed; another day is even now graying the sky above the hill. I was on the point of writing, yesterday: "Now *Cold Friday* cannot be written." All that I have been trying to do in the past year can be summed up as: trying to make it so that *Cold Friday* need not be written. I wished to force no meanings, to leave myself open to all possible meanings, even those that appeared to run counter to my experience and judgment. In this, too, I see that I have been something of the child, though I do not wish it otherwise. To be in part a child, even when nearing 60, is no great mischance, especially if one is so in part only. The mischief would be not to see it steadily. On the practical side (you must bear with me generously in this, too, which touches me so closely), I shall take steps at once to make good what your friend has done for me. They cannot, I am afraid, be completed before the settlement is made for the sale of our old house; and that is scheduled for July, at latest. There is, of course, the obvious way of selling the calls at once; and, if you need me to do this, you must unfailingly tell me so that I can do it. My preference, and my larger plan, was to buy the shares and hold them. But this has no priority now and, indeed, no justification. Mean-

---

[44] As it happened, Chambers didn't profit from the short-term investment in P & R calls. The stock sold in February, 1957, at approximately 26; in April (at the end of the 90-day calls) at approximately 29; in July (at the end of the 180-day calls) at approximately 28. In February, 1958, P & R was at approximately 30; in February, 1959, it fluctuated between 106 and 75. In February, 1960, it was at approximately 78; in February, 1961, a few months before Chambers' death, at approximately 112. The dollar values are given as if the stock had not split.

while, I believe I can make repayment in three parts of which the last should fall in July—provided always that his own need is not urgent. I think this sounds cold-blooded; but I think, too, that you will understand that it is not, that it is only a necessity so that he should not suffer a stringency, or only as briefly as possible, in consequence of your goodness. I confess it still leaves me, organically, a little stunned, and not a little, either; though no more than a stupefaction that I should have failed to grasp at once what your friend had done. How good it is to know that, in this world, he could have done it. I suppose you know that I wanted the shares for John and Ellen, particularly for John, who has the world to face on his own. I did not want them for myself or even for Esther, who is inseparable from myself. Cold Friday is the name of a hill field on this farm, so marked on the title map. It is the hill that rises directly from the little pond. The book begins with an epigraph from Aeschylus: Power (to his companion, Force, and to their prisoner, Prometheus): "We have come to the last path of the earth, in the Scythian country, in the untrodden solitude." I must get on with this book.

May 9?, 1957

Dear Bill,

For several reasons, I must write you though this is, also for several reasons, a poor time. I had to go to bed yesterday; there was no choice. This morning, I am, to put it as flatly as possible, right pokey. No doubt, this is the result of accumulated fatigue and physical excitements. It is also, I think, a direct reaction to the Hiss putsch, which is beginning to seem to me like the Hundred Years' War. I do not know whether, as Nora [Mrs. Ralph de Toledano] assured me last Tuesday, the gentleman's razzia [45] is a flop. Until then, I inclined to think so too. But, at that point, watching developments from afar, I began

[45] His book *In the Court of Public Opinion*.

to wonder. My wonder is increasing. Perhaps I am just between battles, as writers are said to be between books. I know enough about the psychology of war to allow for its distortions; but to allow for is not necessarily to be able to get one's self free of, at the same time. I seem to see that AH has retained a great part of his original base in the community. He is still able to make them work for him, to make the press play his game, not only in the simple course of selling news, but a little more than that; to make the politicians and the political-minded on his general side of the spectrum long to help him, even though they find it impolitic to do so openly. His strength is not what it was. But that it exists at all is stunning. There he sits, and every time that, in the name of truth, he asserts his innocence, he strikes at truth, utters a slander against me, and compounds his guilt of several orders. Yet, in the name of truth and justice, others support and abet him. It is this outrageous performance, this public violation, in full spotlight, of what the West has meant by truth and honor, which is permitted and abetted in the name of truth and honor,—it is this which squirts into my morale a little jet of paralyzing poison. To counteract it, I must bring superhuman—courage is not the right word; steadiness somehow seems more accurate. For the acceptance of the West of this performance, the West's toleration of it, tends to sweep me each time toward despair. How can any community in which toleration and support of Hiss is each time automatic, irrepressible, predictable—how can such a community find the force and virtue (it comes to that) to save itself in greater matters? Such a community is profoundly morbid, in the pathological sense, and precisely at the point where its corruption is mortal to all the rest—the point of intellection and integrity of mind? The fact that a majority, presumably, now believes (with many degrees of qualification, as Burnham pointed out) that Hiss is guilty, does not change the fact that so large and influential a minority does not. Mere numbers is nothing; the size of the body is not at all in point when the mind corrupts; and no lunatic is more frightening, and perhaps dangerous, than the one in whom a deep-seated madness is largely masked by an appearance of what we call normality. It is the American mind that is unsettled with respect to Hiss. It is the hopelessness of counteracting what seems so deeply incurable that fills me and sweeps me to despair. For, sooner or later, we have to face it: why try? I am not Don Quixote, have no talent at all in that way. If the West cannot use the Hiss Case to its own advantage, the Hiss forces will use the case against the West; a kind of historical law of opposite and equal reactions seems to be in play. On the other hand, I never believed that the West could make use of the Hiss Case. My business was only to give it an eleventh-hour opportunity to do so on the outside chance that it might. So I may not complain. I must only try to suppose that, in ways beyond my sight or range of understanding, and along lines that have little to do with me as an individual man, good still works against an evil so insidious. But I am not merely temperamentally impatient of the "all things work together for good" hypothesis. My reason, in the profoundest, most organic sense, is outraged when I am asked to believe that the Nazi massacre of the Warsaw ghetto or the Communist massacre in the Katyn Forest are necessary parts of a process of horrors working together for good. I see that one might believe this on Olympus, that is, quite above the agony. I do not see how the Jews in Warsaw or the Polish officers in the Forest could have believed it; or, if they could have believed, could have cared. It is this problem that the Hiss Case confronts me with at every turn; and, of course, that problem is vastly more important than any turn of the Case. That is why I wrote you once that life is rooted in horror. Tell me that this is not true, but tell me in terms of reality; but me no buts. Tell *us;* for it is this the world is waiting to be told, and this is more important to it than any revolution or other spasm. If it cannot be convinced of this, it will believe nothing though it preserves all the forms and conventions of belief. No, I think that is not accurate; I think it will continue to believe something. But it will insist that that something conform to reality, and where it visibly does not, it will suspect fraud or a failure of mind, even if it chooses to keep its suspicions to itself. Milosz chose to bring his thoughts and recollections of the Warsaw ghetto massacre to one burning point: the image of a young woman, who did not wish to die, trying to outrun the murderers who steadily gained on her while she cried: "No! No! No!" He chose to make a single impression of the Warsaw uprising define his notion of reality in our time: it was the sight of the paving, tilting on edge, row by row, under the force of firepower. Truth in our time must partake of this bleakly delimiting reality if it is to be true for us. What do the fifteen-year-olds of Budapest believe is truth? What does Mr. Knopf,[46] who is among the sponsors of Hungarian Relief? Every path leads to Cold Friday. I never meant to get into this. I began simply to show you why this was a poor morning for me to write letters. Now you see why.

As we rolled away from Wallack's Point, so grateful and mindful of your kindness, my wife said: "We imposed heavily on them (you and your wife). We cannot help it. We are heavy people." It does not help much to explore deeply just what she meant by "heavy," or even to believe that she is wholly right; but I am afraid that there is a truth in it. In the 1920's, it was often asked of anyone who had fallen under the favorable scrutiny of the CP: *"Ist er ein ernster Mensch?"*—Is he an ernster man? The German *ernst* lacks the priggish overtone of "earnest," but means more than our "serious." In this sense, I would say that "heavy" is a fair approximation. At our jolliest, I am afraid that we retain this heaviness of mood. And what survivals, what dated saurians, it marks us for. It is unfair of us to drag our Mesozoic into *la vida de todos los días* [everyday life]. But what a deliverance, among much else, you and your wife were for us. Esther is a touchstone (or I think she is); and I was impressed by the directness with which your wife reacted to her—the more so since Esther was visibly and (to me) frighteningly weary; and seldom less like herself. I thought she was

[46] Publisher of Hiss's book.

covering up one of her heart attacks, but she says not. Esther is as much of a saint as anybody can afford to be and still remain on the human side of the frontier. She is all selfless love and forgiveness, and, in our affairs, has only the most ungrateful (and, in many ways, the most important) part; the part of abiding, uncomplainingly, by the decisions which she does not make, and, left to herself, never would. Both of us feel more and more, tend more and more, to be closed in by a feeling that we belong to an age that is ended, but, for us, not literally enough. We belong to the revolutionary generation of the First World War, the Great War, as its contemporaries used to call it. Both of us grew up on Frans Masereel's "Die Passion eines Menschens"; Barbusse's *Le Couteau Entre les Dents;* Maria Uhden's painting; Toller's *Die Wandlung*. On what? people ask. It clears up nothing at all to remind them that Maria Uhden's husband was commissar of something (education, I think) in the Bavarian Soviet Republic, or that, after the defeat, he was committed to an asylum about which he wrote a very funny book (*Wir Sind Gefangen—*We Are the Captives) of which I remember chiefly that one of the inmates used to mount a scale every day, shake his head and say resignedly: "I've lost another seven hundred and fifty pounds." (Come to think of it, Knopf published the American version of *Wir Sind Gefangen,* too.) Toller's *Wandlung* (The Transformation) was the play in which Death (in the uniform of an officer of the German General Staff) cries: *"Marsch!"* and the dead of the great war rise from their graves and, shouldering their grave crosses like rifles, execute a military drill. Like all Toller's plays of that period, it was dated from: "The Fortress-Prison of Niederschönenfeld, in the century of the great social wars." (There is an echo of this at the close of the Foreword to *Witness;* but no one else knew what it is an echo of.) Toller spent 15 or 20 years at Niederschönenfeld for being Commissar for War in the Bavarian Soviet. After his release he raced Hitler to a haven in New York. There he hanged himself. I remember it vividly because, shortly before, I had met his wife at a publisher's party, one of the few I have ever attended. She was wearing a jacket of cloth of gold and was encircled by the happy pups of the triumphant Left, from which I was in flight. No, Esther and I are Gerontion; not good company this side of Styx. This was behind my desire to see Max [Eastman]; he is Gerontion too. It is not our present viewpoint, but our past, that we have in common. All this is a little context for our "heaviness." We shall long remember here your goodness and patience with us; the beauty and peace of your home and its life; the exhilaration, and the other kind of peace, of the boat on the windless Sound.

We got back to find that we had missed the AP by a scant hour.[47] I went at once to the pond. The apples were in bloom and so were 30 or more dogwoods, self-seeded on the hills. Senator McCarthy [48] was much on my mind; and it seemed to me the strangest chance that I should be seeing these things, and that he could not; that I had survived *him.* It is incongruous. I also felt that there is really no other ending for these ends. It was in that spirit that I tried to write about him. It won't work. Any tribute that shirks an appreciation also shirks truth. Each time, I kept running against the episode of Chip Bohlen, which estranged the Senator and me. Leave it out, and there is a gaping hole. Put it in, however tactfully, and there is a shin-barker. I have told only one other person all that took place between us that night; and that is just as well; for the rest was as bad as the Bohlen business, which was outrageous. If you do not say so, others have a right to ask: "Don't you know outrage when you see it?" If you do say so, they can ask: "Why was such a man a hero?" In the end, it comes down to a simple sentimentality: this man and I fought in the same wars in which he suffered greatly. But he was not my leader. For the sake of the war, I had publicly to say, in effect, that he was trying to use me to perpetrate a fraud on Bohlen. What is left of tribute then? I could not follow him

[47] *I.e.,* a reporter had come by.
[48] Who had died on the day that WC was with us in Connecticut.

living; I could only pity him. Pity of that kind is condemnation of the dead; and silence is more fitting. The Senator never understood Communism or the war on Communism. Hence he never evolved a strategy, but only a tactic which consisted exclusively in the impulse: Attack. That could never be enough, could end only as it did, or in some similar way. I wish it were not so. Trying to write about it made me realize, more acutely than I had let myself do before, how sadly true it is.

This should be thrown in the trash basket. But I promised to mail it, and hence—

Several things in the current *NR* seemed to me uncommonly good. For one, the obit about Roy Campbell; very well done, and better, more effective than using his children's tale. Then the long editorial on the rise of Senator Knowland. I liked it particularly because it notes an emergence without fully embracing it. There will be time for an embrace. More fruitful, editorially, it seems to me, is to chart the emergence and explain the forces in play. The closing reference to Nixon, reminding readers that he is there, is adversary, and yet not bearing down at all, seemed to me admirably done. I claim nearly always to be wrong about American politics. But, like everybody else, I like to make my guess. As of this moment, my guess would be that, if there is no marked economic bust before 1960 (I find it difficult to believe that there will not be), then the Vice President should have a favoring wind. I question whether Americans ever (or only in extreme instances) vote foreign policy. So, they should vote for domestic interests in 1960. But the Vice President also has the chance, an exceptional one, of identifying domestic affairs with foreign policy, following a logic which, I understand, the President is about to stump for on TV. The Right is saying he will get a shocking setback. The Right may be right. I happen not to think so, for, despite my wrongness in guessing the voters' mind (if that is the word), I think it is harder to fool little girls than it used to be. I think that the President will get, substantially, what he wants. As always, I shall find the chief fun in seeing how wrong

I could be. If the President wins, that should be the best kind of victory for Nixon later on. If economic trouble comes, I should guess that it will be neither Nixon nor Knowland, but, more likely, John Kennedy of Massachusetts. Senator Kennedy, I mean; perhaps he isn't John. I may change most of this guess a month hence.

That is a remarkable piece by Frederick D. Wilhelmsen.[49] What feeling and, I must note as practitioner, what writing pace. Where has he been all this time? Or is it just that, as usual, I have not been where I should? But I believe that he is talking, extremely well, about a manifestation, an occasion, rather than a cause. Hungary merely focuses a feeling against Americans that goes much deeper and farther, and is much older. What the rest of the world misses in Americans is something a little different. It misses in them the tragic sense of life. This is much more sundering than any of its manifestations, taken apart. Gottfried Knosperl Rosenbaum (R. Jarrell's character) thought that what was good, but also troubling, about Americans was that they had tried to do something which perhaps cannot be done. They had written into their first charter (though Dr. Rosenbaum does not allude to this specifically) that phrase about the pursuit of happiness. How can the rest of the world look, without wonder and a certain pity, at a nation who believes that one of man's inalienable *rights* is the pursuit of happiness? Tom Matthews[50] told me last year about coming on a magnificent Spanish beggar woman, *vestida de negro, enlutada* [dressed in black, mourning], dirty, wretched, but speaking impassionedly to several others. Tom asked what she was saying and was told: "She is talking to them about the evil of life." The pursuit of happiness, the evil of life. How can peoples who have as a catchphrase: *"No hay remedio"* [There is nothing to be done about it], help seeing [Americans] as, to some degree, children? We think they are looking at our power, wealth, ease, and envying them, and we are right about

<hr/>

49 "The Bankruptcy of American Optimism," *National Review*, May 11, 1957.
50 T. S. Matthews, managing editor of *Time* when Chambers was senior editor.

that. But they are also looking at our minds, our souls, and these baffle them, and their bafflement baffles us. The celebrated difference between East and West, which shall never meet, was Hollywood stuff to the difference between the rest of the world and the Americans. Practicing the pursuit of happiness, we are the mysterious West. So, I thought I noticed that it was with a certain relish that Burnham observed that Europe is finished. Poor Willi, I thought. Poor Europe. Poor Americans too.

As always, and much too much so,
Whittaker

National Review *did not treat the publication of Alger Hiss's book as the occasion for a book review, but as an opportunity to evaluate a political operation. The magazine published (May 25, 1957) comments on the book's appearance from: James Burnham, Anthony Bouscaren, Jay Lovestone, Hede Massing, J. B. Matthews, Frank Meyer, Herbert Philbrick, Richard Rovere, Ralph de Toledano, and Bertram Wolfe.*

May 17?, 1957

Dear Bill,

I have just added up what others have told me about the public treatment of Alger's book, added in some spot impressions of my own, and come out with this conclusion: "The war is over." Our tactic of silence and wait for the whites of their eyes was the right one. Anything else would have played their forfeit game fantastically. We feared (as it was right to do) that this might be a Battle of the Bulge. It was only the skirmish at Turtle Crik, one of those forlorn last follies of the end of the War between the States. There was the tattered leader, perhaps a little schizoid by now and for the nonce, and a following gaggle of loyal lint-heads, barefoot and each with an eye to ducking into the bushes and heading for mammy, the cabin, beaten biscuit and to get me a bear, come harvest. The war is over. But wars never end on the dotted line. They fester. So you have pockets of supuration like Roscoe Drummond, and gestures such as that of Messrs. Cook, Ernst and Daniels. It is a touching ballet of faith to the bitter end (and that is what they mean it to be; for these rats are shrewd). But it is also touched with vaudeville. That trio will not dance for long because they know that the longer they dance, the farther they dance away from reality, and the more clearly they must be seen for what they are (and we have always known them essentially to be)—figures of fun. Was anything more preposterous ever heard than a *lawyer* of Ernst's standing (pretenses, at least), saying, in a matter of this importance, that Alger's book had convinced him of Alger's innocence though he had not troubled to read the troublesome transcripts of what really happened? It is as if an eminent jurist had said: "I have read Bruno Hauptman's book and it has convinced me of his innocence. I am sure he did not kidnap the Lindbergh baby though I have not read any of the transcripts which report the circumstances of the case." This is in no sense an exaggeration; it is simple paraphrase. Alger charged. The old guard would have liked to run interference for him. But he never got halfway up the hill; and you can't run interference for a man whose rifle, which he presents as the latest thing in weapons, is twisted, and whose ammo is sopping wet. What we are witnessing is not support. It is the beginning of the desertions, which must be carried out under various face-saving protestations. The explanations have begun. I understand that the line will be given in next week's *New Leader* by Prof. Hays (is it?) of Columbia, who will explain that the enemies of Hiss were the enemies of the New Deal and progress, at which they shot through him. Therefore, the fight for Hiss was a holy war for humanity, but now. . . . It is, in one of Jim Agee's characteristically devastating line, "The backside hindsight of an upside-down parrot." But it it is true enough* and it is the way out for these birds. All of them will be parroting it ere sundown. (If I remember rightly, it is the line of the ACCF, formulated among the first, in *Commentary*, by Leslie Fiedler, with a hot-dog wrapped in the flag in one hand, and a clasp-knife in the other.) I first became sure of what Alger had done to himself when I saw what the Baltimore Sun had done to him. I did not read the piece, which was not long, I think. But I saw the accompanying picture of him. It was that laughing jackass shot which looks as much like Hiss as he looks like a drooling idiot. It must be remembered that Baltimore is Alger's home town and the *Sun* one of his most venemous supporters. This could not conceivably have happened by chance. They are giving him the picture treatment once reserved for me. I know why. His Baltimore friends really believed in his innocence (believed even after their stirring subconscious told them it could not be so). Now there is the seeping sense that he betrayed their trust in him. Willi's certified gentlemen never forgive that. "He has made us look like fools." Nothing is more vengeful than an oligarchy of which it has been publicly shown that they are men, like any others, dressed in a certain kind of clothes, and who, even as we, must use the bathroom daily. Nothing is more unforgivable by the mystifiers than the destruction of a mystique. Where the mystifiers have collaborated in the revelation, their anger knows no bounds. I would guess that, except for the fever-swamps of the Left-wing magazines, this story, as news, will be dead in another week; and all hands will be joined to lower it into an unquiet grave, whatever deflecting gestures the deed is done with.

* as far as the Liberals go.

Therefore (if I may presume) I believe that NR should handle it this way. A review of the press treatment. I believe (I rather beg) that it should carry this title: The Rats Leave The Sinking Ship. There are times when a cliche doubles the fire-power of anything short of a flash of genius. ("I like the way he writes," a Bureau agent once said to me, quoting somebody's worm-eaten chestnut, "It's so colorful.") The rats leave the sinking ship. This is very sensible of the rats (rats are nothing if not sensible). And how many of them there are! And how desperately they stayed by the ship until, in fact, it was the skipper himself who convinced them that the watertight bulkheads had been stove in, and the moment had come to swim for it. Now they are running up and down among the flotsam of the beach, snarling, squeaking, gnawing flecks of tar out of their fur ("So *adhesive,* my dear!"), and looking around for a new berth. They'll find one, too, preferably one flying the Jolly Roger. Of course, it would never do to admit that they are deserting; that would imply that they could have been mistaken. Some even loved the old hulk and, no doubt, find it hard to believe that even planks must part. So long as one board is afloat, Mrs. Roosevelt, for example, will probably cling to it (Adlai will be pushing one end, but only his nose will show above the water). But Mrs. Roosevelt is only a hybrid rat; she is crossed with goopher. The big act is to scuttle away, letting one's angrily twitching whiskers, cover the retreat. This, I believe, is NR's line. It should be easy to support it with illustrations. But no cries of alarm, such as I myself uttered briefly a few days back. Just a jolly good sneer at the spectacle wrought by Alger himself. That and a glance at the swarm of rats and the mischief they kept up for nine years over this business, which was simply a pursuance, in other forms, of the mischief they managed for years before that. "Vot a bunch," as Gottfried Knosperl Rosenbaum observed.

Ray Moley did an extremely effective job in the current *Newsweek.* The body (Alger) is strapped in place; the guillotine tripped. It drops; the body rebounds; the head drops into the trap and rolls into the basket. Q.E.D. Moley ends by saying something like this. "Who does Alger Hiss think he is? A second-rate bureaucrat who edged close to a sick and dying President. The Hiss Case had little to do with little Alger Hiss but with the effort of Anglo-Saxon justice, the noblest creation of mankind, to see that an accused man had his day in court." Strictly between us, this misses most of the point. I don't know by what standards a former bureaucrat grades bureaucrats. I should have thought that Alger was in the first rank. More important, he was a towering revolutionary figure. He came within an eyelash of subverting Anglo-Saxon justice, that noblest creation of the human mind. I hope I am not too vainglorious in supposing that I was a large part of that eyelash. Still, Moley makes an almost ideal vantage-point to tee off from. No one, to my knowledge, has put it so succinctly. I do not wish to sound exultant. Mankind is seldom meaner than in victory. But it has been a terrible fight; and I believe that, for all practical purposes, it is over. Hiss was convinced even his enemies that his case is preposterous, his guilt not to be gainsaid. Their problem is to get out from under without seeming to do so. You are watching their twists and turns.

You understand very well what the ninth wave had done to Esther and me. There was a point (1948 to 1950) when I meant to die for the West and believed that, one way or another, I should probably have to. I believed that nothing less could save the West than one man's willingness to make himself a sacrifice. Put aside all Christian thinking and feeling. This was the most primitive of religious feelings—human sacrifice so that the cattle may breed, the grain fields yield harvest. It had to be topped by my attempt to destroy myself, so that, having disclosed the conspiracy, I should give the conspirators, as human beings, the chance to live on unharmed by me. That failed; I guess it all failed. Moreover, I never supposed that it could succeed, or the West be saved. But, given my past, I had to make this payment. I had to try to manifest, in its most primitive form, the religious force that made the West the West, if there was anything there at all. So far as I can see, the revolution, the chief fact of our time—and its prevailing form, Communism—produced in the U.S. two men, and only two: Alger and myself. Fate (as if it had been reading Thomas Hardy) brought us together. He was equal to becoming the Communist archetype; I the other. It is largely over now. Is it strange if I think in shadier hours: "It was all for nothing?" Hence my feeling, as I told you with respect to Senator McCarthy, that these ends can have no other endings. For, in a sense, he took up from me and carried on the development to its logical end. It was no good. He knew what it was all about. "Alger Hisses come a dime a dozen," he once wrote, "a Whittaker Chambers is born once in a hundred years." But he did not know what to do with it; in a way, he could do no more. He could not be greater than the forces he manifested, so it could have no other end. Fortunately, John Chambers will be 21 this August. It is almost too pat, like the mop-up in Shakespeare's fifth acts. Frank Meyer telephoned me the other day, and, in the easy exchange of conversation, I think I got at the truth about Brent's piece.[1] I said: "Brent's piece is a moving piece—about Brent." Frost's "We love the things we love for what they are" is too sweeping, like most such embraces. It is at least equally true that "We love the things we love for what *we* are."

You have been extraordinarily kind to me, not least by your patience with my letters. Letters should not leave their recipient "limp". They are for communication, not to move. That is why I destroy so many of mine. Recuerdos a la familia.

As always,
Whittaker

Anent Jim Agee's line, there is something I believe I have never told you. Jim was one of the most understanding of mortals, but he had a high degree of dissembled contempt for Liberals. On one occasion (I have forgotten what), at the end of the week's grind, I thought it would help if I treated all hands to hootch. The whole Foreign News staff crowded into my big office, and soon got tight. Presently Jim, who had an unerring flair for alcohol and the water-hole, hove in. He got tight, too, but talked chiefly about poetry to the assembled colleagues, most of whom were his confirmed admirers. But then that streak of mischief, which often came out when Jim was drunk, came out. He was sitting on the floor, with his back to the wall. Roosevelt had made that speech to the farmers in which he had said, on the strength of his Christmas tree plantings: "*You* are *far*mers. *I* am a *far*mer too." Apropos of nothing, suddenly Jim, who had been staring thoughtfully at his glass, said with a wonderful imitation of the Roosevelt voice, including the aristocratic* quaver: "*You* are *den*-tists. *I* am a *den*-tist too." If there had been a Christmas tree handy, they would have hanged him.

* more properly, Groton, I guess.

[1] Presumably, the reference is to an obituary on Senator Joseph McCarthy (*National Review*, May 18, 1957).

Have you ever read Jim's story: A Mother's Tale? It appeared, I believe, in Bodeghi Antichi (if that is the spelling).[2] It tells how a brood cow on the Western Plains talks to the young stock about what happens to those lowing cattle who go off east in the cattle cars every fall—the great mystery. She tells, too, how there is an old story that one bull, finding himself in the stockyards, managed, after his skin was flayed off, to tear himself from the hooks, and, after incredible sufferings, to get back to the Plains to warn his breed what Chicago means. "But we," she ends up, "are educated cattle and know that this is just an old wive's tale."

In a good novel about the Korean War, of a couple of years back—*Your Own Beloved Sons*[3]—a tough NCO at the front comes on the perennial shy soldier, reading Jim's *Morning Watch*.[4] The NCO sneers, and the child soldier, struck by some need that he does not himself quite understand, tries to defend the author. "He is," he says, struggling with what he cannot quite grasp, "religious, without being religious." He was one of the great souls who are permitted, we do not know why (it seems so unfair to them), to dwell on earth a while; and my beloved friend.

Another Ageeana. He dreamed (his dreams were extraordinary) that he was in a city (he could not think where it was), being pursued by a killing mob. They were after him for something he had under his arm. But he could not, at first, in his dream, realize what it was under his arm. Then the mob cornered him in an alley. At that instant, he grasped both what was under his arm (it was the severed head of John Baptist) and what city he was in. He faced the mob and screamed: "This is Alexandria!" That is, the city of the mind that works though dead. I don't think that the intellectuals, who are now making a cult of Jim, realize what manner of earth-spirit this was. It is a repetition of the scene from Faust, in which the philosopher, having summoned up the Earth Spirit, muses: "Great Spirit, how near I feel to thee." And the Earth Spirit makes his sundering reply:

[2] *Botteghe Oscure*, Vol. IX (1952): 224-248.
[3] Thomas Anderson, *Your Own Beloved Sons* (N.Y.: Random House, 1956).
[4] James Agee, *Morning Watch*, (N.Y.: Houghton Mifflin, 1950).

Du gleichst dem Geist den du begreifst,
Nicht mir.

You are like the spirit that you understand,
Not me.

May 19?, 1957

Dear Bill,

I fear the CP will not like the last *NR*—too much "cult of the individual." The individual, however, read it with some interest. I thought the Knopf piece [editorial] came off nicely. The answers to your wire were journalistically justified, and to me, who know most of the respondents, most interesting as thumbnail self-snapshots. Burnham who, as I think you know, I tend to take very seriously, seemed to me in these few lines to get down just what I hold to be his chief weakness; what I call, sometimes, his "schematism." Whether or not Alger is still useful to the Apparatus is not the point—useful that is, as pilferer. His chief use was never this, but as shaper of policy and mover of personnel. His ability to divide opinion at this moment is a chore almost as important from the CP's viewpoint. This, in my opinion, should have been the accent. For the rest —Bouscaren, J. B. Matthews—ho, hum. Jay—you old fox, not a hair of the brush has changed. Rovere—he can't get off that couch. The really good answers, I thought, were Hede's and Bert Wolfe's. Hede, the old revolutionist, took deliberate aim and shot right through the center of the target. Her revolver hand swayed only a mite at the end by alluding to how mean Alger is to her and me. Bert made the prime point—the lengths I went to to save Alger; for that is at the heart of the witness. Then he clinched the public points, clearly, briefly. But it is Lumpkinova's [51] tale that has most surprised me. [Religion] should be talked, rather than written, about. The picture of me as a Billy Graham of the Left, slipping in and out of the 11th

[51] Grace Lumpkin had a reminiscence on WC in the same issue.

Street house to save Grace's soul, well. . . . Religion, moreover, is a subject that I almost never talk about, not in those terms; and never unless I have been challenged on the subject and believe that there is a strong reason to go into it. By this, chiefly, I mean that the person I am talking to will have some ability to grasp what I am talking about. I used to go to 11th Street to see Grace's husband, who, as I think I told you, was my great friend in the open CP. We almost never agreed on inner CP politics. He was consistently of the Right; I of the Center with Left leanings. He was a child of the slums, almost wholly self-taught, but he had a remarkably good, above all, intellectually curious mind, of great dialectic force. He would smash his way to the root point of any controversy with singular directness, simply sweeping out his way anything that was incidental, distracting and not germane. For this effort, Marxism provided him with a powerful tool, a kind of Magdalenian chipped-flint weapon that he used with extraordinary skill. He swung it brutally. Yet there was in his character, too, a quality that I think we always find in truly strong types; something that is got at most nearly (though not really got at) by the unlikely words, sweet and childlike. With this, a truly fantastic sense of humor. Example. Grace has a bent for knickknacks, mementos, little dolls, flowers pressed in books. To Mike this seemed funny. He had an uncommon tolerance of all human foible and of the kind that was rooted in his amusement at the variety of it; part of his general wonder that the world should be the way it is and he here to observe it all. So he, who ate out of tin cans, roughed his books, cared not a whit what room he might be in at any given moment, used to observe Grace's knickknacks with a rare, contained humor. It was her predisposition to knickknacks that touched his wonder. One day, idly fingering one of Grace's dolls, he broke its neck—not, I suppose Freudians would say, wholly by accident. Then, for a whole day, he worked patiently (he was extremely good with his hands) on something that none of us could figure out. It turned out to be a beautifully contrived little gallows; and from the loop was hanging Grace's broken-necked doll. That kind of humor. In the telling it loses point. But in the context, and at the time, it was extremely funny; it went, without words, to the heart of something. His frightful struggle with the CP (at one point, he begged me for a revolver to defend himself with in the fur market) embittered and cramped him. He was embittered, too, because I remained a Centrist while he was an expelled and persecuted member of the Right. He was already expelled when he first met Grace, though the fiercer struggle came afterwards. . . . The marriage lasted much longer than I could ever have supposed. In this marriage, I was prevailingly on Grace's side. . . . When they separated, I asked Grace to come to my office at *Time.* I have no slightest recollection of discussing religion with her. But I remember clearly urging her to go back South where she would be among her own numerous family, with people of her own kind. This did not go down well with Grace. Then, in passing, I made some amused remark about Eleanor Roosevelt. Grace boiled like a geyser and shot off into the night. Nevertheless, since she was practically penniless, I finally prevailed on her to come and stay with us for as long as she wished. She did (at the house that has burned). . . . I can recall one occasion, when Mike and I were out of the CP, and Grace and Esther were being rapidly drawn in. It was the time when Stalin took over, and the girls were arguing fiercely that the Party is democratic. Mike and I were pointing out that a dictatorship cannot, by definition, be democratic. For several days thereafter, the ladies would not speak to us. But that world shaker took place in a greasy-spoon cafeteria in the Bronx. I write this at length chiefly because it seems so curious a little light on an era that is gone forever, and, with it, types that cannot ever recur because the circumstances will not breed them again. Mike is dead (in the end, he married a girl with some money and died out in the sun that he loved as the proprietor of two profitable apartment houses in Miami). Grace has made of the piece of her life an achievement fairly magnificent in its own terms. Esther and I are what we are. So that is what became of the little group that once meant to man or storm the barricades. What became of the survivors of Pickett's charge?

Another too long letter, saying too little.

As always,
Whittaker

May 29, 1957

Dear Bill,

Herewith, a letter from a California lawyer, which someone in your office (following his alarming suggestion) forwarded to me. Also the envelope and his letter to *NR*. The bulk of the enclosure contains an appreciation of me, and, I presume, of Alger. Presume because I did not get through more than 2 and a half pages. After all, I *do* know who Patkul was, and what the Great Northern War was; and Suvarov; and André Chénier. Not only do accounts exist in English; there are treatments no farther afield than the *Encycl. Britan.*, which is, no doubt, studded with references to all this. This is not the first time that I have been moved to infer that there must be almost as many mad lawyers, as mad doctors, practicing unchallenged among us. Nevertheless, letters like this one do me no good. If others show up, drop them, I beg, in the trash basket.

Every day seems to show increasingly that Alger's book is a dud of some scale. Yet from his (or their) standpoint, it may prove successful in an unforeseen way. It has not so much compelled me to reassess reality; it has disclosed reality to me past any possibility of not assessing it. We may grant readily that such a consequence is always useful, like the excision of a cataract from the eye; albeit an operation performed by doctors who know little about anatomy and most of whom are avowed sadists. I remember, too, a story (Clemenceau's, I believe—

thirty years ago, statesmen were literate) about a Chinaman who longed to have his blindness cured and got his prayer granted. After a few weeks or days of seeing the world as it is, he voluntarily blinded himself again. Perhaps as good a posture as any is Koestler's counsel, affected with much more humor and better temper than he intended: *"Pends-toi, brave Evelyn. Nous avons diné à Blenheim et tu n'y étais pas."* [52]

I find I know less and less about the world, and that little less and less worth telling. So I should like to tell this: I found the piece by the writer with the French name ([Amaury] de Riencourt?) worth reading twice. I wished your editors had condensed their introduction into about two paragraphs. The same with that part of the piece that was warmed-over Spengler (warmed over, curiously enough in the case of a Frenchman, without the German's epigrammatic verve). That would have brought up commandingly what I take to be the essay's chief point (that the Americans are the 20th century's Romans), and its chief insight (that the Americans are organically an old, old, old young people). Here we are trenching on the subject matter of the Third Rome. But it is all in the public domain, and as it seems increasingly unlikely that I shall attempt to show how curiously (dialectically, as they say), Filofei's prophecy [53] has worked out, I feel no itch of claim, or even of regret.

As always,
Whittaker

It strikes me, on reflection, that the California lawyer's essay reads like a deliberate satire of Isabel Paterson.

As an instance of epigrammatic Spengler, I have long been fond of this one: "Rembrandt's landscapes are located essentially in the universe; Manet's near a railroad station."

[52] Hang yourself, brave Evelyn. We dined at Blenheim, and you weren't there.
[53] It was the monk Filofei who expounded the doctrine of Moscow as the Third Rome.

June 7, 1957

Dear Bill,

Will you have someone forward the enclosed letters? I do not have either address.

Your long silence troubles me. It seems to say that I have offended you, though I do not know how. Worse, I fear that I have disappointed you—worse, because there is almost nothing one can do about that: we are what we are. I was never a good agitator because my style is to say: "This is what and how I think things (people) are, and will become. Wait, watch, and see if it is not so; and let the event, and not me, convince you." In general, I think that you and I want the same things from history. But our view of the forces in motion, the values we give them, and their rate of speed and direction—in that we differ widely. Hence, too, about what is to be done, and how to do it; and what we can expect to get of what we want. Such differences are not insuperable. Yet I know that, often, they do not seem worth the patience it takes to live with them. But perhaps I am on a completely wrong trail.

At least, I have at last achieved a short letter.

As always,
Whittaker

Rereading later, as usual, I find the above exasperatingly vague. I suspect (at the risk of being much mistaken) that it is my attitude to the late Senator McCarthy that has disappointed you. It is of this I am saying: Let the event, not me, speak for itself. It is consequences to a cause I have at heart that move me; not a mean obduracy; or any personal animus or petty judgment of a man, the deeper right to which (if such a right can ever make sense) I forgo.

Perhaps, if you have patience, you should read the enclosures.[54]

---

[54] I do not remember the enclosures, and do not remember the cause of my abnormally long silence—probably I was traveling. I do remember that I had not experienced either exasperation or surprise at Chambers' letter on the death of McCarthy, and assume I thereupon wrote and told him so.

June 12??, 1957

Dear Bill:

I have a sense of aiming this letter into space. As Mr. Summerfield rushes it to you, I do not know whether you will be still tossing on the breaking seas or airborne to Omaha. I want to touch first on something in your last letter before skipping on. You mention abandoning your reply to me with a sense of "inadequacy." I suspect that your trouble is the difficulty of exploring and defining a position; and that nothing is so important to you. This is what, for so many seemingly vain months, I have been trying to do about the satellite revolution. It is a painful effort, and I catch myself artfully putting off the daily battle, by walking in the dawn of our garden, or just staring at a sheet of paper. But I, too, find nothing so important as to order my thoughts in this matter, which extends into so much more.

Following your advice, I read Weaver's piece.[1] I remembered, then, that I had begun it earlier and passed on. This is not, of course, because it is not very well done. My resistance springs from what I said to you on the telephone, and which I find difficult to pin down in sensible words. It is a feeling that Liberals and their position, as Weaver goes at them, are no longer on the main target. History is sweeping past these folk, and sweeping them toward something else. What is it? I don't believe I know. But I have a feeling that they are about to be polarized to a degree hitherto unknown to them. If I am right about this, some of the Liberals must hesitate, and review or revamp, their general position; or, what is more likely, drift into a position which is, in effect, no position, but an infertile attitude, posture, habit. The more active ones will probably be drawn, perforce, farther Left, but in the course of a motion (again, if I am right) which will, in effect, make the Left the conservative position of the coming time. The die-hard Conservatives seem to me to be about to be forced into a position like (to grasp the handiest analogy that occurs) that of the Federalists who manned the Hartford Convention. The analogy is merely handy because I find no precedent for what is about

---

[1] "The Roots of Liberal Complacency," *National Review*, June 8, 1957.

to happen, is now in course of happening. The pundits (press and political) are having great silly powwow with the two great hooks of Khrushchev's TV talk. These hooks are his remark that the USSR wishes merely to "compete" with the U.S. and that our children will live under socialism. The two hooks are, in fact, one hook. They are Nikita's private joke—private because, while all the data are right before us, the pundits miss the point completely. Khrushchev's point is that, if disarmament comes on any great scale, the shrivelling of military industrial orders, a chunky prop of the economy, are likely to produce a situation which must tend to one or another of two sad effects: 1) depression; 2) deepening socialism, swiftly invoked, to cope with the slump. This is the point of the twin hooks. The point of the joke is that nobody, or almost nobody, in the West, even dares to present the dilemma in those terms. So masses here do not see it, are baffled, complacent, and, therefore candidates for an eventual disillusionment of some scope. But Asia and Africa can see the point. Hence those hundreds of millions of smirks. Leon Volkov of *Newsweek* is a former Red Army Air Force officer of the type called, in German, Gefreiter (NCO), and in Russian, Yefreiter. But even Volkov, because he understands Russian, and so caught many shadings that Oleg Troyanovsky's translation fudged in English, for once grasped the animus, though he missed the heart meaning of what Khrushchev was saying. If I am not mistaken the satellite revolution represents Asgard. That, if you have forgotten, was the rainbow bridge whereby the gods, at such cost, at last marched triumphantly into Valhalla, completed at last. It is the tragic irony of that triumphant music, that they must hear, but cannot know the meaning that we know, as the Fate-motif, the Gold-motif and the Curse-motif soar through the Valhalla music. There is a passage from Hegel's Preface To Aesthetics which says: "Now, the essentially tragic consists in this: that, within such collisions, both parties to the contradiction hold themselves to be justified." Paraphrasing my rough translation, this can be simplified to say: Tragedy is not the conflict of right with wrong, but of right with right. The same formulation can be found on the second or third page of the Foreword to *Witness* (Alger v. myself), though I did not come on the Hegel passage until some time after that was written. It is simply the dialectic, of course. This devilish dialectic appears, dissembled like Khrushchev's invocation, and for reasons not too different, toward the end of the Foreword where it is said, for those who can read, that in the struggle of the West with Communism, the struggle itself is its own solution. That is, out of the effort of struggle, the West will develop those energies indispensable to its survival—provided it still includes within itself forces that permit necessity to breed such energies. Of course, the West that went into that struggle will not be the West that emerges from it. The struggle will change it. I am weaving, in my roundabout way, back to Weaver. I am trying to say that vision at this moment consists in grasping history as tragedy. That is now how it can be dispensed weekly, journalistically. But that is the vantage point from which the weekly breakdown of facts must be made: history as tragedy, the tragedy that we have seen, worked in, lived through. It has not its like in history. That is greatness of grasp. It marks the limitations of Knowland. It is, oddly enough, what gives Nixon his special advantage as, intuitively, gropingly, seriatim, he tries to confront reality. I have just had a long, and, to me, fairly astonishing, talk with him. He knows what is at stake— in his own terms, which include several that lie quite outside my interest. There is in him the seed of growth; and that is uncommon indeed, regardless of where it leads or fails to. I tell you in confidence that I have seen him. I have not told anyone else, not even Ralph, though I suspect he knows.

I must break off here to go "top out" the larger lambs for market. I will resume after the lamb break. Poor lambs! (Later.) Well, they're Baltimore-bound: and I, washed and reclad, still smell like a tallow end. This [as I have explained] is a team job. Esther stands on the truck and opens and shuts the tail-gate for each entry (lamb). Mr. P. and I wade in among them in the pens. He catches and weighs most of them. I am along chiefly to say which lamb is a candidate, and for the little-boy chore of opening and shutting pen gates. But as I am also quick and shifty (I learned it all on the Columbia wrestling mats), it helps if I catch whatever I can stalk, too. So we get through this hot, slow, laborious work-out. It's a twice a year nightmare. We do not enjoy sending lambs to butcher. And, later, there are the ewes (or yoes, as all sheepmen say). At first, the mothers do not miss the lambs. Then they come back to the barn to look, and the lambs are not there. The yoes look in each pen. Nothing. Then they know. They know they will never see the lambs again. Their blats are terrible, deep, heart-rending, Asian grief. We hear it, but we do not listen. Among the GPU, as Walter Krivitsky pointed out, are many deeply humane men. They hear; but they do not listen. Life, at the instant, in the circumstances, in which life befell them, does not permit them to listen. Let no one tell me what is good and evil who has not lived under necessity, actuality, in this time, whether it was in organizing an economy, or only so tiny a facet of one as that which gives us, this day, our daily lamb. But then, all I am saying is that only the priest, the soldier and the poet have ever known reality. I would say the peasant, perhaps should say the peasant; but the peasant, in our time, has lost his power to generalize reality. Moreover, the machine is liquidating him as a class. The peasant who could grasp reality has become a farmer or left the land. Most of the rest who have stuck it, are the goons who stuck because they are incompetent for anything else. My observation is that, in the American countryside today, there is a surprisingly high incidence of mental cases. By "farmer," above, I mean, of course, a businessman who farms. By "peasant," I mean a social rank (Stand, in the German sense), shaped by a thousand-year-old special way of life, intertwined with the view of the world, life, fate, that it breeds. Therewith, a dedication, organic, irreversible.

I hope the swells abated a bit donde desemboca el rio Delaware, and that the rest was plain sailing in the plain sense. I was embarrassed to tell you why we could not come aboard.[2] That morning was the bottom of a trough—the trough of a swell. By noon we

[2] The reference is to an invitation to WC and Esther to join me in a trip aboard my cutter, *The Panic*, from New York to Annapolis, stopping at Cape May.

sold some stocks, which, of course, was what we disliked to do. Now the trough has risen, for the nonce, to the crest of the next swell. There is nothing you can, in your kindness, do about this; so you must not "brood upon it." It is almost squarely up to me, and I have not been doing well at my task. There is an area in which I owe you some explanations, and more. When you first introduced me to the subject of "calls," my ignorance was oceanic. Innocence here was a function of ignorance. I now know just a mite more, enough to see, I hope, what I must do and how, and when.* ((HANDWRITTEN FOOTNOTE: *Misleadingly phrased, but not worth laboring)). I am working to relieve you of a burden that I never meant to inflict on you; did not dream of inflicting on you. Later on, we can laugh at me, writing off the laugh to education. Few things have ever interested me so much as the stock market. If I were younger, I should home on it, like a bee on a hive. By such things, rather than by the annual rings, we know what age is. But don't you suppose that, despite the syntactical bobbles, I could get me successfully down the carretera panamericana? Incidentally, I said that my cousin is clerk or treasurer of Cape May. The parentesco is somewhat more complex than I have means to Spanify. My cousin is Stanley Skellinger. His mother was my great-Aunt Alice, (somewhat in the old bigoshes, bucolic style). Cousin Stanley's uncle was my Grandfather Chambers. There was Cousin Stanley, Cousin Paul and Cousin Irving. I saw them last in 1909 or 10 or 11. Paul and Irving were then active young men; and so I picture them. They would now be in their late sixties or early seventies. There was a 10 or 15 year age-spread between Stanley and the other two. They were different in other ways, too. The elder boys were blue-eyed and fair. Cousin Stanley was olive-skinned, black-haired, a gypsy type, and, I felt then, curiously farouche. Cousin Paul was then a Cape May postman. Later, I am told, he went with Dupont and did well; that is all I know. Cousin Irving became a locomotive engineer on the Pennsy or the CRR of NJ. He died young. From those far off days, when I played with Cousin Stanley among his mother's hen coops, until the Hiss Case, I never heard a peep from or about him. About 1951, he wrote me. He had married a Quaker and become one. After *Witness,* he ceased writing. I suppose my account of his uncle Jim scandalized him. It is quite possible that he knew nothing of that side of my grandfather. I have a lot of these Philadelphia kinships. Most of them I do not know even by name. Philadelphia, almost as much as the South, though very differently, is a nation within the country, with a distinct national type. I never found the type so interesting as the Southerner. I am afraid that, about Philadelphia, I feel as D.H. Lawrence did about Chicago: Philadelphia delenda est. (P.S. After I have exercised my option on those "calls".)

I am sure there is something else I wanted to chat with you (at you) about. But, fortunately, I have forgotten what it was.

As always,
(Whittaker)

Above, I see I have written: "It has not its like in history." This is a phrase that I used in my last *Life* piece, and tried to play variations on, like a musical theme. Would you like to know where it comes from? There was no way, I found no way, to explain in *Life,* though I hoped some might remember. Let me try to do so here by way of a section of the forever-uncompleted satellite piece, because I believe this section has been killed by this beastliest of editors. Here begins the threnody.

I was thirteen years old when Sir Edward Grey (surely, among the least imaginative of Foreign Secretaries) stared into the evening of the day, in 1914, when Britain declared war on Germany, and summed up for his age: "The lamps are going out all over Europe tonight. They will not be lit again in our time."

I was 16 when, on a raw day in Petrograd—the rain wind beating in from the Finland Gulf—Antonov-Avseenko (surely, as grotesque a figure as history ever turned on) rushed the Winter Palace at the head of the Red Guard. Therewith, all power in the former empire of the Tsars fell to Communism. In the Petrograd Soviet, Leon Trotsky rose to announce the revolutionary victory. As if, for once, at a loss for language, he stood for a moment, staring at the jammed mass of booted, great-coated men, who stared up at him. Then he found the words equal to the event: "Comrades of the Soviet of Workers and Soldiers Deputies, we have this day begun an experiment that has not its like in history."

That is where the great phrase comes from. Trotsky closed an epoch with a phrase just as telling: "Lenin is dead. The words are like great rocks falling into the sea." Whether we like it or not, only the spirit speaks so. If ever you should come on the *Life* piece again, read it with that counterpoint in mind. I think you will see why I say that what little I know of writing I learned from no writer, but from Beethoven. Pity, that I am the least disciple. In the same piece, there is another counterpoint worked around Antonov-Avseenko. It hinges on knowing that Khrushchev liquidated, or helped to liquidate, Antonov, whom at the 20th Congress, he reinstated. On that, and on that scarecrow figure— Antonov, the former Tsarist officer, with the long hair crowned by the battered hat, the old pipe; an inveterate chess-player and co-planner (with Trotsky and Podvoisky) of the coup d'etat. But this was a ciphered counterpoint and only old revolutionaries could find it, or were expected to.

June 29, 1957

Dear Bill,

I can scarcely tell you with what relief John's parents learned that he was to pass his last night in America with you and your wife. It was a sense (which life does not often allow) of: There is nothing now to worry about; scarcely even any need to think about. Thank you both; and for the letters you have armed John with, and the pains (very inconvenient at pre-sailing time) you took to write them. It sounds too formal, written so. The quality of our gratitude is tied to the fact that this trip of John's to Europe, ordinary enough in itself, is felt by Esther and me to be one of the last two or three things we can do for him; heightened by our sense that he cannot know this, or will

understand only much later, if at all, what looks out of our
eyes at him during these days. Our feeling of thankfulness to
you is in that context.

A manila envelope came from *NR*, which I supposed to be
Ralph's copy. I put off reading it all day, not from lack of
concern, but because I can be of no use in this connection
unless I am editorially ruthless. This is never pleasant; and I
am not sure that I am competent in this particular matter. So I
took the envelope to open in bed and read there. Of course, it
contained your *Saturday Review* piece.[55] I imagine that it could
scarcely be put more directly or simply. The conservative position invokes and defends those great truths which the mind of
the West has once for all disclosed. "And this is the whole duty
of man." It is the end of Ecclesiastes. I could say: There is also
the Book of Jonah, whose three or four pages are among the
most marvelous in the Bible. And at its end occurs one of the
most marvelous colloquies that have engrossed man's mind.
God asks Jonah, who, most unwillingly, under compulsion, has
performed by acts the whole duty of the man, Jonah: "Do you
well to be angry?" Jonah answers: "I do well to be angry." It is
well to mention this because almost no question and answer
of record is so worth a lifetime of reflection. But I want to come
a little closer in time, our time. Two items.

Item I. Czeslaw Milosz, my old friend, notes (simply in passing, if I remember rightly), the curious position of
those members of the Polish security police who are
practicing Catholics, and are commanded to murder.
I do not remember that he draws conclusions from this
casual note. Two are obvious: (1) if they obey, they
retain their power, at least the possibility, of mitigat-
ing other horrors; (2) if they refuse in the name of
truth, they will be destroyed without anybody's ever
learning of their stand; and the murder will be carried
out anyway.

[55] On the meaning of conservatism (a symposium).

Item II. This requires a little preface. During the Great Purge, many foreign Communists were quartered at the Hotel Lux in Moscow. Day by day, there occurred there a piecemeal massacre. At two or three in the morning, the soldiers would come and take away another victim. There would be the hammering on the selected door, the shout: "Open! Here is Authority!" In all the other rooms, there would be the silence of those who have wakened and wait in terror.

In the Lux lived Alice Abramovitz and Frieda Rubine (it is pronounced: Rubina). Both were longtime, and highly intelligent, German Communists. Frieda Rubine, in particular, was a writer of force and much learning. Alice Abramovitz had a young baby. In such cases, it was the custom for the baby to pass a day alone after the mother's arrest; then it was taken away, too—where is not germane here. All these people were comrades of the closest intimacy. But no one dared to take the abandoned children since this was in itself a ground for liquidation.

The soldiers came for Alice Abramovitz. With the baby in her arms, she dodged them and rushed to every door on the floor, begging each inmate to take the child. And, you know, it is interesting, the soldiers just stood there and did not interfere. When the frantic knock came, Frieda Rubine opened her door a little, and Alice Abramovitz begged her to take the baby. Slowly, Frieda Rubine closed the door. It was this that Frieda Rubine could never forgive herself for, never, never, never in all her life; and, it seems possible, in all eternity.

Of course, she could not forgive herself (more truly, she could not endure herself) because she had sinned against a great truth. Woe unto that truth by which comes the meaning that to bear witness to it is to die for nothing. That is why I once wrote you: All life is rooted in horror as every field of springing grain is dunged with filth and death. Yet, in that sentence, the meaningful word is "springing." For, if we ask about the above incident: "who bore witness to truth?", we are almost compelled, and with astonishment, to answer: "The soldiers," who were, in fact, the agents of murder. They were guiltless because they were powerless, so that their inaction, in that instant, became the highest mode of compassion possible in that situation. It is not whim that has brought certain Catholics to seek to reconcile Thomism and Existentialism. It is reality and the age. It is not the truths, but the little power of man, caught between them and a reality which crushes him, that is in question; so that, in our time, it is given each of us to understand what was said from the Cross: "My God, my God, why hast Thou abandoned me?"

It is not so simple as Frank Meyer would like to be able to think.

As always,
Whittaker

During the month of June, it became clear that policy and personal differences among the senior staff at National Review *would soon result in the resignation of William Schlamm. During the same period, Chambers had expressed interest in at least reopening the question of joining the staff of* National Review. *I told him that nothing would please me more. And I wrote him at length, making him privy to the commotion within the magazine.*

July 7, 1957

Dear Bill,

Our letters crossed, which makes my (for me) rather brief one particularly inadequate in the light of your long one and its contents. Where to begin in response? I think, for everybody's sake, as far as possible off center.

Almost nothing moves me so quickly to anger as the charge

that Burnham is a "concealed Communist." [56] Every former revolutionist is open to it whenever stupidity or perversity chooses to make it. In this case, it is a nonsensical lie, preposterous on its face. First, Burnham is a man of honor. My brief talk with him, everything I have heard about him for years, or ever read of his, admits no other impression. That is, there are things he will not do. No, *cannot* do, since honor is much less a code than a condition, much more organic and reflexive then persiflage can imagine. To the degree in which honor can best be divined by honor, let those who make the charge look to themselves and see where their own slips are showing. This does not mean that honor is an unbreachable mail when pressures become ferocious enough, and the world being what it is. Milosz (again) notes that the satellite mind became somewhat skeptical of the consolations of philosophy after watching philosophers fight each other for scraps of garbage in concentration camps. Honor is no more proof than philosophy. But, further, Burnham never was a Communist. He was a Trotskyist, precisely at the moment when Trotskyism was worn to a shadow by reality. To have been a Leninist required a commitment about reality, in philosophy and act at once, which I should have thought B. by temperament incapable of (this is not a criticism but an observation). He isn't the type. More exactly he wasn't, in my opinion, the type then. He most certainly cannot be tempted that way in the world of 1957. If by the charge it is meant that B. refuses to suspend his assaying of reality, and it tells him that the socialist trend in history is irreversible, then "admit me Chorus to this history." What other conclusion is possible when, to reach for the handiest exhibit, it is seen that the Republican Party has been able to rule only by becoming a socialist party, and there is a strong likelihood that it will be voted out of power in favor of the more knowingly socializing Democrats? I should suppose

[56] A charge leveled by a reader who insisted that no other hpyothesis could explain the so-called Burnham Proposals to a Great Power evacuation of continental Europe.

that, in a historical earthquake, a fixed position was a most unhappy, and rather useless, one. I should think those who make the charge against B. were in danger of finding themselves in the plight of Jim Agee. After a severe earthquake shock, down he rushed out of his California hotel with dozens of others. To the stranger he happened to find himself beside, Jim observed what strange pieces of clothing people snatch up to cover their nakedness at such moments. "No stranger," said the man, looking Jim up and down, "than running out with nothing on at all." Then Jim glanced at himself and saw that, in fact, he had run out naked. Let the chargers of B. look to their own attire. Khrushchev is leaving them little choice. The plain fact is that history's latest turn has forced Burnham, exactly as it has forced me, to re-examine reality, and therewith our own position with respect to it. What are we to do—act as if nothing has happened? Abdicate intelligence on what grounds? What do the Burnham critics say: that what is happening in Communist lands is just more of the same, that Khrushchev is a new edition of Stalin? Perhaps he would like to be. Unhappily, for him and for those who will not probe reality coldly, circumstances will not let Khrush be another Stalin. This is not 1932. An era has ended. If Khrush cannot give form and force to the new period and its problems, he too will go, whether it takes two months or two years. But to recognize what he is trying to do, is compelled by circumstances to do, regardless of personal motives, is not to revert to Communism. The greatest drama of the great century is in play. This is the moment of spin-out of the age. No moment for more stupidity than we are naturally gifted with. Whether we like what we see is not in point. To see is in point. Burnham is trying to see. . . .

I am going to pass over [your remarks concerning] the conservative position simply because it is too much for me at this moment. I will simply quote something: "Quietly, something enormous has happened in the reality of Western man: a destruction of all authority, a radical disillusionment in an over-

confident reason, and a dissolution of bonds, have made anything, absolutely anything, seem possible. . . . Philosophizing to
be authentic must grow out of our new reality, and there take
its stand." The words are Jaspers'. But, except that they are
better put, and that I would not speak of "philosophizing,"
they might be my own. In fact, I have said as much. Yesterday,
[Russell] Kirk's (and, I suppose, Henry's [Regnery]) *Modern
Age* arrived. I looked through it to get the flavor, and noted
one or two pieces that I would read—later. What came into my
mind (I suppose because by the same mail Koestler had sent
me his latest book) was an incident from *Arrow in the Blue.*
Koestler tells us how his Jewish uncle and his Gentile aunt
had lived, for years, a happy married life beside a lake when the
Nazi extermination of the Jews began. One night, the aunt
missed her husband and rushed down to the shore, calling
him. Quietly, his voice answered from a boat on the lake:
"Don't make it more difficult." What do Kirk and his Burke
have to say to that voice from the water, or to that woman on
the shore, or you or me or even the corpse of the unlikable
Molotov; for I believe him to be dead? Philosophizing to be
authentic must grow out of our new reality, and there take
its stand. Burke and High Anglicanism have the least possible
to do with that. They, too, are chips, tossed on the blackly
running stream, now a torrent. Only the Catholic Church has
dared to look steadfastly at that torrent, and measure what it
costs a man's soul to make its passage, not in terms of deflecting
hope, but in terms of what cruelly is. Of course, the Church is,
by no means, at one on this. But the tide has set—or I am no
judge of tides (there are a lot of things I am becoming less and
less sure about).

So I have got, by carefully wandering stages, to the center.
Out of your goodness and sensitivity, you are seeking to help
me—to save me, even; I think you know what is at stake. (At
this point, I got up and left the typewriter; in part because I
was tired; in part, because I felt unequal to laboring what I am,
etc., which is, above all, so tiresome. A few minutes later, you

telephoned and I told you that it could not be.) Only you (and, in quite different terms, one other) have tried to help me in this meaningful way. I hope you understand that my rejoinder is, nevertheless, filled with a gratitude that I simply cannot express. Meanwhile, I have thought it over. Let my no stand as a tentative no, if you will.

Let me try to put it quickly and simply because, for certain practical reasons, this letter must be mailed. Within the next 30 days, at longest, I must decide what is to be with me. This involves the kind of considerations that the world calls practical (most of them in the narrowest form). It also involves considerations of quite another order, high among which stands the question: What can be done with a shattered life at the age of 56; or is it worth trying to do anything with it? Day and night are beautiful experiences, but, at the candle end of time, do they make a justifying fare? One has lived through so many days and nights; what price repetition? A man must stand on his own feet. He cannot be propped or lugged by friends the most devoted. He must be what German calls: *selbstständig*, literally, selfstanding. Otherwise, he is no man, but dead weight. I have never been dead weight. I have always been a *selbstständiger* man, no matter how exiguous the ledge I stood on. Circumstances have me trapped. Some of them are so effective that a way out seems as unlikely as anything I ever tried to solve. Above all, because a way out raises the question: way out to what? If, within the coming weeks, I cannot devise a feasibly planful way out, which can, at the same time, give a tentatively satisfying answer to that question, why, then I must acknowledge that I have reached a point that has been reached before me by thousands of better men—thousands and thousands of them. "A long time ago the world began...." The problem is heightened because, with the years, deception becomes more and more difficult to entertain in its favorite guise of hope. A kind of rudeness to hope sets in, a quite unrepentant incivility, so that we find ourselves simply getting up in the midst of the endless conversation, pushing back the chair and saying, not unkindly but finally: "If you have nothing more to say, nothing more actual, let us not waste each other's time. You will be better entertained by sprightlier heads. And I have, before nightfall, one or two things to do which will take all the breath I can hoard from conversation." So we find ourselves saying ungraciously to hope. "Show me a purposeful way," we find ourselves adding, "to a meaningful end. Either that, or let us say good day, for it is getting late." Hope answers, for hope is patient and itself infinitely civil: "Find the way yourself, and, if you find it, you will find me there, too, and, in fact— for you are quite right—nowhere else." That's it as baldly as I see it. I beg leave to make my no tentative so that, if, in these days ahead, I find some answer that seems to make a point, equal in meaning to the effort involved in reaching it, I may then come to you and say: "This is what I have concluded I should do. This makes as much sense as I think I see. Do you think so too?" If you do think so, if my way seems practical, however tenuous the practicality or long the course, then I can say: "Help me, if you will, to reach a point where I may be able to repay you, not for the spirit that moves you (that cannot ever be repaid), but in the world's way." That's it, I think.

Now this must go into the mail with all its faults. I hope that all of you are recovered from that beastliest of sicknesses, the summer cold. I will return, too, to the Conservative Position. I began a long essay on the subject, appended to my last letter. But I removed this appendix before posting, as unfinished, and worse, too luridly arresting, and the ally of insomnia (the words are the Incomparable Max's).

As always,
Whittaker

How right I was to feel, when I knew that John was under your roof: Now there is nothing to worry about. I hope he wasn't a damned nuisance. I swear to blow off steam because there was no reason in the world why he should not have got to Quebec by train with time to spare. His parents begged him to set off two or three days before sailing date. There come moments, even with a beloved son, when we are moved to nod assent to what Carl Brandt once said to me: "Don't you know that boys at that age are poisonous, simply poisonous?" Thank you for getting him off. It's clear that, otherwise, he would never have made it.

July 15, 1957.

Dear Bill,

We have had our first letter from John. It was sent off his ship by lighter and posted from Southampton, stamped officially: E.R. "Eduardus Rex," I thought, "how can that be?" A hint of how far I live in the past; then I updated. John, if not eggstatic, is clearly exilirated. (It would be disloyal of me to share his wonderful rendering of: cognac.) He has been practising his German (this, too, must make for some wonderful renderings and rendings) on German and Yugoslav bar-keeps. (Bar-tends, John says, so I presume that that is now the mode.) He finds it a bit strange to be hearing the names of Liebknecht, Luxembourg and Bebel, "not from students or teachers", but from, I gather, real people. One lives and learns, even if one has been to Kenyon. Most of the passengers are not "real people"; they are chiefly teachers on vacation. They are "boring". I am afraid that I, too, would listen with less interest to vacationing teachers than to a German bar-keep who, when the American officer shouted at him (just post-War): "*Why* were you never a member of the Nazi Party?", answered: "Why are you in the American Army?", but who was not really hurt, when the officer swung on him, because "he ducken". I am sure that John will have a lot of things to sort out later, and, indeed, that is largely why I sent him. I have little doubt that he will sort them out right, given time. For there are ways in which John is many strides ahead of me at his age. It is not only that I should never have found my way to the ship's bar in the first place. He carries, in addition to your letters to Erik v. Kuehnelt-Leddhin and the others, a letter to the rector of the

Louvain Seminary, which, no doubt, you know, is a center of somewhat advanced Catholic thinking. One of my good friends will be attending there this autumn; another, the priest who gave John the letter, will be going there after a hitch on the West Coast.

My last letters have been somewhat grave. So this is chiefly one to reverse the current. I have been meaning to draw your attention to R.H.S. Crossman's review of Alger's book in the N.S. & N. It is the absolute summit. Beyond this one, not the clouds, but outer space, takes over. The review falls into two fairly neat parts. In the first, Crossie begins by saying that, of course, he has read none of the relevant documents (this is not the first time I have noticed this fabulous disclaimer, like saying: Of course, I know nothing about the matter, but let me tell you). He then says that Alger has adduced "sensational new evidence"—"Evidence"!— about the pumpkin papers (he means the Baltimore documents) and the typewriter. He cites the usual about a conspiracy of the Congress cum FBI cum Chambers to frame Hiss. He says that the four jurors who voted against Alger's guilt in the first trial, thereafter lived "in terror of their lives". He finds that since a duplicate typewriter *could* have been constructed, this amounts, ipso facto, to a judgment of "not guilty" for Alger. It seems to me like arguing that, since an earth satellite *can* be constructed, I have constructed and launched one. I have seen some mad leaps of the mind in my time. But I imagine they send people to asylums for less than this one. Then occurs the switch. Crossie discovers that, in fact, Alger has conceded the political indictment. "Chambers was right. There was a Soviet espionage ring in the Government, and it included New Dealers." What a world of choking emotion is crammed into those two little words: New Dealers. And, of course, the leap of the mind, or mere stupidity, is almost as striking here as before. As if an array of testimony by members of the ring, from Wadleigh to Pressman, needed any "concession" from Alger. This concession, which takes the form of Alger's saying that, not he, but certain others, were the real agents, stirs Crossman to the crack which must be most of my excuse for going into all this: "If Dreyfus's defense had been that three other

Jewish officers spied for the Germans, Zola would have been considerably deflated". But the ending, the conclusion, is a wonder of its own breed. I quote from memory, but pretty closely: "I ask myself, as I put down this remarkable book, can it be that Alger Hiss was both unlawfully convicted *and* guilty?" The Liberal mind can do no more. When I first read this conclusion, I was appalled. But then humor got the upper hand. It is one of the funniest twists I ever read, and one of the most extraordinary. Not the least of the jest is that Crossman wrote me, not too long before the Hiss Case broke out, to ask me to contribute to *The God That Failed*. I had been recommended to him, he said, by—no, no, it is much more farcical than anything you could ever expect to come up with—C.D. Jackson.[1]

In the spirit of the new blitheness, I enclose two clips. The smaller is my candidate for your wife's book.[2] On second reading, it seems less than at first. Still, it has its touches, including that "clean". It comes from the NS & N.[3] But my favorite is Congressman Kearns' comments which I take to be the opening shot in the outclass struggle.

As always,
Whittaker

[1] C.D. Jackson (1902-64) was an official of Time Inc. from 1931 to 1964. WC and Willi Schlamm thought him a philistine.
[2] The reference is to an informal scrapbook in which clips were kept, recording unintentionally amusing news events.
[3] The cartoon is not available. Ed.

IV

September, 1957, to November, 1959

I wrote in Esquire *(September, 1962): "Eisenhower ran and was re-elected. Nixon was safely Vice President. Six months later Chambers wrote to say he wanted to sign up with* National Review. *Having made the decision, he was elated. After years of isolation and introspection, he was like a painter who had recovered his eyesight. He felt the overwhelming need to practice his art. How many things he wanted to write about, and immediately! Mushrooms, for instance. Some gentleman, in an act of supreme conceit, had recently published a ten-dollar book on mycology, heaping scorn on one of Chambers' most beloved species of toadstools. Camus. What a lot of things needed to be said instantly about the* Myth of Sisyphus! *Djilas'* The New Class *was just out, and most of the critics had missed the whole point. . . .*

"I rented a one-engine plane and swooped down on him at Westminster to make our arrangements. I was to leave the next day for Europe, had to make the round trip in one day, and wanted to act immediately on Chambers' enthusiasm. He met me and we drove in his car to his farm. He told me the last time he had driven to the little grassy strip at Westminster, on which reckless pilots venture occasionally to land, was to greet Henry Luce, who had soared in from Washington to pay him an unexpected visit some months after Hiss' conviction. I remarked that such, obviously, is the traveling style of very important publishers. If he would not acknowledge that common denominator between me and Mr. Luce, I added, then he might recognize this one: such is the style of publishers who employ Whittaker Chambers. He laughed, but told me my manner was grossly imperfected. When Luce arrived, he said as we bounced

195

about on the dusty dirt road in his open jeep, he had waiting for him at the airport a limousine to drive him to Chambers' farm. I made a note for my next landing . . ."

In the issue of August 31, 1957, was the notice: "We are honored to announce that Mr. Whittaker Chambers will re-sume his career as a journalist to join the staff of National Review. *Mr. Chambers will write regularly, beginning in the next few weeks."*

Sept. 4, 1957

Dear Bill,

Here is Djilas, Take I.[1] It may appal you. I, writing in my basement, presently lose all ability to take an objective view of copy, which almost comes to seem to me "stuff that could ne'er be writ by any man alive." If you think so, too—to the trash basket with it. If it seems less of a disaster, I beg you, do not think of publishing until Take II is finished.

I'll leave anything else to a later letter or conversation.

I am sending a copy to Frank Meyer.

Yesterday we sold all our cattle. *Dieu! que le son du Cor est triste le soir au fond du bois.*[2]

As always,
Whittaker

Oct. 8, 1957

Dear Bill,

Yesterday I mailed Suzanne [La Follette] the top copy of the enclosed offering, my first to *NR.*[3] As I believe I have said to

[1] WC began by assigning himself to a two-part review of Djilas' *The New Class.* He did not complete it, and would not authorize the publication of the first part.

[2] God, how the sound of the horn is sad at night, from deep in the woods (Alfred de Vigny).

[3] "Soviet Strategy in the Middle East," *National Review,* October 26, 1957. The article was datelined Westminster, Maryland, and the opening read, "Talk, here in the farmlands, is chiefly of the heaviest frost of this date in a decade, and what it may have done to stands of late corn. Yet it cannot be said that we are wholly out of touch with the capitals of the mysterious East—Cairo, Damascus, Baghdad, New York."

you before, I never know, when I have completed a piece, how horrible it is. I usually suppose the worst. Yet, rereading this, in the freshness of this early morning, it seemed to me to have spots that made readable copy. And, heaven knows, readable copy would be a boon to *NR* readers. I mean just literally readable.

This done, for good or ill, I am back to Miss Rand.[4] I have brushed her for a couple of pages while penciling the attached. Frank Meyer has been silent for a while, no doubt from a scruple not to harry me. But the good Brent has telephoned several times. From his tone the last time, I gathered that the feeling in N.Y. is that I have given up writing. By now, he may know (possibly with loathing) that I have not. Djilas, of course, has been a shocking stumbling block. No doubt, the editors in N.Y. are appalled by the degree by which *NR* has missed the news break on this one. I, acting from a different kind of journalistic experience, am not. If the piece is well done, according to my code, missed news pegs mean little. What counts is that *NR* should have had something effective and summary to say. This presents difficulties of several orders, which I shall spare you here. Djilas, and what he implies and relates to, will be with us a long time. No doubt, I shall be with him a long time. The nub of the problem is to locate him (and much more, therefore, and many others) in this moment of history. It takes some doing; and I am, at the best of times, a maddeningly careful writer, going back and over and over, throwing away reams (quite literally reams) to have left a handful of copy. If what is left reads easily, I take the effort to be worth it. That is why, perhaps, like my friend, T. S. Matthews, "I do not like to write, but I like to have written."

To switch the pattern, and keep readers happily uncertain, I should like my next Westminster Letter to be made up of short items, end to end. So far, for my grab bag, I have chiefly the cryptic news that the Aneuran Bevans, on a recent Crimean

[4] A review of Ayn Rand's *Atlas Shrugged, National Review,* December 28, 1957.

trip, were the house guests of Mrs. Nikita Khrushchev. I find this a little nugget—one of those unnoticed bits of living history which, like a bead of radium, light up shoals of darkness, even though radium itself remains a riddle, and even what we see by that curious light perplexes. There is also a possibility of using the energy wherewith the Vice President and James Hagerty jumped on the San Francisco *Chronicle* for Miller's mischievous gossip note.[5] I have the correspondence about it. But, in this area, I must have Mr. Nixon's permission to write (especially to quote); and if he should feel that it is better to let the matter die, I am afraid that I should have to agree with him.

You were right in supposing that I have not written you because I am ear-deep in work; and when that is done around midday, my head is heavy. Even my son has not had a letter from me since he got back to college. But, in your case, there is also something else, rather odd. I feel as if you had disappeared over the horizon and that you cannot be spoken to intimately for the duration. I hope you are both having a good time [in Europe]. Only one renter has appeared for our house; and he (a violinist of some note, who works at the Peabody in Baltimore), though clearly attracted, dreaded the daily commutation. I am still fixed here.

Meanwhile, the earth satellite. TV interrupted a World Series game to amplify the first terse announcement. [If I had had to explain my reaction] I think I should have had to begin something like this. In 1923, I was sitting in a restaurant on the Kurfürstendam in Berlin, either at a big window or at a sidewalk table, I have forgotten which. What did the mark then stand at—40 million to the dollar? The exact ratio of catastrophe is unimportant. There walked past a handsomely dressed, extremely dignified woman. It would miss something to say that she was crying. Tears were streaming down her face; tears which she made no effort to conceal, which did not even distort her features. She simply walked slowly past, proudly

---

[5] The gossip columnist reported that Nixon was badmouthing Eisenhower among intimates.

erect, unconcerned about any spectacle she made. And this was the terrifying part: nobody paid the slightest attention to her. The catastrophe was universal. Everybody knew what she signified; nobody had anything left over from his own disaster to notice hers. She became one of my symbols of history in our time. With this unknown, slowly walking, weeping woman, as with something else that occurred a few weeks later (of which I think I once told you), I felt, with Karl Barth; at that moment, "I found my hand upon the rope, and the great bell of prophecy began to toll." Does it sound wildly irrational to say that, when the newscaster interrupted the ballgame, I laughed because this woman walked again across my mind's eye? It is so. With her began the prophecy; the circling of the scientific moon was incipient in her walk-past. Something of this is what I was trying to express in some lines I scratched off, a month or two ago (I have the secret vice of versifying):

> *As I was crawling on the floor,*
> *I heard a groaning in the wall;*
> *Here, as well as in the town,*
> *Everywhere the walls were down;*
> *This was just before the Fall.*

I got a little farther, but I cannot remember where. To have known this as a possible reality for more than thirty years, and to have been unable to communicate it sensibly to others, that is the heart of loneliness for any mind. Cassandra knew. It works out, too, in the simplest, most immediate ways. As soon as Esther and I were alone, I said: "They still do not see the point. The satellite is not the point. The point is the rocket that must have launched it." Of course, the scientists and the ranking military chiefs must have grasped this obvious implication at once. But it took three or four days for the organically stupid press to catch on. Consternation, of course. Add in this datum: The satellite passed over Washington. One minute later it passed over New York. We have entered a new dimension. Like Goethe after the Battle of Valmy, we can note in our journals: "From this day, dates a new epoch of history; and you can say that you were there." Doubtless, the Americans will soon launch bigger and better moons. That, too, is not the point. Again, the point is: the battle for space is on. Foster Dulles, in a recent radio broadcast, dropped some casual, unintelligible words about the struggle for space. I said to Esther at the time: "That is the most interesting thing he has said. What do you suppose he means? What does he see that we don't see?" There is a wonderful line in the *Journal of the Goncourt Brothers,* wonderful for its date, which is something like 1890. I shall not be able to quote it exactly from memory, but it goes something like this: "We have just been at the Academy where a scientist explained the atom to us. As we came away, we had the impression that God was about to say to mankind, as the usher says at five o'clock in the Louvre: 'Closing time, gentlemen.' " None of us knows whether this means closing time; none of us can fail to see that closing time is a distinct possibility. Unlike Goethe, I doubt that any of us can feel a particular elation in being able to say: "And you were there." I suspect that the best we can muster will be like the historic first words uttered by the King of Greece, on landing after the German occupation and the frightful civil war: "Nice weather we're having."

Our best to you both,

Whittaker

Oct. 23??, 1957 (Mon.) [6]

Dear Bill,

Naturally, I was pleased by your letter (it arrived last Sat.), saying that you liked the Middle East job. Curiously (perhaps you will suppose, perversely), your belief that *NR* is full of readable copy troubles me most. But I'm not going to plague you with that here.

[6] A letter dated October 10 is lost.

One thing chilled me, though: your suggestion that I was raising a shorthand signal to RMN [Richard Milhous Nixon]. I'm sure that you know, on swiftest second thought, that that couldn't be true because it isn't necessary. There is always longhand.

What would I say of all this [7] in sum? At first, I should have said: disquieting. By now, I think it is: saddening. Saddening because, in these short weeks, I have come to enjoy writing for *NR*, greatly. It has given me a new lease of life; and I have felt my mind turn over as an engine turns over. I have been grateful to you in a way that I could not express without courting extravagance. Yet, every day, I say to myself: Don't let yourself go; it can't last. Many factors enter into that feeling. I try to weigh them with the same detachment, even cold-bloodedness, with which I should try to weigh greater factors elsewhere. I think it unlikely that I should react impulsively about any of them. But I think, in the end, I shall be overborne. I shall try not to be, because I wish not to be; and that is a new development. I shall try to give the development its chance.

I am reasonably sure that you have your share of cares these days; and this seems the unkindest kind of letter to send you during your last days abroad. So poor a man am I.

As always,
Whittaker

The usual footnote: Yes, it's a poor letter. But I mustn't, mustn't, mustn't take time to write another. This has been a day when a number of unrelated bricks fell on my head. The collective impact is felt in the tone above, and should be discounted. My mind keeps spinning on your Nixon remark. I should expect our (his and my) position to be loosely similar on most issues. Yet I shall never be speaking for him; while I, like him, reach my conclusions independently. Conclusions I reach

[7] Of the whole of his experience in writing and publishing his first article in *National Review*.

that may be of any use or of any interest to him, I freely submit. His rejection or concurrence is not my affair. We disagreed "sharply" at the outset, that is, in 1951 or was it early '52? He was judging in political terms, and, in those terms, was absolutely right. I had looked at General Eisenhower when he was still General Marshall's boy. I have never found any reason to revise the opinion I reached then. In that sense, I hold that I was right in 1951. He was thinking tactically. I held to a judgment that I could not yield on. I respect him for his tactical thinking and skill. I feel that he respects my refusal to yield. He knows that I will always tell him the truth as I see it. Intelligence can ask no more; and power seldom gets as much and seldom knows how to take advantage of it. I think he does. Besides, he has nothing that I want, and what he wants I would not want for him if he didn't want it. There are great areas, by which the world sets much greater store than I do, where I am as flexible as a snake. There are a few matters where my joints are calcified. These matters have to do with truth and reality in contexts that make them seem to me important.

Some sense of what is fitting made me feel that I should not mention your Spain piece in this letter. It was, of course, an admirable piece, one of *NR*'s high spots overall. A piece like that, once a week, as a spine to shape the magazine around, and you'd be a long way to having it made. When you can count on two such pieces a week, as a matter of course, you will have a magazine. My mentioning this means that I have worked a little out of the mood I began with.

There is a rumor (reaching me by way of Suzanne) that ———— is turning East. I cannot believe it, and would not mention it except that I have heard something similar from somebody whose carefulness I trust. This matter touches me closely. Can you ask discreetly (that is, without furthering the rumor) over there? Do you know the story of Lenin and Malinovsky? The latter was the Okhrana's agent in the Bolshevik Central Committee. When the charge was first made to Lenin, he denied it furiously. This happened at Zinoviev's house (they were then all in Austrian exile). The Lenins had to go home by way of a long bridge. In the middle, Lenin suddenly stopped, grabbed Krupskaya's arm, and said of Malinovsky: "But suppose he is!" And what a horrid confirmation that would be of certain warnings in the *Life* piece on the 20th Congress.

Oct. 24??, 1957

Dear Bill,

"Did the Loved One pass over with gas?" asked Miss Thanatogenos. "No," said Dennis, "he passed over by a deadline with Ayn Rand cinching the knot." That being the case, I should never take time to write again next day, if a practical editorial matter had not come up. I attach a letter, just arrived, from Father Victor J. Donovan, C. P. (no, no, the other CP). That ragged line you see forming up behind me at the door of 211 East 37,[8] is not a rising of the proletariat. It is that knowing section of the Right, the Catholic Left. My good old worker and peasant seminarians. They know. And each knows that the other knows. What do we know? That: "It's the third-class carriages will save us." The author of that inflammatory line? Mr. Rudyard Kipling. I hope you realize that this is my notion of good clean fun. Anyway, I have spared you Father Victor's sermon which was attached to my attachment. And what do you suppose His Eminence made of that?

Now to what justifies this truancy from Miss Rand. My piece about Bevan, etc., lies in the office, unable to make its way into the next issue for space reasons. After all, I may be a sheep at times, but I musn't be a hog all the time. The piece deals, inter alia, with the revision of Labor Party tactics and aims whereby outright nationalization has been dumped in favor of the socialist government's buying, as majority stockholder, into fated industries. Clearly, this is a shift of historic importance, East as well as West. In the *New Statesman,* Oct. 12 (it came with Fr. Victor's note), is a wonderful cartoon of

[8] *National Review*'s offices at the time.

Vicky's, captioned: "Workers of the World, Invest!" I should like *NR* to buy this classic and run it with the Bevan piece. It will make a smart editorial flash. Or so I suppose. Will you look at the cartoon, and, if you agree, get it, and call upon *NR* to act accordingly? I will say nothing to them. In your absence, my role with the interesting personalities at 211 is to be as gracious and accommodating as possible; no words wasted. Perhaps I should be precise. I would not trouble you with this simply to dress up the Bevan piece. I think Vicky's cartoon will make an issue of *NR*, make the difference between a magazine, and a magazine well turned out. If no one agrees, I shall get on with Miss Rand, about whose review I like nothing except the title: "Du Calme, Madame!" Frank will change that. But, by then, I shall be getting on with something else. As I wrote yesterday: I am enjoying myself!

Note from my son on the Mideast piece: "Full of subtility and written as God meant pieces to be written." Who could fail to swell up like a turkey wattle—not for the praise, but for the son and his giving it?

Our best to your wife.

As ever,
Whittaker

Second thought. I had better write Suzanne about the Vicky cartoon, and that I have written you about it. Thereafter, it's out of my hands.

Nov. 1??, 1957

Dear Bill,

No farce so good as any day, and this morning's drollery won't keep. The mail brought a letter from the press attaché of the Israeli Embassy in Washington—"pleasure," "interest," *"National Review,"* will I meet him, Washington, N.Y., etc.? I think I am about to be corrupted. Does General Yadin need a seeing-eye? Articles about the horrors of the Khora and the

Khkhkhalutsim [?]? These people are amusingly on their toes. The tricks and the troubles that ensue can be read about in Vincent Sheean's *Personal History,* which makes curiously good rereading 25 years later. Of course, you know what they really see in me—I am Israel's secret weapon against Utley.[9] Brent tells me that, at mention of the Mideast piece, Freda had a tantrum and had to be roped to the stair rail. I don't think she can have understood what I said. I more and more have the impression that people do not understand what I say. They see the flower but not the adder under it. Perhaps it results from years of speaking the Aesopian language, not as Mr. Budenz [10] imagines it to be—a kind of cipher—but as an art of conversation which is very much about one thing, but seems to be about something else. I submit that the statement: "Israel, as enemy, is Communism's indispensable piece in the Middle East" is hair-raising. It means that the situation is hopeless. It should enrage the Israelis and charm the Arabs about whom nothing even remotely so shocking was said. (Incidentally, it was precisely because I felt this appraisal to be so blood-chilling that I performed my anti anti-Semitic ablutions; and never imagine that this is thrifty hindsight.) Yet here is Ibn ben Utli, frothing like a dervish, because she cannot make out the lineaments perfectly visible under the Turban Of Invisibility. The upshot is obvious: overseas editions of *NR* in Arabic and Hebrew. Peace be on your house!

It's a relief to be able to spoof directly without having to go via APO at 211.

As always,
Whittaker

Need I say that, for me, there will be no rendezvous at the Wailing Walls of N.Y. or Washington?

9 Freda Utley, author of, among others, pro-Arab books.
10 Louis Budenz, the former managing editor of the *Daily Worker*, who turned anti-Communist.

March 1, 1958

Dear Bill,

Here are some paragraphs. They are merely promissory. I do not see how you can very well make much out of them. What you may be able to make, you may not like. But I think you can see, at least, that I am trying to strike out across a new region. That is inexact; it is an old region in which, to the eye, many relationships seem new, or distorted, by reason of a change of light common in partial eclipses. I have not enough mathematics to plot my course, even if I had the instruments. I have only a pocket compass, and intuition. So, as always, there is the trash basket, an editor's best friend.

Should you decide not to use it, certain possibilities are clear. You could publish the first eight pages of this copy, ending with the Milosz quote, and my comment about Milosz' Law. I think it would make better editorial sense to wait for the completion of this Take, whose point is really made in its closing line: "This century is of a greatness whose meaning we cheat ourselves out of continually, by refusing to know it as a whole." In that completed version, Take [number] I will include a further, clinching consideration of X. In polishing it (it is written, of course), I may well radically trim down the section on X that I am sending you. I sense that pace, and the danger of boring readers, make this necessary.

Two minor points. I suspect that "Lalique" is misspelled. That it should be spelled with two l's, not one. But I cannot find the word in any English or French reference. The other point is the quote from Conrad. I cannot find *Heart of Darkness,* though it must be somewhere around the house. I am sure that the quote occurs in [F. R.] Leavis, but John seems to have made off with my Leavis. Can somebody up there check the quote? I have an uneasy feeling that it reads: "Mr. Koertz—he daid." I suspect that my dislike of Patois has made me remember it as "dead." [11]

[11] WC's ms. was correct: "Mistah Kurtz—he dead."

The whole effort falls into five related, but self-contained, pieces. I. What you have here plus its ending. II. The year 1957 seen as a turning point ("Not to see that the rockets are a specific form which the mind has taken in this time is to miss something. Nothing like the mind in this form, at these velocities, has ever been known before"). III. The satellite revolution revisited. IV. The culminating crisis ("Is it not possible to see this as a radical readjustment of reality, a crisis of a kind such as occurs once in a thousand or two thousand years?"). V. Hope ("Hope in this time is not something that can be taken by the hand and invited into the house. Hope can only be taken by the throat"). Etc., etc.

I should take it kindly if you do not show this effort, until it is completed, to anyone else. I am only incidentally writing for my generation. I am trying to speak to the youth. You have been wonderfully patient.

As always,
Whittaker

There is some very big news in the making, which I am bound not to hint at. If and when it breaks, I hope we may talk it over; you will recognize at once what I refer to. I think it will induce some severe stresses at *NR*. I also think that "Toward an Examination of X" will abruptly have a topicality less evident now.[12] Of course, I began writing it long before this music crept by me over the water. I think I can, and must, say this: the first stages of what I refer to have already taken place, and been widely discussed. Only no one sees what is implied. So look, if you are interested, at seemingly minor news of the past fortnight or so.

I guess I may say this too: the President's news conference disclosure of an arrangement with No. 2 [Nixon] was not an accident, though the succession is not the big news.

12 The reference is to an article written by WC several months earlier whose publication he did not, finally, complete.

March 2. I saw my first robin this A.M., sitting, huddled, fluffed up and chilly on a bare branch, just like, I thought, a Republican candidate in 1958.

Aug. 14, 1958

Dear Bill,

This morning, according to schedule, we should be in Delft and Alkmaar. We think about it as watchers on hilltops watch people trudging the hot and dusty roads at noon.

In fact, we're almost back to old times. A couple of days ago, I burned a seven-page letter to you; a few days before that, another, shorter, but not much shorter. I set out to tell you certain simple, and as it seemed to me, faintly amusing facts— and lo, we were orbiting with all that cosmic debris "5000 miles (or was it feet?)" as Nietzsche said, "above time and space." This is not a good mean epistolary height—so, to the fireplace!

First, I wanted to apologize once more for the "we're not going abroad this year" rumpus [13]; and all the nuisance we were to various people. Then I wanted to say: thank you, but it's a little hard to know where to begin. So I started chronologically (this was what seemed amusing to me). For Mrs. Vogt's [14] letter and its enclosure arrived after the great cancellation crisis was over. I telephoned to cancel the booking. You telephoned, Ellen [Chambers' daughter] telephoned, Nora telephoned and even arrived on her magic carpet to reconnoiter. A special delivery from you arrived—a 24-hour feat never before known to man. There I was, feeling a little weary, not at all disappointed, but much disgusted at myself, when the mail was brought in. Idly I opened Mrs. V's letter, saw that it enclosed a bill and a check, of which I thought without glancing at it: "Why a check?" I did not, in fact, take the contents out of the

[13] WC had planned a trip to Europe with his wife, which at the last minute he canceled.
[14] WFB's secretary.

envelope, and went to bed, unenlightened. Next day, to continue the epic, I sank below a sea of typhoid and smallpox germs, for both E. and I had beautifully positive reactions. When I returned to life, the word *bookkeeping* flashed through my mind (some impression must have been nibbling there, like a mouse in the wainscoting). The plane bill, and whatever that check was, must go back. So I looked and saw what the check was for. How wonderfully kind! All the more so in view of *NR*'s hard times. It was at this point, though, that I began to smile. For, if I had grasped its meaning when I should have, we might even now be in the land of cheeses and tulips, unblooming at this season. I should not, under any circumstances, have accepted that generous check: I no longer feel myself able to justify it. But had I seen it, it might well have given the psychological fillip that would have sent us across, anyway. This is my sole thin excuse for laboring all this. Money was the true reason for our canceling out. But it was true within a context. The context was Esther's worry about money. She is beset by outstretched hands, presenting bills, as Odysseus was beset by the ghosts. E. had worried herself into a heart spell. She told John what was wrong; he told me. The next day I cancelled. What else could I do? How could we run around Europe to any point when one of us is tormented at every turn by the specter of bankruptcy upon homecoming? Yet we could have done it—paid our way, I mean. We have the money; that is why I liquidated when I did—a very poor move as it now turns out, since it was unnecessary. Yet Esther's relief was enormous and instant; and nothing else really matters to me. My point about Mrs. V.'s letter is simply this. If I had studied it a psychological moment sooner, I think I should have said: "This money hubbub is really all nonsense; the thing to do is to bundle E. on that plane even by stretcher." But I didn't; so here we are. No doubt, it's all for the best. Travel is a dreadful fatigue (I don't see how you, 20 years younger than we are, can possibly sense our organic weariness). Add into this a lot of incidental factors, and you have the outlines of the mess—on one side.

There is another, of course. In cancelling, I quite consciously closed a door. I do not know that it gave on anything. In any case, I closed it. It is at this point, in my earlier letters, that I rocketed into space. I do not want to do that again. But I must note, in honesty, that I no longer seem to be of the slightest use to you or to anybody else. This should be thought on. I am a casualty of the times, an extremely minor one, of interest even to myself only to the degree in which, as artist, I can get above myself, look around and draw some conclusions. To others I am simply a burden, gratuitous. Perhaps I can risk some pawings, and thereby land this letter, like the others, in the fireplace. The thesis implicit in *Witness* is that, for the West, the struggle is its own solution. Out of the struggle itself, the thesis goes, the West may rediscover in itself, or otherwise develop, forces that can justify its survival. Lacking these, the West is specifically described as "a dying world," or "the losing side." The deeper counterpoint is orchestrated around my brother's suicide as one logical act in face of this world bereft of meaning; and my own rejection of suicide in a deliberate effort to act meaningfully upon that dying world. Thus, in personal terms is set forth what Camus has argued theoretically in *The Myth of Sisyphus* and *The Rebel* (without, necessarily, accepting his conclusions). In *Witness,* too, I declared myself a counterrevolutionist by express contrast with conservatism, which I found incapable of coping with revolution, for reasons given. So I invited consideration of counterrevolution as a course of action. Invited because I myself was uncertain. In this time, the modes of counterrevolution are defined, of course, by rigorous realities. I was uncertain whether a counterrevolution à la de Gaulle (as we might now say) was possible. This I might have accepted *then.* Otherwise, the question was: are there humanly permissible variations on the other alternative (I believe there is only one other)? Senator McCarthy, as much as anyone, convinced me that there are no permissible variations. I became convinced that de Gaulle is no answer to anything, even before the event. By 1955, it seemed clear past question that the thesis of *Witness* is no go: for the West the conflict itself is not going to be its own solution. At least, the West is not going to rediscover in itself, or develop, any justifying energies—at any rate in terms meaningful to me. So far, it has responded in nothing but power terms whose logic (whether or not it ever comes to that) is simply apocalypse. Certainly it is not a solution of anything. Mr. Eisenhower's great speech (of yesterday) on Arab slum clearance sniffs at some solutions; it is late, but the bazaar may keep open late for a bargain. (At this point, mercifully for both of us, you telephoned.) I should probably have rambled on for pages. But all I was going to say is this: counterrevolution will not work—its solution is a bad one, and, if tried, must come to a bad end. The West keeps piling up weapons systems, which lead, of course, to two bad alternatives: (1) to retreat whenever there is any danger of using the weapons; (2) the temptation to use them, which is catastrophic. The East, at least for people like me, is a horror. This leaves me, sitting in my rocking chair, or tearing out to shoo the kingfisher away from eating my goldfish. I can't even indulge moral indignation at his expense; I'm a fish eater, too. Certainly I'm of no use to anybody. It is true, of course, that I also hear what Sisyphus listens to as he descends the hill—the little voices of the earth. I am afraid that, much against my will and to the embarrassment of both of us, I must agree with Sartre's charge that Camus finds peace by subtracting himself from history. In my rocking chair I think of what Sisyphus thinks of when he descends the hill. But I also hear: All day the din of battle westward rolled. I want to struggle toward that sound. Then I see that I am disarmed and that the battle is for nothing. "You are dead, of course?" the Mayor of Riva asks the Hunter Gracchus, who is lying on the bier in [Franz] Kafka's fable. "Yes, of course, I am dead," the Hunter answers. "But you are also alive?" asks the Mayor. "Yes," says the Hunter, "in a certain sense, I am also alive." "A terrible fate," says the Mayor. In my American way, I should say: "Put up or shut up; fish or cut bait." That's the point I am at, and which you must think about. For I am simply a burden to you.

As always,
Whittaker

The Russians must have been misinformed as to which KLM flight we were to be on.[15]

September 2, 1958

Dear Bill:

Thank you for Lolita, who has come to our house to stay. So far, I have met only three words which I did not recognize; and, as I cannot remember what they are, I must muddle through without them. If *nictating*[1] puzzled you, that is perhaps because you did not learn, as a child, the meaning of a *haw*, that is to say, "the nictating membrane or third eyelid of a horse." The grandeur of this definition, together with the fascinating fact that horses have three eyelids, has caused me to remember nictating all my life. Perhaps *phocine*[2] stumped you? If so, it is probably because the *ph* caused you to forget that Spanish calls the same thing: foca. (The French word for it is *phoque;* but, as we know, the French, they are a funny race. It is a quite innocuous word.) So much for lexicology.

I have met Mr. Nabokov before. I have his brilliant study entitled: Gogol. I say "entitled" because it is a brilliant study of Nabokov, but I am not sure just where it leaves Gogol. Not in any shape readily recognizable by me. Now, Gogol happens to be one of my oldest and dearest Russian friends. I could not have been more than 14 when I discovered Dead Souls, nor 12 when I read Taras Bulba. It was the entrance upon a universe. In a famous line of Pushkin's: Tam russki dukh—tam Russuyu pakhnet (*There* is

15 A day or two after WC was to fly KLM to Amsterdam, the plane (same flight number) went down in the Atlantic, no survivors.

1 Nictating membrane: "a thin membrane found in many animals at the inner angle or beneath the lower lid of the eye and capable of extending across the eyeball." (*Webster's Third New International Dictionary*)

2 Phocine: "of, relating to, or resembling seals." (*Webster's Third New International Dictionary*)

the Russian soul—there it smells of Russia). And when one says smells in this connection, one means *smells*. Gogol meant *smells*. And besides, chort ne znayu, who has read that opening scene in Dead Souls, and gotten up, shaking with invisible laughter, and ever been the same man after; or failed to laugh again and again, no matter how many times he rides with Chichikov up to the inn? Tam Russuyu pakhnet. Gogol has on me the effect of laughing gas, and even in anticipation. When I think of the title: *Ivan Fyodorovitch Shponka And His Aunt,* I am off. I nominate it for one of the world's most marvelous titles. All the futility that used to be east of the Vistula, and many other things, besides, are in that ridiculous title. But my case is even worse: others, I find, are quite unmoved by the postscript to Aunt Vasilisa Tsupchevska's famous letter—"PS. We have a most wonderful turnip in our kitchen garden. It is more like a potato than a turnip." I laugh inwardly at what I know too well to laugh aloud about. And this is not helped by Shponka's reply to his Aunt: "Dear Auntie Vasilisa Kashporovna, Thank you very much for sending me the linen. My socks, especially, were terribly old and my batman had to darn them four times as a result of their having shrunk. . . . Pigs are mostly fed here on brewer's mash which is mixed with a little stale beer." I know one laughs, or one finds it pretty stupid. I commend it beyond all learned works to those who would know what Russia is all about.

Nabokov does not think too highly of Shponka And His Aunt. He is pushing a thesis, namely, the Gogol is not a realistic writer. So Dead Souls and The Revizor etc. are not pictures of Russia, but refractions of Gogol's genius, which is true, naturally, up to a point. A somewhat similar line is pushed about Shakespeare: he was simply writing melodramas of blood according to a well-worn pattern of his time, and we are simply reading things into the plays when we think he consciously wrote four or five of the greatest tragedies of the will known to man. Nevertheless, some of us continue to think so. And thousands who laughed themselves blear-eyed, or wrung their hands in happy despair, over Dead Souls and The Revizor, saw in them the old Russian reality, and still do. They smell of Russia. Nabokov has his reasons, I suspect, for holding otherwise. He is a free intelligence, and stands superior to Tsars and Commissars, whom he sees to be alike stupid and malign, from his vantage point. It is the vantage point of the man who, having lost his land, has found haven, with a little scorn, in the only realm open to a superior intelligence, the realm of Art. He is a superb artist. But, at bottom, he is saying: There is nothing. It would be a rash man, who, at this hour and day, would choose to gainsay him. True art usually runs a little ahead of reality. He is the fall-out before the fall-out. Which makes me wonder: now that paperbacks are here, why does no one translate and publish Paul Bourget's Essays In Contemporary Psychology? I was 22 when I first read them, sitting in the sun on a balcony above the Vereeniging Straat in Brussels. They made a powerful impression on me, and I have the feeling that, unlike much else, they have a lot to say right now. I suspect that the essay on Turguenev bears somewhat on Nabokov. Glancing back, I see that I left something dangling. I said that Nabokov is saying: There is nothing. Deep within me, I resist this. I take my stand on something else, which Nabokov would laugh to scorn, and not only he. I stand on what Ehrenburg said, a couple of years ago, in defense of Pasternak: "If the whole world were covered with asphalt, one day a crack would appear in the asphalt; and, in that crack, grass would grow." This forever divides me from the Nabokovs. It also divides me from the easy optimists. But it is also why, though I may sound bleak in the great night, it is unlikely (as the shallow imagine) that I could ever be a man of despair, as, I suspect, many of them may prove to be. And this touches what I mean by saying that only those who speak to men 100 years from now (when perhaps the crack will appear) have much to say to me. My hope lies beyond the walls of darkness. They are real, but so am I. I live, therefore I cannot despair. Of course, I am speaking of despair in terms of history, since it is at our throats.

Turning to something certainly related—do not build too much on my editorializing. I shall try; I am not sanguine. Out of your goodness and generosity, you incline, I think, to brush aside my saying that the differences are great between NR and me. They are great. Nothing is so likely to disclose them as editorials.

I should guess that the differences will paralyze me so that I cannot write; or that what I may write will not suit. Once, when I was younger, I could play the game, write all kinds of shorthand, take all kinds of short cuts, trusting truth to emerge somehow, faintly, through all compromising journalese. I am older; much more important, so is the age. I want reality now; have no time left for anything else; have little patience with anything short of this effort. We actually do stand before the thermonuclear apocalypse, for there is a visible impulse, on both sides, to break the weapons stalemate by a calculated taking of the consequences. This defines the reality of this moment, as I see it.

As always,
(Whittaker)

Next day: Up at five this a.m., to see that my son got hot coffee in him before I drove him to his draft board; and to give him, too, at least the illusion, that there was someone quiet and strong beside him up to parting, and, thereafter, behind him. If the time ever comes (as I pray it never will) for you and your son to take this journey, I think you will consider with a quite new urgency what Jaspers meant by writing: "Quietly, something enormous has happened in the reality of Western man: a destruction of all authority, a radical disillusionment in an overconfident reason, and a dissolution of bonds, have made anything, absolutely anything, seem possible. . . . Philosophizing, to be authentic, must grow out of our new reality, and there take its stand." Other parents were sitting in parked cars near the draft center, waiting—for a last look, I suppose. I did not wait.

Shortly after writing his August 14 letter, Chambers told me that he wished to change his work habits, and to come to New York and work there with us putting out the magazine on Tuesdays and Wednesdays. Accordingly, on alternate Tuesdays (NR is a fortnightly), he took to rising early, driving to Baltimore, and catching the train that brought him to New York in time for the editors' lunch at 12:30. After that, the editorial meeting

at which assignments were given out to the editorial writers,
of which he was one. We would work late, until about eight
o'clock, and then would go out, the four or five of us, to dinner.
Thus it went for four or five months, and then one Tuesday he
did not come. I telephoned and learned that he had been struck
down again and was held in bed, immobile, by his doctor's
orders. In the anxious discussion with Mrs. Chambers I learned
that it was her impression that it was I who had suggested that
Whittaker come to New York. I was very anxious to correct the
record, and wrote him.

I hope you can read this.

Nov. 23???, 1958

Dear Bill,

Going to N.Y. was my doing, and nobody else's; and there
should be no more laboring of that. Up there, no one could
have been more kind to me than you were. My current condition was coming to me for a month or so, as I knew well enough.
Usually, I sit out the symptoms. I tried to sit out the last one.
But it proved too strong. First night was rather poor. Next day,
I was still alive; the following day even aliver. I intend to get
up as soon as possible. As to N.Y., I shall return, though perhaps
more cautiously at first. This heart business is much misunder-
stood, it seems to me, by the spectator. You can have some
felling twinges, and quite extravagant pain, and get up, and go
about your business. The real outsizers are warning, of course,
that you had better go to bed or else. But the net virtual effect
is that of an apparently bouncy soul who, nevertheless, claims a
special illness. People feel cheated. You can see forming in the
eyes of sympathetic onlookers an expression which means:
"Why, he's not really dying." They want to go to the box office
and get their money back. They do not know about the im-

mortal fatigue or the tiny edge of stamina that keeps all this brave show going. No reason why they should.

I hear that you have turned thirty-three. Birthdays fill me with wonder that anyone should have survived so long in a world where so much is against that likelihood. I see that in this sense, they are occasions for surprise. Whether they are rightly occasions for rejoicing, I am of two minds. Granted that consciousness is the most wonderful thing that ever happens to a creature, and its extinction the most brutal violation.

I am much content with my cheerfulness of mind in this spin as contrasted with those in the past. Several factors contribute. But I shall claim something for the course of re-examination and retesting of all ground for firmness, which set in with the crisis of 1954–55 (I think it was).

Some editorial matters. Ralph tells me that Edmund Wilson has done (*New Yorker*) something about Pasternak in the general direction that I was moving. Too bad I didn't move faster. I propose to move, anyway; this kind of thing is timeless. Wilson (from what Ralph tells me) has certainly got hold of the right string to pull. But I shall pull it rather differently. So I am doing a Pasternak piece. I am also picking away at another piece on the Republicans. Trouble ahead here, I am afraid. It was the Old Guard the voters wiped out in the last election. If anyone supposes that my published reaction thereto was a lament for the Old Guard, anyone has completely misread the piece. If the Rep. Party cannot get some grip of the actual world we live in and from it generalize and actively promote a program that means something to masses of people— why, somebody else will. There will be nothing to argue. The voters will simply vote Republicans into singularity. The Rep. Party will become like one of those dark little shops which apparently never sell anything. If, for any reason, you go in, you find, at the back, an old man, fingering for his own pleasure, some oddments of cloth (weave and design of 1850). Nobody wants to buy them, which is fine because the old man is not really interested in selling. He just likes to hold and to feel. As your eyes become accustomed to the dim kerosene light, you are only slightly surprised to see that the old man is Frank Meyer. So you see I am as always

Whittaker

Nov. 31, 1958

Dear Bill,

I have graduated to John's portable. It is a sullen machine: and neither of us trusts the other an inch, so I am not quite sure how it will turn out—the letter, I mean.

Last night, I had a number of jottings in mind. But they seem to have vanished, mostly. I now recall only these shreds:

In Warsaw, they are saying: "Thank God, we have a buffer state between us and the Chinese."

If you have not heard Victor Borge reading, in the "inflationary language," a story which begins: "Twice upon a time," you have missed a moment, minuscule, but pleasant, of our time. In re Borge: how much even a little intelligence helps; after listening to his rather usual European cabaret, the lone and level sands stretch far away. The sands are everything else one is likely to be exposed to. The enemy is within the citadel; that is, the TV set now stands on the chest beyond my bed. What bilge most of it is.

In re that piece about Fate and Freedom which F. Meyer's correspondent finds apocalyptic in its choice, yesterday, for the first time ever, I came on this quote: "The laws of social life and the principles of party . . . are also a force not second in its grandeur to the antique Fatum. Social principles in their pitiless compulsion, not less than Aeschylus' Fate, can grind into dust the individual soul if it enters into conflict with them." The author: Leon Trotsky, writing in Siberian exile for a local paper, 1902. I was then one year and several months of age. It took several more decades for us, each in his own way and scale, to illustrate the brilliant seer's text.

I am very eager to review for *NR* this book: *Germany and the Revolution in Russia, 1915–1918: Documents from the Archives of the German Foreign Ministry;* edited by Z. A. B. Zeman; Oxford Press. This is a field that is of peculiar interest to me; and one in which I have done a good deal of special reading. I also have a special devotion (I believe religious folk say) to two of the main characters involved—Karl Radek and Parvus (A. L. Helphand—of whom I have written you before). Perhaps you can get Frank Meyer to route me the book; I doubt that I should have much luck.

Herewith, too: Bishop O'Gara's very human response to your beautiful tribute to your father. Also, Mr. Mooney's [16] letter to Meyer. I don't quite make it out, largely, I suppose, because it refers to a past conversation between them. I have the impression that Mooney is trying to be sensible in the presence of eternal verities—usually a troublesome business. But I am not sure; it is all through a glass darkly. If I were Meyer's keeper, I should commend to him the therapy suggested in this line: *"Pour atteindre la vérité, il faut une fois dans sa vie, se défaire de toutes les opinions qu'on a reçues; et reconstruire de nouveau, et dès le ʃondement, tous les systèmes de ses connaissances."* [17] Quote from memory, so, no doubt, the usual errors. I would also add something: not *une* fois dans sa vie, but as often as there remains in the daily perishing creature any principle or energy of growth.

I have no intention of remaining in bed much longer. But I hope the interval has given me a time out for some stock taking (stock, not profit, taking).

As always,
Whittaker

[16] *NR*'s advertising manager.
[17] To attain to truth, one must, at one point in one's life, undo all the opinions one has received and reconstruct anew, from the foundations, the whole system of one's knowledge.

Dec. 8, 1958

Dear Bill,

Some repairs. First, Bishop O'Gara's letter, for which over-sight my apologies. Second, a ten-dollar bill which Mrs. Vogt has sent me (probably at Brent's request) to repay $10 I once lent him. But I had already been repaid. Third (one can smell the brimstone!), Mrs. [Isabel] Paterson's letter. *Saxibus ululant nymphae.*[18] I wore myself out, the other day, writing you a tightly typed, five-page commentary on this letter; or, more exactly, on the dilemma of the Rep. Party. This has now been, wisely, burned; and I do not want to repeat the exercise. But, of course, I am tempted to scratch some notes. Mrs. Paterson seems to feel an extreme need to be a pythoness (of course, I do not mean a female reptile of great girth and length). She seems to crave 100% score in prophecy. This, in addition to being of little moment if only one keeps a clear view of lines of force and directions, is extremely difficult to achieve. History tells us that no one has ever succeeded. But I am heartened to learn that she knows that a party represents "a substantial interest." From the underscoring, I gather that she feels this to be a discovery. And so, no doubt, it was several hundred years ago. But, soon, later, or when you will—it matters little so long as she has this little truth firmly in her mind—it can lead to the most illuminating (not to say, lurid) insights. But it can't lead Mrs. Paterson. For, from her discovery that a party represents "a substantial interest," she makes the as-tonishing mental somersault that neither party (Dem. or Rep.) any longer represents any interest. Each does, though; the pathos, indeed the crux of the Rep. dilemma, arises from the fact that it represents a very definite interest (or set of interests), but not one that stirs so many eager voting hands as the Demo-cratic interest. I have not the advantage of knowing what Meade Alcorn [19] said that so raised the lady's wrath and bent

18 The nymphs are wailing by the rocks.
19 Republican national chairman.

her logic like Einsteinian light rays. But I think I could reconstruct what he said (or meant to say) with the slightest effort. He said (of course in much more winsome words): "Republicans have got to win the masses or sail up the creek." I deduce that something like this, too, brought Mrs. Paterson to the sunburst thought that original sin, politically speaking, consisted in giving the vote, in the first place, to the unpropertied helots. Some old ladies con dream books or tea leaves; Mrs. Paterson divines the future from the past wickedness of giving men human rights; and dreams (I can only infer) of a sweeter, better time when this old error may be undone. The No. 1 problem for the Rep. Party is to win back the masses for the only objective history has left the Republicans in the running for: to win the Executive in 1960. All else is lost for about a decade (that is, taking the most optimistic view). The problem is to win the masses: and this, I presume, is what Mr. Alcorn senses, and perhaps even dimly sees. In this effort, the Republican Right, so far as I can see, is not of the slightest help, and, historically, probably can't be. Yet the masses must be won by the Republican Left while keeping the Republican Right within the family. Once I hoped that Mr. Nixon could perform this healing bond, holding the Right in line, while a Republican Left formed about him a core. By Republican Left, I do not mean Liberal Republican. Theodore Roosevelt would know exactly what I mean. But what *I* mean is of little moment. The Republican Party will win the masses, or history will find for it a quiet, uncrowded spot in the potter's field; the grass will grow greenly because no mourning foot will ever tread it down. Besides, people will dread the spot because of the banshee screams, heard there even at noonday—Isabel Paterson, of course.

I thought that, in the circumstances, you answered Max Eastman well. His resignation [20] is extremely disquieting to me

---

[20] Max Eastman, the inveterate atheist, resigned (amiably) from the board of contributing editors to *National Review* on the grounds that *NR* was too religious.

personally; not only because it seems to have been precipitated by two pieces about which I felt great concern. Your piece about Father Halton [21] was, of course, well done and generous; so that, while I deeply questioned the saying of anything about him, I could go along with the thought: "Poor man, somebody should say a kind word for him out of simple charity." Max's emphasis is different, of course. I always fail to see why an atheist should get excited about "unseating Him," if he believes (sic) that He isn't sitting there; and since, if He is, nobody can unseat Him, anyway. I even wonder if Max *is* an atheist. I bet he believes that E equals MC squared. In the age of the rocket and atomic plane, that's getting perilously close to faith. (By the way, if *NR* doubts that the Russians have the atomic plane * I suggest that at least you, Jim [Burnham] and John [Chamberlain] should not rely on secondhand press clips, but read *Aviation Week* and its editorial. I found that it stirred (not just for the Russians, but for humankind) something like the only question which Mr. Beerbohm thought Mr. Benjamin Jowett likely to have asked Dante Gabriel while he was painting the murals at the Oxford Union: "And what were they going to do with the Holy Grail after they found it, Mr. Rossetti?")

Max's second aversion (to get back to that) was *NR*'s attitude toward Djilas. So far as I know, *NR* has slapped at Djilas only by way of a book review. This was a nasty little job, sophomoric and vicious. If you are going to roast your victims when they are strung up by the thumbs over a slow fire, at least it should be done with some dash. I seem to remember complaining to you about this review. Certainly, it disturbed me enough so that I decided to check; I read the book. I see exactly why the reviewer disliked it; the review remains sophomoric and vicious. I imagine that while Jim, Meyer and I all distrust the Djilas business, each of us puts on it a quite different personal emphasis. My own distrust stands on three legs. I.—There is no

21 The Catholic Savonarola who, briefly, terrorized Princeton.

charisma; Djilas seems to me now exactly what I said of him when he first swam into view: "The perpetual YCL [Young Communist League] leader." But he no longer knows (or at least won't say) whether he is still for the YCL or half of it or none of it. This, I think, is why there is no Djilasism in the world. Neither the Old Guard nor the Youth greatly care what Djilas is doing in Sremska Mitrovitca—except as a symbol, not well defined. And this leads us to II.—That, in consequence, the Djilas fad is a hop-head dream pushed by the socialists, liberals, etc., and their pals in the intelligence services. Perhaps it is of some use; perhaps not. But my deepest objection to Djilas is (III.—) that he is an intellectual misrepresentation. There is almost nothing in *The New Class* which has not been said infinitely better, long, long ago, chiefly by Trotsky. I used to suppose that the term New Class had added something helpful to vocabulary. One day, I discovered that Victor Serge had used New Class in 1937—less emphatically, it is true. I hate to see the work of a brilliant mind (Trotsky) dulled and labored by a high school boy (Djilas). Isn't it odd that the translator and biographer of Trotsky [Eastman] should not feel this even more intensely?

All of which leads me to wonder, by no means for the first time: Why do you want a lug like me on *NR?*

As always,
Whittaker

* (prototype)

Dec. 23, 1958

Dear Bill,

I can't think of a happier way to open the New Year (and perhaps distract you from your painful hand) than to share this information that I have recently come on. The first European translation of *Das Kapital* was into Russian. The St. Petersburg censor looked it over and passed it. *Das Kapital,* he said, was much too scholarly and technical a job for many to read it. But with the clairvoyance of censors, he confiscated the whole printing of a work which, at sight, he recognized to be inflaming—Adam Smith's *Wealth of Nations*.

The best to everybody.

As always,
Whittaker

Perhaps the censor was himself inflamed by Adam Smith's celebrated insight: that corporations have no future.

This is a fragment of a letter which I began the day before the one you have just read. I began it directly after our telephone conversation, which gave me no hint of what your coming letter would say. I have reflected some time about sending you this fragment. Still, for reasons that I do not claim quite to understand myself, I am sending it.

Christmas Eve, 1958

Dear Bill,

Yesterday, I wrote you a note meant to be a light-hearted opener of the New Year. There I should be happy to leave it. But more, much more, needs to be said. I want to thank you for your great kindness and goodness to me, and your infinite forbearance and patience with me, sometimes in matters that may offend you; even more often, perhaps, puzzle you. Certain of my views and stands, even my general habit of mind, may seem to you perversely ungrateful. It is not so. But there is a deep division in my mind, as there often is in minds of my special breed; though, in this case, the division is grooved deeper by the age in which we live. The true quality of my mind is poetic. So far as I know, I have nothing to do with it. I was born this way, and could not change if I wished, at least without violation. By nature, without taking thought, I write poetically (that is, in images, tones, cadences, always, when they come true, related to the mystery and the tragedy of man and life). Often I speak this way, scarcely noticing, myself, the effect whose true nature goes unnoticed by others. I wrote in *NR*, about the moon rocket: "The earth has become a shore of space." Good or bad, this is a purely poetic line; it is almost nothing else; in fact, it runs counter to the subject (scientific achievement) because it calls the mind back from it to the universe. I first spoke this line. It tumbled out in discussing with Jim [Burnham] how I was going to treat the moon shoot. I had the impression that he was a little dismayed (Jim is not essentially a poetic mind; he is a first-rate mind of another breed). But he could scarcely have been more startled than I was when the line slipped out. Where did it come from? I have not the slightest idea. An instant before, it did not exist, and I had not thought of it. An instant after, it was there. This process is essentially me; it is curious that the only image I can find for it is a technical one: the process seems a kind of overdrive. At any rate, it is largely unconscious, intuitive, instinctive. I am continually surprised to read what I have written. I cannot recapture how I came to write that way. It is as if somebody else had written it. But it is not a matter of phrasing. At the core of such minds is the tragic sense of life. It is a sense that one is born with (or is not). Deep in the interior mind, it is like an ever-flowing spring ("nor loud nor harsh"), but perpetual. All the vegetation and the landscape of such minds is watered by that unstaunchable spring. In Greek fable, there is a monster, whose name escapes me, who disposes of his human victims by binding them to a pair of bent saplings, which he then lets fly up, so that the victim is torn in two. So it is always with the poetic mind. Ravished by the beauty of the external world and life, horrified by the frightfulness of the human lot, that mind is torn apart. It seems as if, by the fretting of the raw edges, there arises a peculiar music: we do not know how.

Precisely at this point, Esther brought in the mail with your letter. There was no point in completing the fragment. But I think that I must try to rough in the general direction. I was going to say that the side of my mind which I have called poetic is defined by an extreme individualism, which feels any unusual restriction of freedom to be a killing frost. Freedom is its mode; it simply cannot live in an enjoined conformity which kills it by suffocation. But this same mind is also capable of an intellection that craves irreducible reality as the sole ground from which to generalize a little truth. It cannot ever settle for less, since, ultimately, this reality is all that matters in life, as you find at the last frontier. Reality tells me that freedom, as I meant it above, is ending. The world, for identifiable reasons, is freezing into one of its ages of conformity. And this is true West, as well as East, though the forms and degrees differ. The last decade has taught me that I can do nothing whatever against this trend; and neither, presumably, can anyone else. All I can do is try to fight a rearguard, delaying action. Thus I am in constant revolt against conforming forces, which I see encircling us even in benevolent guise. But what I want, and what reality is, I must keep carefully distinct. I cannot force reality wishfully. Intellect cannot, without self-violation, permit itself to be misled about the nature of the forces in play, their true strength or eventualities. Errors are inescapable; but the mind may never abet them. Often, I believe, this makes others conclude that I am conniving, intellectually, at the very powers that seem to me most killing—because I insist on seeing them without softening, for what they truly are. No doubt this impression is strengthened, in turn, because I gird at the conformities which I think I clearly see entrapping us in the West itself, often in the name of its preservation. Much too much of this.

Then your letter came, and came as a great surprise. It seemed to me a *hic Rhodus; hic salta* letter, which left me no choice but to resign from *NR* at once. The great question in my mind was whether this was your conscious intention, or whether, unconsciously, you had simply added up the factors that brought me to the jump. I did not want to jump. No need to labor the several reasons, though I should like to cite two. One is a sense of gratitude, highly personal, and I should think, quite immeasurable to anyone else, that when my grateful colleagues of the American press (among whom I was not, surely, the least practitioner) slammed the door tight in my face, *NR* offered me a place at its board. Across all differences, so long as it is humanly possible to do so (and even sometimes a little longer), I stand with the men who stand with me. The second reason was that I greatly enjoyed working in N.Y.— greatly. Many words usually make such matters worse. During Christmas and half of the next day, I was trying to say in as few words as possible, as simply and unplaintively as possible, what the problem was. While I was brooding on it, Nora telephoned to say that you had written *Newsweek* about their paragraph.[22] I think the first thought in my mind was: "I'll be damned!" The news seemed to dispose of the question of

22 *Newsweek*, December 22, 1958: "Westminster, Md.—Whittaker Chambers, the onetime Communist agent and former magazine editor who was Hiss's main accuser, lives here quietly with his wife in an old brick house on the same 200-acre farm where he turned over the famous 'pumpkin papers' to House investigators in December 1948. It has been a nonworking farm since 1952 when Chambers suffered a heart attack and there is not a pumpkin in sight. He supports himself from his savings, is now writing a second, non-autobiographical book about the Communist system. His hair is somewhat grayer, but otherwise, at 57, he is still the heavy-set, round, and rumpled figure who dominated the Hiss trials."

WFB letter to editor: "Why on earth do your editors write 18-month-old news about Whittaker Chambers under a Periscopic rubric (current issue, p. 10)? Whittaker Chambers left off writing his book on Communism in order to join the staff of *National Review* in August 1957. He has worked for us full time ever since, and was coming to New York regularly until his most recent physical setback three weeks ago. The story of his joining *National Review* was carried in full by AP, UP and the New York *Times*."

intention in your letter. It also left me with another feeling
for which I must give a little background. The *Newsweek*
piece upset me not chiefly because of its timing, which implied
deliberate mischief, or its muddled reporting. It seemed to
say past question that Alger had, in general, in his conduct
been right, and that, by so much, I have been wrong. Alger has
for Americans in general an annihilating contempt, which he
has dramatized by getting a considerable body of the most
intelligent of them to believe in, and connive at, a lie, which
so far as I can see, has no parallel in history. Why should he
not despise such dupes? For his lie which is aimed at their
lives, they love him and openly or surreptitiously, heroize him.
And this the *Newsweek* piece clearly implies. The man who
sought to help them, they openly or surreptitiously despise and
have, in fact, outlawed, though the means are largely invisible.
It was this contrast that upset me about the *Newsweek* caper. I
felt that for reasons of truth, as well as for reasons of tactics,
somebody should have torn into *Newsweek*. You did, and
without any solicitation from me. There is something else.
For a decade, I have had to be my own defendant. On me
almost alone has rested the burden of defense. The few who
have come to my aid have, in general, done pretty ineffective
jobs. This, too, is a sundering fact that I had to look at and
draw conclusions from. So your rejoinder gave me a great lift.
I am afraid that my pleasure was disconcerting to Nora, for,
while your letter delighted me, it got Ralph into trouble. Like
this: Ralph tried to fend off the *Newsweek* piece, and, failing
at that, to fudge and deaden his answers to the questions which
the N.Y. office sent him. He meant to spare me, and, for the
same reason, did not consult with me about how to handle the
matter. So when you fired into the mischief-makers, and caught
them flatfooted, they caught Ralph with his copy down. Nora
called to get me to agree to a formula that would help Ralph
off the hook. It was not a very sound formula, and I agreed
reluctantly; but the first need was to rescue Ralph. All this
seems to point up something that I have long brooded on—the

lack of consultation among us. Few in numbers, we face an outnumbering enemy that is cunning and extremely cohesive. I think we must consult constantly on any public act. To get away from this particular instance, to another example: when Jim bolted out of the Cultural Freedom Committee, he told neither Ralph, John Chamberlain nor me. If we had consulted, the rest of us might well have gone out with him (I almost certainly would have, and I was then a member of the Central Committee). His action would have been much more effective. In the *Newsweek* matter, I feel sure that Ralph will weather the blow; and I remain delighted that you acted.

By such detours we get back to your letter about which your *Newsweek* thrust so abruptly changed my feeling.[23] Still, the problems from which that feeling arose remain, and I should like to try to set out what I think some of them amount to. I have long feared (have sometimes cautioned) that you suppose me to be something which I really am not. At the risk of offending you, I am going to try to rough out crudely the situation out of which I think the trouble comes. First, you stand within a religious orthodoxy. I stand within no religious orthodoxy. The temptation to orthodoxy is often strong, never more than in an age like this one, especially in a personal situation like mine. But it is not a temptation to which I have found it possible to yield. Forgive me for saying this, but we must get ground under our feet.

You also stand within, or, at any rate, are elaborating, a political orthodoxy. I stand within no political orthodoxy. You mean to be a conservative, and I know no one who seems to me to have a better right to the term. I am not a conservative. Sometimes I have used the term loosely, especially when I was first called on publicly to classify myself. I have since been as

<hr>

23 I could not, even on receiving this letter, recall what it was in my own that prompted WC to write of it as he did. I had no copy, and still cannot imagine what was the subliminal provocation. I wrote and asked, but he did not allude again to it.

circumspect as possible in using the term about myself. I say:
I am a man of the Right. I am a man of the Right because I
mean to uphold capitalism in its American version. But I claim
that capitalism is not, and by its essential nature cannot conceivably be, conservative. This is peculiarly true of capitalism
in the United States, which knew no Middle Age; which was
born, insofar as it was ideological, of the Enlightenment. Hence
the native effort to rest in the past always makes us a little
uneasy, seems merely nostalgic, antiquarian, futile and slightly
fraudulent. England was the first great power in which capitalism seized the State apparatus; begun in 1640, consolidated in
1660. France was the second. In both powers, the medieval
vestiges, which had slowly to be assimilated or co-existed with,
formed a conservative continuity that was valid, and persists
even into 1958. America was the first capitalist power that
started from scratch in a raw continent. We are something new
under the sun. Only the American South sought to persist in
the past, as an agrarian culture, resting on slaves instead of
serfs. To wipe out this anachronistic stronghold, above all to
break its political hold on the nation as a whole, the emergent
capitalist North fought with it what amounted to a second
revolution, that took form in what was (up to that time) the
bloodiest (and first) of modern wars. Here, for the first time on
such a scale, were used the products, turned into weapons, of
Northern industrial capitalism—railroads, telegraph, machine
guns, submarines, armored ships, etc., etc. In sum, the South
lost because it could not match the North in those products,
whose fabrication it scorned in the name of a superior culture—
the fatality of history. You know the rest. From the ruins of
war, in direct consequence of war's industrial needs, U.S.
capitalism burst into such growth as the world had never seen
before. Moreover, as the contending capitalism of Europe (and
Japan) destroyed themselves in war, American capitalism grew
massive as the unassailed arsenal. At the same time, with the
favorable trade balance, it freed itself from Europe's financial

grip and became itself the guardian of the hoard whose symbol is Fort Knox.

There is in this history not one single touch of conservatism. How could it be otherwise? Conservatism is alien to the very nature of capitalism whose love of life and growth is perpetual change. We are living in one of its periods of breathless acceleration of change. The Church did well to distrust Roger Bacon. Science has been, from the beginning, the ideological weapon of capitalism, and is now asserting (even though it may not be interested in doing so) an exclusive dominance. I am saying that conservatism and capitalism are mutually exclusive manifestations, and antipathetic at root. Capitalism, whenever it seeks to become conservative in any quarter, at once settles into mere reaction—that is, a mere brake on the wheel, a brake that does not hold because the logic of the wheel is to turn. Hence the sense of unreality and pessimism on the Right, running off into all manner of crackpotism. Hence, on the other side, the singular manifestation (or so it seems) of prime capitalists (a Rockefeller, a Harriman, a Mennen Williams) turning, as we say, Left. In fact, whatever political forms their turn cloaks itself in, they are chiefly seeking to pace, in order to continue to dominate, the new developments to which the logic of capitalism itself is giving rise, now at tremendous rates of speed. I, too, am a fly, clinging to that violently turning wheel, in the hope of slowing it by what a fly's weight is worth. But I am pro-capitalist; I would only retard for an instant, seek to break the fearful impacts of change, hold back lest the rush of development (in a multitude of frightful forms) carry us to catastrophe, as, in fact, seems almost inevitable. But, above all, I seek to understand what the reality of the desperate forces is, and what is their relationship in violent flux. Thus, I am very much on a line with Jim, though our readings of many things are probably radically different. I have almost nothing in common with the effort of Meyer or Kirk, whose rationales, no matter how formally logical, seem to me, by contrast with the total reality, chiefly an irrelevant buzz. There will be a time when the mode that preoccupies them may again be relevant. But, unless I am greatly mistaken, that time lies on the far side of unimaginable changes, which must be assimilated and generalized before a new synthesis can have any wide meaning. We are in the middle of a universal earthquake. If we survive it, then there will be something to reflect on. It is perfectly clear that we may not survive. At that point, I lose interest.

Forgive me, if you can, the primer history lesson, the discursive superficiality of all this, from which so much is left out. So much that is relevant. But, poor as it is, I think I owe it to you as a crude chart of my view.

We look forward to your visit.

As always,
Whittaker

Dec. 25, 1958

Dear Bill,

This has been an unusually beautiful Christmas. Our Connecticut family stayed home. John and his parents spent Christmas together—the first time the family has been so divided. In prospect, it looked very sad. As it turned out, it did not matter. It was a wonderful day outside, cold but sunny. There was a tree, which we trimmed and found our handiwork good. In its presence, the three of us drank our morning coffee in almost stately detachment—none of the usual rush to tear open, claw open, gifts—the children's hour. John gave me the *Journals of the Goncourt Brothers,* a book I had wanted for years. I gave Esther a book of superb icons, and I gave John Rostovtsev's great work on the Iranians and Greeks in South Russia. (At college, John did East European history with von Solomon, one of Kenyon's best, and one of the best in his field, which John will probably continue in if he goes through with his MA work. Hence Rostovtsev.)

So the day was one of great tranquillity and rare affection, made rarer by the knowledge which each of us has reached in his own degree, that, in life, tranquillity is always precarious and fleeting. Life works always to do its worst to us. We seek constantly to outwit, or at least outlast, it. One learns that about all life has to give are moments; and we must be grateful for what is given. If this was the only Christmas, or the last Christmas, we should have to say that life, by so much, had been very good to us.

We hope that it was as good to you; and that the coming year will be too.

As always,
Whittaker

January 3, 1959

Dear Bill,

You might say to me (like Dr. Hasselbacher): "You should dream more, Mr. Wormold. Reality in our century is *not* something to be faced." The italics are not the author's.

Don't you understand, Bill—my anxiety with respect to you and your letters is rooted in a fear of disappointing you. It is specific with respect to you. If it were somebody else, it would be a matter of some indifference to me. You have offered me something that is very precious—friendship; and you deserve better than to be disappointed by me. But I see that disappointment is threatened by strong differences of viewpoint on important things. In honesty, I have tried to rough out certain differences that seem to me pretty central. You seem to feel that they can be lived with; I am certainly willing to make the effort. So, for the time being, I propose to stop there. To push particulars, especially in the religious area, seems to me to court hurts, and quite unnecessarily. What appeared to me necessary was not to mislead you, or let you, as I feared you were doing, generously mislead yourself about my views. They are explicit in *Witness'* central statement on this side: "God is the Wholly Other—*Gott ist ganz anders.*" I am quoting Barth, of course. And, of course, time has made me uncomfortably aware that people read into this proposition their own accepted meanings, and stop short of its true implications, which might seem rather cheerless. But let us drop all that, if you will, and turn to other matters.

The doctor sentenced me to two months in bed. I got up in one, and I see why the doctor said two. But I am resolved to get back to N.Y., at least in time to try to help out Jim while you are away. If that goes well, in several senses, it would seem to remove certain problems. If not, everybody's course should be clearer. I shall simply do my best to be helpful.

Herewith is the ———— piece about *Zhivago*. I can offer an opinion on it as journalism: it seems to me rather awful. I cannot yet give a final opinion on *Zhivago*. But I have at last driven myself to take up where I left off, about midway. I should finish soon. The book is not exactly a bore. Reading it is more like taking, under compulsion, a very long journey, about which you begin to suspect, from the general route, scenery and comments by the way, that, after you have got wherever it is you are going, you will not have got much of anywhere. Of course, Pasternak is a lyric poet of talent, and you rather itchily suspect, too, that much of the book's quality was lost in translation, which must have been extremely difficult. As you might expect in the case of a lyric poet, the landscapes and their evocative moods are much the best thing; much better than the characters, which have a way of dissolving just as you expect them to take firm form. *Dr. Zhivago* is, in fact, the only real character (as we use that term about fiction) in the book. This does not help a novel much. Still, this vast slow-moving flux must be building, just by accumulated weight, toward some culmination. When I have reached and experienced it, I may revise, even reverse, some of my opinions about it. So far as I have gone, I have not come on anything to support a notion that Pasternak is essentially, let alone explicitly, Christian. Perhaps that, too, will turn up later. But I must confess in advance that I shall be greatly surprised to come on the "inescapability of resurrection." It sounds almost like a threat. That kind of thing may be quite in place in a denominational magazine. Elsewhere, it has an air of finger-shaking assertion that doesn't quite suit. I think Mr. ——— misses a point, or perhaps it is just the point that arouses him. To wit, it is not that thousands of minds in the West do not *believe* in resurrection. It is rather that they do not want resurrection. For most of them, one life is quite enough, is a little more than enough. With Camus they can say: "I want a closed door." But perhaps Pasternak doesn't. I shall be most curious to see.

Forgive us our trespasses.

As always,
Whittaker

Pasternak inspired Ilya Ehrenburg to make what seems to me one of the memorable utterances of the time. I have long disliked Ehrenburg to the point where I would simply turn away from anything he had said. This was not only because he was one of Stalinism's most abject literary time-servers (of that, one might have said: "Poor man, what could he do, how can I judge?"). But I believed, too, that he had condoned, if not connived at, the purge death of a man who had been most kind to me—the Polish writer and editor, Bruno Jascienski. So it was astonishing, when Pasternak was under official fire before the *Zhivago* business, to hear that old time-server, Ehrenburg, rise to Pasternak's defense. This is what Ehrenburg said, inter alia: "If the whole world were to be covered with asphalt, one day a crack would appear in the asphalt; and in that crack grass would grow." It wrings the heart, and suggests that resurrection may be of more than one kind. Incidentally, it was those lines that closed the long, three-part piece [24] which began with the account of TV's *The Price Is Right* program—the mink-upholstered sofas and all that. I offered the lines as the irreducible terms on which the mind can have hope in our age. I have not changed my mind, so no doubt it was just as well that I shelved the piece.

[24] Chambers did not complete it.

Feb. 8??, 1959 (Sun.)

Dear Bill,

I am afraid you will be jetting back before I can jet off a
letter to you. I have been writing pretty steadily; and, when I
am not writing, I am a washout. This will be only a phrase to
you, one whose meaning, happily, you will not overtake for
many years. You and Jim were most kind about the Lunik
piece; others whose judgment I trust tell me that, as it appeared,
it was another basket case. I chose not to see for myself. Anyway, I have sent Jim a thundering 13-pager; and I am waiting,
somewhat curiously, for his reaction. I believe that it is pro-
vocative; I imagine some would find it hair-curling. I lift my
adjectives from the mode. I also have 3 other pieces, one
completed in rough; one half done; one on the way. The half-
done is topical, and must be put ahead. It is about TV and
Education; perhaps I can crash "From the Academy," [25] at least
on the slight pretext that I am an honorary Doctor of Laws. If
only I had the strength, I could be writing day and night, if
only. . . . I have seldom been so beset by subject matter; I slap
at piece-ideas, like a man batting off mosquitoes. There is a
reason for this, of course. I seem to be clarifying and firming
up a position, from many sides, of many strands; and, of course,
when we grope toward a position, there is a bracing sense of
outlook, if not actual height. Anyway, there lies the world,
always at such times disclosed afresh, because, though it is the
same world, the perspectives and the relationships appear new,
yielding a new landscape. It is the year-long, knee-deep slogging
through the lowlands, with their mucky sloughs, that wearies
body and mind. Of course, I have long had a sense of direction
(direction here converts to hope); it was destination, or perhaps
just resting place, that baffled. But the world, through which
this commonplace journey must be pushed, is, these days,
shaking and tumbling, while "brightness falls from the air"—

[25] A department in *National Review* relating to educational matters, written
by Russell Kirk.

often an utterly deluding brightness, and, ultimately, perhaps, lethal; or heading that way. And the position, if indeed there proves to be one? Not, I think, a position in which multitudes will throng to join me. But who wants multitudes? It is my feet, mine alone, that I am responsible for, and need to feel firm ground beneath. If, here and there, one other finds this ground firmer than some other—why, I am middling courteous and the mind knows no monopolies. But, as I say, I shall not be crowded. Etc., etc., etc.

I did not thank you at all for the "Goldberg Variations." Somehow that got lost (unpardonably) in the din of the Erinyes, who are also much on hand these days, though I shall spare you all that. I love this intellectual counterpoint with its horizontal certainty (destination beyond question here). But though I love it, and love to listen to it, I would be untruthful if I said that this music is mine. It is not, though it has taken me some time to understand why, for I am fearfully unlettered in this field, as in so many others. I have been able to get at it, as usual, only historically. Brooding on this recently, I was much caught by what seemed to me a consistent point of departure in your thinking and mine (a subject that has much preoccupied me of late). You tend to take off, or so it seems to me, from a mainland of established verities. I am the horrid brat of historicity. Faced with almost anything, my first questions are: how, why, from what cause through what lines of development (in flux) to what effect (in flux)? No judgment entertained here; just a distinction attempted. But I could not help thinking, sadly, that my letters would not be of much use to you in winding up your book, for the same reason (to snatch at grand symbols) that Bach cannot be Beethoven, however much B2 fulfills the disciplines of B1, which B2 is, nevertheless, fated to end. The other day, I heard L. Bernstein "explain" and conduct the "Egmont Overture" for young people. Yet his explanation did not "explain," did not mention, who Egmont was. Like trying to construct an arch, I thought, without dropping in the keystone. Historicity.

I hope the book marches. Do you have a small room to write in, with as few windows as possible—always my first requirement (and what fun the Freudians would have with that)? As for skiing—*Hals und Beinbruch* [Break a leg!], the curious Austrian way of wishing you Godspeed; perhaps the Swiss have their own style. Which, in turn, reminds me that neither have I thanked you for Mark Twain on the German language. Poor man, he did not live to read the first Duino elegy, which I quoted in *Witness*. It goes: *Wer, wenn ich schriee, hörte mich denn aus der Engel Ordnungen?*

> Who, if I cried out, would hear me than from among
> the orders   Of the angels? And suppose one of them
> were to take me Suddenly against his heart. I would
> fade out against His stronger being. For the Beautiful
> is nothing   But the beginning of the Terrible, which
> we are just able to bear, And which we adore so, be-
> cause it disdains, serenely, To destroy us. Every Angel
> is terrible.

So Rilke is my poet, and Lorca with his *Tierra seca/Tierra quieta/de noches/Inmensas*—so different; so same at root; for, of course, we are all talking about the same thing *en attendant* "with a little patience" *l'ange noir.*[26]

Already we are expecting your return soon—much too soon, I suppose, for you.

Our best to your family.

As always,
Whittaker

And what does the B.O. [Bernese Oberland—Ed.] in [your] address stand for? Surely, not, *um Gottes Willen, nein!* [For God's sake, no!], not among the Swiss. Though Saanen, one re- members, is a notable breed of goat. Then a worse thought

[26] On awaiting, with a little patience, the black angel.

occurs . . . have the Russians, can it have happened already—
B.O.—Bernski Oblast? [27]

March 12, 1959

Dear Bill,

I thought you might want this [28] back quickly. Thanks for
the privilege of a peep on three counts.

I. If the *New Statesman* is "a muck heap," I wish that General Grant would tell me what whiskey he drinks so that I could
send the same brand to the other generals.

II. So Miss West has discovered that "the Welfare State is
an inevitable result of the machinery that has to be set up to
deal with the huge urban populations which are a feature of
our civilization." I love that "deal with"; and I'm sure that
there's a term in logic for this particular, amusing scramble of
it; but she's got the root of the matter in her. Twopence gets
you a £ that she'll never find her way along the root. This is
not said meanly. I think you know that I admire her as writer.
Besides, she has brilliant insights. Come to think of it, there's
something more special: she's the only writer that comes to
mind whose insights are *brilliantly* wrong—sometimes, not
always. But when you think back—how superb *Black Lamb and
Grey Falcon* was; and when you think a little farther back, you
think: But what a taffy pull! She's wonderful at catching bits,
sharp bits, like the Croat calling to his wife on the station
platform, early in *Black L & Grey F;* and in juxtaposing them
with other bits to form a big burst of meaning. What an eye for
relationships, you think. Then you think, one day: But it's all
Roman candles! You see the process in the raw in that curiously
illogical sentence about the cause of the Welfare State. Don't
let me seem ungenerous. Miss W. is a writer of the born-not-
made breed; for these mercies, let us give thanks.

III. I was struck by her compassion for Alger; and, for
once, I think, I was pinked. I don't quite know why; just,

27 A Russian province.
28 A letter from Rebecca West.

perhaps, because my rather circumspectly reverential mind does respect her, and her compassion does command my attention, I feel that the compassion might be a little more catholic. And, of course, my thought disgusts my mind; but then the human creature does so many disgusting things, any day. Ralph took out after Alger recently; and I said: "I have no rancor against him whatever. Judge Murphy was right in saying of the Hisses: 'If they came back tomorrow and said they were sorry, you'd resume the friendship.' " Ralph said he simply could not understand. I said that my compassion, apart from the purely human consideration, sprang from the fact that I understood, as few others can, the rules of war that Alger fought under, and the tactics the rules (and the situation) dictate. A silence followed in which I found myself thinking: "Nevertheless, if you take your eye off those peculiar rules for an instant, there is nothing left to say but that Alger has behaved like a complete swine." Not a very bright swine, either. Then Ralph spelled out in some details certain of the swineries. Perhaps this is too fresh in mind for Miss West's *"Dieu, que le son du cor est triste le soir au fond du bois."* I must sound this way at times to other people. Besides, I'm getting crankier and crankier, surlier and surlier. My writing's all snarled up too. Do you know why? I've always known why.

Since I know A. Koestler, and sometimes we write letters, and I've read almost everything he's written,—now that *The Sleepwalkers* must be appearing, one of these days, I suppose that Frank. . . . And how right he will be. *I* should *not* review *The Sleepwalkers*. I should not write at all; I've long known this, too. This isn't the posture that people imagine; Rimbaud *knew* why he went to Africa and traded in calico, though the literati are still perplexed. Calico clothes savages; and trade brings calico and a bit of a profit; but words are nonsense; and so are these words.

It's really a rather pleasant day outside.

As always,
Whittaker

How extraordinary, it suddenly strikes me—but the one thing in my life of which I can think with a certain calm that "is the bliss of solitude" is my one dabble in business: P & R. The only thing I can see that has really helped anybody else, either. One raw day, when I was sitting alone in Ellen's little house, writing that *Life* piece on the 20th Congress, I could see Mr. Pennington, grown old on this farm, working around outside in the weather. I watched and I watched, and I thought and I thought; and all the rules said: Don't. So I called him inside and said: "I take no responsibility whatever, but if I were you...." But you know what I said. And Mr. P went the next day and sold all his government bonds and.... But you know what he did. For a year or two after, when we were stringing fence together, I would catch him looking at me, wonderingly. I knew he was wondering how, after a lifetime of hard labor and hardheaded common sense, he had ever let himself listen to me. He thinks himself a pretty rich man today. Now I feel better. Let us hope capitalism lasts our time.

April 8?, 1959

Dear Bill,

"If"—my subconscious kept mumbling between its stainless steel teeth—"if it's *auspice Teucro,* how can it be '*Teucer dux'*? Better check." So I did just now; and of course, it can't be. The line should read: "*Nil desperandum Teucro duce et auspice Teucro.*" [29] Nothing more horrible than to be caught with one's shirttail showing in a literary affectation. Will you correct?

The line is Horace, of course; Book I; Ode 7. It's the one that begins with the haunting:

Laudabunt alii claram Rhodon aut Mytilenen
aut Ephesum bimarisve Corinthi [30]

[29] Never despair under Teucer's lead and Teucer's auspices.
[30] Let others praise famed Rhodes, or Mitylene, or Ephesus, or the walls of Corinth.

and ends with the crashing: *Cras ingens iterabimus aequor* [31]—
one of my favorite quotes. For I am, improbably, a Horace
fiend. "I should have thought Catullus was the better poet,"
Mark Van Doren once said to me reprovingly. Perhaps Catullus
is; sometimes I think. . . .[32]

Overnight interruption at this point, which included negotiations with some artisans at the Summit, and a telephone
call from a Phila. newscaster, asking if I had a comment on
the State Department's issuance of a passport to A. Hiss. My
comment: "No, no comment at all." I am sure that it lay entirely within State's discretion to give, or not give, the passport,
since Alger has a prison record. But State saw a chance to arouse
people against the Supreme Court's decision in these matters,
by claiming that it had no choice, under existing rulings. This
is an issue on which I feel very strongly, and on the Court's
side. The right to travel freely on the necessary papers is a
fundamental *right* of citizens; and it seems to me to make little
difference who the citizen may be. The spectacle of an artist
like Paul Robeson, denied a passport by his own government,
makes us traduced of other nations. More immediately, it puts
you and me and the next him in jeopardy. Today you deny the
pass to Robeson or Hiss. Tomorrow, with, oh, so slight a shift
in the turning political wheel, and their crowd or some other
denies it to you; with good precedent, which you established.
Much better, in my view, to keep these lines absolutely free.
Only under conditions of actual war, or special legal circumstances (a case in being or in prospect), should government
have the power to trammel its citizens' rights of free transit.
But it helps the Communists by letting them go abroad for
instruction and whatever it is it helps them to do? This seems
to me very close to 100% nonsense. First, how many travel
abroad in this way, for such purposes? They teem, no doubt,
in the minds of the police or certain readers of *American
Opinion*. I remain unconvinced, for I have seen no shadow of

[31] Tomorrow we will take again our course over the mighty main.
[32] WC did not complete the sentence.

evidence that the numbers, the figures, or their missions are
of much moment. Second, if they *are* numerous and of moment,
and if we are on our toes, why, let them travel, and let us
shadow their travels; they will take us to their leader, and
many interconnecting persons, to boot. In fact, it's mostly rot;
and gives those who have an interest or a frenzy at stake something to scare the wilder citizenry with. My telephone caller
of yesterday (self-identified as a friend of ———) surmised that
Alger was free to go behind the Iron Curtain. How stupid can
you get? Alger's business is in London; some flowers on the
grave of the Lord Chief Justice [33]; some understanding moments with his (the LCJ's) friends, heirs assigns. So much for
broadening travel. In fact, this is another move in Alger's
careful rehabilitation. No manager ever nursed along a fighter
more tenderly than the pro-Hiss faction nurses AH, or got more
intelligent cooperation. Nobody has believed me, but I continue to say: "This Cataline is on his way back. *Quōusque
tandem abutere nostra patientia,* * *Catalina?*" [34] To which, he
has the right, I think, to answer: "Just so long as you en-
courage me."

So I get back to Latin tags. I learned, the other night, that
Lenin's speaking style was consciously touched by an enthusiasm for Latin forensics. I also came on this passage: "Sunset.
On the great, springtime pools in the fields, wild swans were
swimming." Five hundred guesses who the author is. I also
learned yesterday, via *Newsweek,* that Krzhizhanovsky died last
week. One of the first made and lastest left of all Old Bolsheviks;
he was in the earliest circles, dating from the last years of the
last century. I did not know he was alive. And then the wailing
died along the mere.

As always,
Whittaker

* But why isn't it: *hastram patientiam?*

33 The Earl Jowitt, Lord Chancellor of England.
34 How long will you continue to try our patience, Cataline?

April 12, 1959

Dear Bill,

For the Order in Council forbidding *NR* editors to write for the *American Mercury*—to thee from me, the *zemnoi poklon*, the Eastern obeisance. Now we are cut loose from that dragging filth; it is a liberation. How good, and how strong, it is to take a principled position. It defines, and defining, frees. Now what is good and strong outside us can draw to us, about whom, there is, in this connection, no longer question, equivocation. The dregs will be drawn to the dregs, and sink where they belong.

In general, in my opinion, we do not discuss enough, within the cadre, about principled matters. We are too considerate, fearful, politic, precisely where we should be bold and free, and, above all, unafraid of the gods of the copybook maxims. If we were to be more freewheeling, we might be surprised by the attraction our freedom might exert on the youth, on whom continuity, if nothing else, depends. No youth, no future.

But such discussion would bring into the open the tenderly evaded, just dissembled, lines of cleavage among the group as a whole? Yes, it would; and so is not to be ventured on rashly—not at the moment, anyway.

For example, to come back to a current matter on which I feel sure I stand alone, the restriction of travel of American citizens is, from a *Rightist position,* wrong in principle. Even if (for cause) we compromise editorially with the expediency, in my opinion, we should, at the same time, make clear that any encroachment by government on the citizen's freedom of movement is, in principle, wrong. Tactics can be extremely flexible so long as the principled position is jealously defined, asserted, iterated.[35]

In defining positions in principle, one always risks losing,

[35] WC expanded his thinking on this point, and on his current attitude toward Hiss, in "The Hissiad, A Correction," published in *National Review,* May 9, 1959.

anticipates losing, the fuzzy, the foggy, the fainthearted, the geese, etc. But in this matter, I have never abandoned Lenin's phrasing of it: *"Luchshe menshe, no luchshe"*—Better less, but better. Besides, the best of those who fall away at first impact, reconsider and return, clarified and strengthened on the point of principle. And that, precisely, is a function of a journal of opinion.

Where is the ms. of your book?

As always,
Whittaker

April 28?, 1959

Dear Bill,

I hope this is not too disheartening. For me, it is becoming a simple necessity of candor to make clear certain positions I hold off the main line of the Right. Otherwise, a blurred or untrue image persists. For the most part, this may not matter. But soon it does. Moreover, I am strongly unwilling to let the Liberals, by default, preempt the humane and intellectually sound positions, when it is precisely the Liberals who, in the name of freedom, are inviting the Total State. Let us have no curtailment of freedoms, they say in effect, so that (though this they do not say) we may more freely construct the Octopus State. I think the Right is playing into their hands, and that the time has more than come for those who claim that general position for themselves to examine and define with a special scrupulousness the civil liberties field. By right it belongs to the Right. Unless the Right willingly forfeits it, the Left falsely preempts it; and when this field is stoutly held it is seen to run counter to the necessities of the Left Liberal position, which force on these folk a tightening and strengthening of the State's coercive powers, beginning with taxation, which is the crux of the Revolution in the U.S., just as the tax police are the true secret police here. But all this is the subject of a very thorough and careful analysis of real forces, together with a most cool-headed appraisal of the comparative weight of the inner (Total State) and outer (Communist) dangers. The inner Communist danger was great in the recent past in the degree, of course, to which its secret cadres were numerous and strategically placed. Those cadres have been pretty thoroughly smashed; and, what is more important, the historical climate does not favor their growth or operation (though, admittedly, a change of overall weather might also change that, and the change might be sudden). Nevertheless, as of now, there seems to me a certain unreality about the Right's general treatment of this subject as if no drastic change had occurred. It leads to faulty emphases, both in what we are for and what we are against. Why, for example, should we leave it to the Liberals to give tongue against the frightening developments in wire-tapping—though that is much too crude a term for the refinements which science is introducing in this practice which the Right has even more reason to fear than the Left? *Ecrasez l'infame* [Abolish the infamy], the Right has every right to say, and much prescient reason. That said, the debate on principle is freed of much hampering and ugly impedimenta. The West, I am more and more convinced, has two main goods to offer mankind: freedom and abundance. They interact, of course; and what we are chiefly saying is that our form of interaction is the best so far evolved. If it isn't, the argument may be long and harrowing, but the upshot seems fated. We help ourselves little, if from one or another kind of anxiety, we abate or curtail freedom. But this is a subject for another piece. Grandmother, how long-winded you are! The Right, I feel more and more, must find its conscience, and make it explicit, first of all to the Right. Until it does, the Liberal monkeys will chatter from the treetops, having them to themselves.

As always,
Whittaker

Automation and what it is doing, and (more important) what it is likely to do next, and the meaning of this in the world context, seems to me a subject screaming to be explored. Jim, I should think, was born for this task.

May 7, 1959

Dear Bill,

I have finished your book,[36] and suppose (with a good chance of being mistaken, of course) that I understand some of your problems in winding it up. It seems to me that they must swarm a little around that chapter which (in my copy) excerpts a letter of mine and indicates only that commentary cometh. This excerpt fascinates me, not only—not at all, I believe—for In Love With the Sound of Your Own Voice reasons. It is the date (1954), above all, that interests me. In the autumn of that year, I went down, unloading hay bales; and, in the long rest in bed that followed, went down and down to where the bedrock begins. Between Christmas of that year and New Year, 1955, I woke, one dawn, from a dream in which I had been singing (in German, but not aloud, of course) a marching song. In my half-waking state, I continued to sing the song to the end, which goes: *Hell aus der dunklen Vergangenheit/Leuchtet die Zukunft hervor*—Bright, from the darkness of the past/Beacons the future. From what depths had this song risen, which I had not sung (or heard sung) for decades? But the song was only a signature. What was wonderful, incredible, was the sense of having passed from one dimension into another; a sense of ordered peace, together with an exhilaration ("At last, I am free"). I had touched bottom and was rising again to the surface; and, to rise, I had cut loose a drowning weight of extraneous this and that. Rather, it had been cut loose for me by my dream (or in my dream), the main lines of which I can remember quite as vividly now as then. I will spare you them. But I lay there in the dawn, listening to that song sound soundlessly through my mind while I savored that unhoped-for release and new freedom. The dream was, in fact, the turning

36 *Up from Liberalism.*

point of my late years. I take it that such a dream is a recapitulation; it prepares itself, as Camus says of suicide, "like a work of art, secretly, in the heart," without the artist's being aware of the process. One day, the secret, subconscious preparation finds expression; in my case, in a dream; other men, other forms. This does not mean that, from that moment forth, I knew where I was going and went there; not at all. Many ups and downs and zigzags followed; much aimless beating around. What I had learned was of two paths, the one I was not going to take because I was not fitted to take it (and, of course, that breaks down into many other factors, too). What I knew thereafter (and this is my excuse for laboring all this to you) was that I was not a Conservative, and that, if I insisted on trying to be one, the only result must be a profound deformation, ending in falsification. I had to face the fact that for me the machine is *not* the enemy. I had faced it once before, of course, with profound reservations. Now I had to face it in quite other terms. The wonderful thing is that this liberation (or work of demolition, if you prefer) having been effected, the practical means of translating it into action presented themselves almost at once, in ways that no one could possibly have foreseen. They would, of course, have presented themselves anyway; that was implicit in the real situation. But if I had not been inwardly prepared to act, they would have meant nothing, a shadow's passing. But I was, at last, prepared to act, and acted. All the rest followed. For practical purposes, I had accepted the world. Let us not push this too far. But I had never before done anything like it. So my first firm act, in this sense, was to liquidate this farm as an operation, and, therewith, all that grotesque resistance to the real world of which it was last stand and symbol. It would be incorrect, I think, to say that I made my belated peace with the real world; but I think I began to see its reality more clearly. This in no sense implies that I was not aware of consequences of all kinds. Some I simply filed as untimely, for future reference and observation. Some I simply moved over for. Etc., etc. Then I waved a little sadly (the pathos of parting) to Frank Meyer and Russell Kirk, silhouetted in a death struggle against the door to which I had left the key under the "Some simple tears they shed," the great reporter of our First Parents tells us, and then, "with something [wandering] steps, and slow, from Eden took their solitary way." From the heights, Burke spoke eloquent invective, to which I had no better answer than: Onward to automation! One chiefly judges by side effects, and I should say that the last two years of my life have been, by all odds, the best. For whom the executioner waits? He always waits; the great thing is to meet him with good spirits and a clear eye. And be prepared to take the consequences? And be prepared to take the consequences. Are you? One never knows for sure. But what makes us feel that we are seems the next best thing to being sure, and about all the certainty we are likely to know.

But I think you must know what lies on the other side of that excerpt, whose meaning remains constant, in the sense that I hold the machine to be the enemy of Conservatism. As I have said ad nauseam, I hold capitalism to be profoundly anticonservative. I have met capitalists who thought otherwise; would, in fact, be outraged by such a statement. I have concluded that they knew their craft extremely well, but not its implications; and that what they supposed to be a Conservative Position was chiefly a rationalization rooted in worry. The result is the oddest contradiction in terms. But, then, the world is full of august contradictions. After all, capitalism took over the world in a century or so of the bloodiest wars, which it supposed were about religion. So they were, so they were—only, not only about religion; and Americans are probably the only people in history who have had the simple forthrightness to face the fact and put it in blunt terms: taxation without representation is tyranny. *They* knew what it was about. The history of the Americans has never yet, to my knowledge, been written. What uncomplicated eyesight. No wonder they suspected Jefferson, the dreamer (and what a dreamer!), the reality of whose dream was to be Jackson. So here we are back to dreams. But it seemed to me that I had to fuzz this in though it will not, I imagine, prove wondrous helpful.

As always,
Whittaker

I wrote in Esquire *(September, 1962): "In the summer of 1959, Chambers felt well enough to indulge a dream, more particularly his gentle wife's dream, to visit Europe. She had never been there, and he had been there only once, in 1927, the trip he described so evocatively in* Witness. *We drove them to the airport after a happy day. I noticed worriedly how heavily he perspired and how nervously his heavy thumbs shuffled through the bureaucratic paraphernalia of modern travel, as he dug up, in turn, passports, baggage tags, vaccination certificates, and airplane tickets. His plans were vague, but at the heart of them was a visit to his old friend Arthur Koestler."*

Innsbrück, O. [Österreich]
June 24, 1959

Dear Bill,

How to begin at all is even more defeating than where to begin. Hop-skip seems indicated. The ocean crossing was some 8 or more hours of wholly supportable discomfort. Amsterdam was briefly jolly. Paris was cold, dirty, vast, engulfing, but, above all, cold. (The Hôtel Palais d'Orsay is not one to be warmly recommended.) Still, we had a room with a view of the Seine and Tuileries, and a balcony wherefrom to do the viewing. From there to Zurich where we merely touched down en route to Innsbrück, in a small Swissair plane that, as the Alps bumped us up & down over valleys, and brushed monstrous mountains, soon turned into a vomitorium. We, the Americans, sat un-upping and generously permitted the weaker-tummied Europeans to whisk off our paper bags—the ones neatly folded in the boot of the seat in front. Curiously, I found myself unable to reach Arthur Koestler from here. But, after we'd gone to bed, he got through to me, with news. Alpbach, where AK lives, is some 40 miles higher into the hills than Innsbrück. While we were flying from Paris, the worst landslide since 1908 (I am only quoting) had destroyed several miles of the only road up. Nevertheless, we got through, by jeep, on a road just wide enough for a jeep, and not always quite that. On my side, without leaning out at all, I could see straight down several hundred feet. Happily, the Austrian army was at the wheel of the jeep. K, waiting at the point where our trail emerged (the army had just hoed it out much higher up the hills than the old road), was thinking of the most amusing headlines: "Whittaker Chambers Crashes Over Alpine Trail on Secret Visit to Arthur Koestler / British Intelligence Questions Surviving Writer." There in Alpbach (of all places) we spent some days about which I cannot possibly write fully. Perhaps, some moment being right, it will seem proper to try to recover certain moments. Perhaps. Then K had the idea to wire Greta Buber-Neumann: *"Komme schleunigst. Gute Weine. Ausserdem, Whittaker C."*—"Come quickest. Good wine. In addition, WC." Two days of unresponding silence. Then, just as K went out to hold the bus so that we could all go gawk at this or that medieval something, Greta stepped out of the bus. In case you do not know, Greta Buber-Neumann is the daughter-in-law of Martin Buber (who is grandfather of two of her children), widow of Heinz Neumann, most dazzling of German CP leaders (shot without trial), sister-in-law of Willi Muenzenberg (organizer of the Muenzenberg Trust, killed by the NKVD while trying to escape the Gestapo). Greta herself spent three years as a slave in Karaganda. By then the Moscow-Berlin Pact had been signed, and the NKVD handed her (and many others) over to the Gestapo on the bridge at Brest Litovsk. Then she spent four years in German concentration camps, mostly at Ravensbrück. Impossible to tell here this story of our own lifetime, which makes the *Odyssey*, for all its grandeur, somehow childish. By comparison, Dante's Hell is contrived. Here, only one sampling. In Ravensbrück, the SS was using Polish women prisoners as guinea pigs, for bone and flesh transplants, etc., etc. The other inmates supposed that, after the experiments, the survivors were released. Greta, working in the camp commandant's office as a filing clerk, discovered that the women were being shot. From the desk she stole the lists of the condemned, changed the numbers of the condemned to fake numbers. Then she organized a faction among the Poles, who grabbed the next lot of victims, tore off their numbers, sewed on new ones and hid them among the 60,000 women in the camp. This is just skimming: the story is much more complicated. But this will give you some idea of it, and of Greta B-N, and what our talks were like. A night or so before, AK got launched on his escape from France after its fall. He was in Marseilles and had to reach Lisbon. He was with Benjamin, the mentor and analyst of Bertolt Brecht (*The Punitive Measure, The Caucasian Chalk Circle*). Benjamin planned to walk across the Pyrenees. K could not go through Spain because of his death sentence during the Civil War. Since neither expected to make it, Benjamin shared his most precious possession with K: a massive dose of morphine. In our time, I think, it has become true that there is no greater love than that a man share his poison with his friend. Benjamin with two women refugees crossed the mountains. The civil guards seized them, kept them in jail overnight to send them on to a prison camp in the morning. In the morning, Benjamin was dead: he had taken the morphine. A little later, the civil guards came in and told the women: they sympathized with the refugees, and had agreed, on their own, to let them escape. Have you read Sartre's story *Le Mur*?

So there we sat, and talked, not merely about the daily experiences of our life. Each of the two men had tried to kill himself and failed; Greta was certainly the most hardy and astonishing of the three. Then, we realized that, of our particular breed, the old activists, we are almost the only survivors —the old activists who were articulate, consequent revolutionists, and not merely agents. Of the latter, there are some around. Utter defeat. Not even the French Revolution, surely, yielded so complete a human disaster. I do not, of course, know all that the others thought, in the intermittent silences, though I know from words that emerged that our thoughts ran rather close. This conference on the Alpbach summit fed a great hurlyburly of my own impressions, quite impossible to sort as yet. Europe is visibly decades behind us. I cannot possibly know whether (as I hope) it is at a point of great sudden change; or whether (as I fear) it is beyond saving. I seem to see, only, that it is pretty desperate, and looks to me all but hopeless. At the same time, I had the impression (I must be wrong, I suppose) that my companions could not bring themselves to draw the practical and theoretical conclusions that follow from the European failure. But, in Paris [Manès], Sperber [37] cautioned me not to foreclose on Europe too quickly. He told me this about the moment, in 1939 or '40, when he joined the French army. He was "poorer than a dog." From his window he could see Notre Dame. To himself he said: "Terrible is it to kill anything, and there is almost nothing worth dying for. But those stones, just those stones, are still worth killing for and dying for." He also said to me of myself: "It is not important that you find the truth, or that you think you find the truth. It is only important that you want always to continue to seek the truth." And this, which is obvious enough, was somehow wonderfully heartening and quieting. So, for the moment, I shall follow Sperber, and hope there is something great left in this once greatest, now almost extinct-seeming, volcano of man's creative energy. Surely, these three Europeans, once my comrades, are great spirits; it would be hard to find their match in the dwindled world. "It is that," K said after the account of Benjamin and the morphine, "that makes it impossible for me to take the beat generation seriously." Yet all of us held long and grave conversations about the beat youth (the Halbstärke, Half-strong, as Germans call them),

[37] Author of *The Burned Bramble.*

echoing and amplifying the conversation that Jim and I had one day at lunch.

To get away from all this, which a letter can only brush exasperatingly—in Amsterdam I found a German edition of Jim's *Machiavellians,* and began to read it at a sidewalk café on the Rokin.

Tomorrow, we fly back to Zurich, spend a night, get on at once, via a touchdown at Milan, for Venice. Two days there. After that, I am much in doubt. But soon after, we get to Rome, where my holding address for the present will be: Am. Express, Piazza di Spagna 38. Sperber has asked me to come to him in Provence. We may do so. After that perhaps, Paris, where K plans to join us for another old-home week.

I find letter writing en route almost impossible. So please bear with me. My best to your wife. To all, too, at *NR.*

As always,
Whittaker

Venice, July 1, 1959

Dear Bill,

Has Europe addled my wits? Anyway, I find the enclosure extremely funny, and offer it as candidate for your kind wife's unkind clipping book. I hold the last two lines to be classic in their simple sequitur. When I read them, I laughed out loud, to the disapproval of the Italian waiter, who held that such bursts did the house no kind of good. It's from the *Daily Telegraph* of June 30. I would send also the Commons debate of Sir Somebody Peacock and a Mr. Hare about a pig and two cats, undergoing radioactive experiment. Sir Somebody Peacock explained that in "parts of the experiment no anesthetic was needed"—surely, another lapidary line. Last night, the English woman sitting next us at supper said musingly: "They make good waiters, don't they?" Then, feeling, evidently, that there was a chance her meaning was not clear, she added: "The Italians." Her sweet parochial voice carried distinctly to every

Italian ear in the place. Sir Somebody Peacock reminds me of that. I started to say above that I would send you the clipping, except that, traveling, there is nothing to cut out things with, to do anything with. And no time, no time, no time, except for Thomas Cook and Sons.

If you get time, yourself, will you drop me an in-filling line to American Express, Piazza di Spagna 38, Rome? What is happening to Canada Southern [38] in which I have a certain interest? Tell me more.

As always, but more stormily,
Whittaker

Venice
July 17, 1959

Dear Bill,

Of course, Am. Express forwards my mail; so your letter followed me to Venice. There I got it this morning by bullying the clerk (he had already told me that there was no mail for me) to go through the heap plainly visible at his elbow. But that is how one gets anything done in Europe. Your letter was most welcome, and came just in the nick of time: tomorrow we go to Paris. The thought appals me. It involves a four-hour train trip to Milan (I know this Milan run, having done it on the Feast of St. Peter, along with the rest of the Italian nation who shared our compartment). Then to Malpensa, the Milan airport; and never was an airport so happily named. Not only does it lie somewhat nearer Munich than Milan; it was there the Constellation blew up just as we entered Italy. The landing of our plane cleared the field for the TWA takeoff. If and when we reach Malpensa, four air hours to Paris. I am very nicely fed up.

Behind this there are some easily guessable reasons. In Rome, I had to ask Esther for the nitroglycerine I had been needing since Zurich. Since then, I've been living on the stuff. Florence

[38] Ltd., then listed on the American Stock Exchange.

ODYSSEY OF A FRIEND   256

was the worst. I came back to Venice chiefly to rest. If it were not for my children, I should try to spend the rest of my life here. Other cities are greater or less great than something or some other city. Venice is incomparable. It is the only city I have ever loved. And the days here (it is our second visit) have lessened the nitroglycerine eating; they haven't ended it.

The result of my physical state is, of course, a fairly rancid mental state. True, I did not particularly want to come here in the first place; and my surmises have proved right. Europe has almost nothing to say to me, and almost nothing to tell me that I cannot learn just about as well from the European press and occasional European tourists in America; or correspondence. The big thing was that Esther should see with her own little eyes and fulfill the life dream. And I think she has. I think that, once she gets back and begins to dream back, it will all seem rather wonderful. The accent of our interests is quite different. I have little sentiment about the Europe that is (the Europe I knew in the past, and which gravely shaped my life, is gone forever). I should offer as modest proposals that: (1) three-quarters of Europe's hoarded art be destroyed, so that art could start again from scratch; (2) that most of Europe's quaint cities be bulldozed, not so much to introduce the navigable street and decent living quarters, as to get rid of the Ye Antikee Shoppee neurosis forever. Europe belongs in the 20th century. In fact, it's getting there at great speed. Though I do not quite agree with Forrest Davis' optimism on the political or economic federative score (the certain tempo of it), that is the direction. I disagree with him decisively about the future joy of Pan-Europe for us. Give them the means, and these dear friends, that noble Third Force, will cut our bloody throats. As people, they are stronger than we are, and they know it—I mean as individual people amounting to a mass, they are stronger. In the mass they loathe us. At another level, their disdain for us is withering. At their most understanding or compassionate, they neither hate nor loathe; it's just that they cannot help being conscious of a difference that superior breeds feel in the presence of others. Often they show it most by their effort not to show it. Give these superior breeds the economic power to see us "at eye level" (I think was Forrest's phrase) and they will see right over us. They have been seeing through us for years. Don't imagine that this prospect pleases me. The anti-American climate here enrages me. It is immensely part of my being fed up. On the other hand, I feel as if I shall be leaving a Europe which in many ways I dislike acutely, for an America that is visibly a madhouse.

You can scarcely blame even a well-disposed European for getting this impression just by reading the American press here. On top of horrifying, utterly incredible stories (and pix) out of Louisiana (with the governor of a sovereign state [39] urinating on the carpet in front of a throng)—on top of that comes the art to Moscow idiocy.[40] How, even the well-disposed European, like any other sane man, asks—how did it happen in the first place? How could a great government, sending an art exhibit to the key fair, get it loused up so? Then he asks, quite naturally: Is it really so? How many of the artists are Communists? The answer comes, of course: It's not sure that any were. But there is a report that —— *was* (what meaning does the past tense have—the European wants to know that too). But —— is precisely the worst name (from an American viewpoint) that could have turned up. For, if a European knows anything at all about such matters, he knows that precisely —— is one of the few artists in America who can really paint. If —— has ever painted anything remotely political, I have never seen it, and probably few Europeans have. In view of the solidity of what he *has* painted, the European doesn't give a hang, doesn't think it has any bearing on art, if —— held ten Party cards. And neither do I. And bang on top of this preposterous mess (not bettered by the President's mouthings) came a really stomach-turning démarche of [Senator] Eastland

[39] Earl Long, D.-La.
[40] The reference is to the selection of American art to be sent, under the cultural exchange program, to Russia.

and some other worthies about *Lady Chatterley's Lover*. You
can see why a land where such things happen in rapid succession looks to even the well-disposed European like a lunatic
asylum. And so, at this range, it looks to me. The European
infers that where such things can happen, there is something
radically wrong. And so do I. He looks at the tourists in their
thousands, since these are the Americans he sees most of. Even
if the European has never seen the President's letter (it comes
free with every passport), explaining that each tourist is, in
effect, an ambassador, the European's notion of Americans is
not likely to be edified by tourists. Not that they are all alike,
or particularly noisome. Rather, they huddle, like bemused or
bored cattle. But when they reach one of those godawful
havens, set up just for them (like the one I am writing this in),
then the tourists caper. The tourists, feeling at ease for once
in this international compound, caper and act themselves; and
the hired help, in their obsequious and mendicant thousands,
do everything to promote the capers—and, in the guise of a
smile, to sneer at the caperers. I am convinced that it isn't
so much the capers, as the fact that the victims don't see through
the forked smile that fills the Europeans of this order with
contempt. This makes me feel sorry for my countrymen, and I
try to help them when I can. Usually, it is quite wasted effort.
They don't know what's happening to them, how they are
being conned, frisked and sneered at at every turn; they are
happy. This, too, the European grasps, and it hitches up his
sneer a little higher. There are exceptions to all this, of course.
But, in general, this Europe I am in is of a poisonous climate.
This is where Esther's spontaneous goodness helps out. Last
night, we were crossing a stepped bridge up which a woman
was trying to drag a loaded baby carriage. Without second
thought, Esther picked up the free end of the carriage and,
between them, she and the woman carried it to the top. The
woman, who had first been astonished, blushed with gratitude.
Things like this have happened several times. It's like fresh
air in a fetid room. But then, they seldom take us for Americans.

Esther's dark complexion is puzzling. But from certain small signs, they guess she is not Italian. Generally, they decide we are French (I can pass for a Norman). As you know, Americans are unusually kind as peoples go. But they are inhumanly stiff and seem completely unable to communicate their natural kindness. At least this seems true of the genus: tourist. I hope I don't sound too hard on the tourists. I find the mass of Europeans, by contrast, disgusting.

I've got to nip this up. So some quick notes. If I survive the Venice-Paris hop, I think I must go to West Berlin. I feel as if I had some kind of moral compulsion to go there at this time. It's not particularly rational. But it's a feeling sufficiently strong so that I shall try to act on it. After that, I don't quite know. I think we've pushed our luck, healthwise, almost to the breaking point. I shouldn't like Esther left here with the debris. What would she do, alone, not knowing six words of anything? But we'll see. In Paris, by the way, we shall be at France et Choiseul. But mail goes Am. Exp.

Time's review of Rovere's book [41] almost convinced me that it was good. Brent's review (excellent from its viewpoint) shook me. But I deplore the whole McCarthy ruckus. You cannot defend a man who was, basically, not defensible. You only weaken your position when you do; you weaken your future power to defend others. The Senator, in my opinion, did the Right more mischief than he ever did the Left; and he keeps right on doing it. It does no good to plead (or prove) that the Left was (is) mean to him. What did he really accomplish? I would say: very close to nothing but noise. Bob Morris [42] really accomplished most of what the Senator is credited with.

I don't know whether Rovere ever attacked me. From others, chiefly Ralph, I gathered that Rovere is no friend. But I think he has used a certain discrimination. ———'s plan to call in Rovere is outrageously stupid. Tactically, he could scarcely achieve a better blooper. When will they learn?

41 Richard Rovere, *Senator Joe McCarthy*, 1959.
42 Chief Counsel, Senate Internal Security Subcommittee.

Of course, ———— should be told nothing: I assume you're joking. Here tactics call for saying nothing, since whatever is said can only feed his little fire—if it is one. He lives on the public reaction to the public jab. If he does it again, if he gets more particularized, then we'll see. P & R, by the way, is acting rather creepily. That market is way, way too high, and I only hope that, when the adjustment comes, P & R is as counter the down trend as it is now counter to the up. If I had the means, I should make a monster speculation in Canso—say, 10 shares. No, I don't mean that; I mean 10 thousand shares. If I get home in time, if I find the ways and means, I may do something yet. Assuming, of course, that Canso does not begin to climb. If the prospect is truly good, I'd like to see the little shares stay around 4—any little shares—for as long as possible. It gives Mr. Pennington a chance. My daughter is rumored to have made a fabulous killing in oil. But she won't say what it was.

My best to everybody. As always,

Whittaker

September 20, 1959

Dear Bill,

Herewith Jim Burnham's letter, with my thanks. It might be commented on, but I think I will not. I may be immensely mistaken, but I sense the root of much of Jim's motivation where few look for it—not qualitatively far, I should think, from much of Malraux's. What a genius *he* was before he began to research Berlioz' arrangement of the *Marseillaise* for 75 trombones! We are told, you remember, that when, at the end of their Long March, the Marseillais reached Paris, what made their singing of the new song so memorable was that they seemed to sing it from their chests, rather than their mouths; less a chant than a groan: *"Egorger vos fils et vos compagnes!"* Would Jim give up that for 75 trombones? In life, one must choose between Maxfield Parrish and M. Angelo. Nothing, however, against the noble Berlioz, who is clearly on the side of the Angelos.

I am on record as saying to Esther: "Khrush is here for peace.[43] At UN he will offer total disarmament à la Litvinov." Yesterday, we watched it all on TV. No more wits than a gnat needs were needed to see that this must be, since there was nothing else K. could offer. The situation precluded all else; so, for once, we find necessity, strategy, tactics and longing lying down together. They will not, I am afraid, beget more than embarrassment laced with perplexity shaken by a fall in the stock market until the nervous traders realize that all is well; nothing will happen. "Between this and this morbidity in matter," the historical pathologist of the future will say, laying his pointer at a point toward the end of the first decade of the second half of the 20th century, "occurred the lesion on which turned the fate of humankind." (There is an echo here of *Darkness at Noon.*) If I were a Vice President of genius, I should, after regretting that the kickoff fell to others, grab the ball and start running until I was President by a shoo-in. I will say no more, except to quote a piece that appeared once in *NR:* "America has always secretly despised the mind. Now mind is taking its revenge. We need it desperately, and it simply isn't there."

Your letter about the new-minted typesetter includes some odd bits. For the first time, I am moved to wonder: "What *is* going on there?" I have a feeling that he [Hiss] did not go to Europe, after all. If he is, indeed, jobless, that seems to suggest a rift with orthodoxy. But where only speculation is possible, it is idle to speculate.

You are too kind in commenting on my return to school.[44] Most people incline to laugh. I think they feel that it is such a waste on all sides since I shall not be around long enough to put it to any use of the kind people call "good." I've considered

---

[43] Khrushchev had come to the United States to meet with Eisenhower.
[44] Chambers had enrolled in the University of Western Maryland College.

that. I do not wish to die an ignoramus. If I can bring it off in terms of health, energy, time, application, then I think the world should let me try. The world is desperately ignorant at the moment when it has most reason to know with some exactitude, and there is more than ever before in history to know about. But I am going to have little time for anything but study henceforth. So I think my separation from *NR* is in order. I daresay it will be an occasion for relief, if not rejoicing, with all but you and Jim. I cannot say that the rejoicing will not be justified: I have never been more than a burden to the magazine, and Brent was quite right in saying, long ago: "You really *don't* belong on *NR*." He did not mean it unkindly; he was just summing up, perhaps betraying a slight surprise. But he was quite right. Jim and Brent are poles apart; represent, reflect, quite different bases; yet this is not often noticeable and they are able to work in fairly close harmony. In my case, this is not true. I feel my differences with Brent to be at root an age difference. (I dwell on Brent as spokesman for a majority, of which I take F. Meyer to be the theoretician.) Brent is likable on sight, and what we like is what we feel to be an instinct for honesty. Yet I always feel about him that he is a young man, and a most troubled one at that; so that I have constantly to correct a surmise that his intransigence is, in fact, an evidence of his extreme uncertainty about various matters. I did not mean to say, above, that my differences with Brent are solely an age difference. They imply a different way of viewing experience. I can imagine a situation in which Brent, having reached my present age, and looking back, will say, one day: "So *that* is what he meant." Then he will grasp that the roots of true compassion are reality, and not the feeble "goodness" that sicklies o'er most manifestations of compassion. But compassion also interacts with the reality that breeds it, and makes for the steady glance and slow and rigorous conclusions, never easy, never swift. But I am running off at the mouth. This is, of course, because I feel that *NR*, faced with a great test, did not serve its readers very well.[45] The same may be said of almost everybody else? Yes, I think so, though my concern is chiefly *NR*. Perhaps, the London *Economist* came out best—no great shakes at that. It gets back to my old theme song: Nobody knew enough. The almost continuous press coverage of Khrushchev is technically superb; intellectually (most of it), for retarded children. One or two exceptions apart, most of what was intended for analysis has been pawing, rather clumsy to boot. So the TV press has presented Khrushchev in terms of not being the scarecrow they had hitherto presented (and really imagined he was). But the tone is one of literal intense resentment that he should not be. Result: we know from these worthies no more about Khrush than we knew before. Happily, there are other ways of knowing, at least attempting to know. Not that I am happy with Khrush. If I may borrow his own felicitous phrase, he "sticks like a rat in my throat." Those pig eyes, that shark's face—they are not my dish. But this does not make me suppose that this is not a fateful man, and that I had better be at better business than dreaming up animal terms to describe him. He is no monster, either, in the sense that Stalin *was* a monster; and it does much disservice to say he is. It blurs where we need clear windowpanes. His speech to UN was also a de-Stalinization speech. That bears brooding on, too. And I must get home tonight.

As always,
Whittaker

I have just come on something I wrote a few years back, and thought I had destroyed. It goes like this. "All that we really know about Tamuz [more commonly, Thamus] is that he was a pilot, and an approximate date, on which he heard his name called three times: Tamuz! Tamuz! Tamuz! from all the edges of the sea. Then he was given his message: that his age had reached its end."

Curious? In the reign of Tiberius, Tamuz' ship seems to have

<hr>

[45] In its handling of the Khrushchev visit.

been standing off Ostia [Paxi] when the voice called: "Θαμοῦς, Θαμοῦς, Θαμοῦς, ὁπόταν γένη κατὰ τὸ Παλῶδες, ἀπάγγειλον ὅτι Πὰν ο μέγας τέθνηκε"—"When you come opposite to Palodes, announce that the Great Pan has died." The incident is reported in Plutarch's *De Defectione Oraculorum* (I trust I have got the title right). [*De Defectu Oraculorum*—Ed.] Others think they have a better explanation of what they think Tamuz thought he heard. The doubting Thomases, of course.

And I have said nothing about Willi! [46] Never speak German around Esther if you don't want her to understand. She understands a surprising lot, but her pronunciation is vile. So slowly and painfully she read out the cover line under Willi's picture: *"Krieg muss riskiert werden"*—War must be risked. Then she fell silent: Our Willi! I suspect that the cover line, after the fashion of cover lines, rather misleads as to what Willi really said; and I have not yet got to reading what's inside. Yet I also suspect that a line of cleavage lies somewhere in the neighborhood of: *Krieg muss riskiert werden*. The line that marks *die Grenzen der Gefahr*—the limits of the danger. Ah, Willi. Or as Sperber said hesitantly: "That book." Or as mad Ophelia has it: "But our beginnings never know our ends."

No, no, come to think, that's mad Eliot, not mad Ophelia. She's much better: "Lord, we know what we are, but we know not what we may be."

John's address is:

A/B John Chambers
ANG 83, Box 1510
Lackland AFB,
Texas

A/B means Airman Basic; ANG must mean Angry Young Man. Soon the PS will outrun this letter. I have also come (I am burning, burning) on a thick ms., which again I thought I had

[46] I had sent him the issue of *Der Spiegel* with a cover story on Willi Schlamm.

destroyed. It is the almost book-length ms. of *The Third Rome*. I found it good reading, at least some of the included quotes are. Writers are such vain idiots. I know I should burn at once; and I haven't.

Oct. 4, 1959

Dear Bill,

It is Sunday, about 4 P.M. Since about 9 A.M. (with a noon hour recess) I have been studying. I am far from finished. In practical terms, that is perhaps all the answer there is to your letter. Of course, the answer can't be only in practical terms. But, in any other, it's difficult. It is so kind a letter, it sounds churlish to say that you overrate me. Besides, I really don't know what the answer is, and, with time at my throat, can scarcely pause to consider. So I am going to do what people often do in such cases—put it off.[47] I seem to have sat this one out, much against my better judgment; and to get upwrought now has a touch of anticlimax. So I propose to do this. First, to leave it, for the moment, wholly in your hands; mine are too full. Then, something else. Recently, a young under-graduate in a Southern college wrote me a brief, but fulsome, letter. Unlike President Robbins (in our favorite book[48]), I have not yet discovered that any day has 32 hours in it if you only know where to look for them. But if, somehow, I can whittle and chisel enough time to write for *NR* an answer to the young conservative, I think a great many points will be covered, or inflamed, and perhaps that will be all to the good. For example, the term "young conservative" has always, if I may borrow the lyric phrase of a recent speaker at the National Press Club, "stuck in my throat like a dead rat." It is a contra-diction in terms. In the course of telling the young man why I think so, much might be stirred up, profitably—and quite apart, of course, from whether I am right or wrong, or anybody will

[47] *I.e.*, put off the decision whether to resign from *NR*.
[48] Jarrell's novel, *Pictures from an Institution*.

ever know. Then the young man tells me that both in high school and college he has waged war on Communist teachers. I am strongly moved to counsel him to stop wasting time, to get back to his books and try to learn enough so that he can tell a Communist teacher from one who merely disagrees with him, or (as is more likely to have been the case) lets slip the truth, by now rather worn, that the sun of *unrestricted* free enterprise has set, never to rise again. Not only undergraduates are guilty of certain lapses, his letter implies. But this poor lad, who shall be nameless, makes a handy whipping boy. If I bring this off, then, perhaps, I can decently make clear a position (foreign policy enters, too); or, all the boys with a happy heave can heave me off *NR*. What do you say?

Of course, the recent business [49] was no mere flap. Something very serious happened. *NR* committed itself to positions, and, above all, in a way, a style, that has given pause to more than me. The pertinent comments are not from the Left (with which *NR* found itself in mutually repellent accord). The real brush was with the Right, the Right that exists out beyond *NR*—i.e., the larger Right. The foreign policy turn is theirs, and all that goes with it. Brent (again) sensed this Right *v* Right effect perfectly well, when he said, early in the game, something to the effect that: Now we will see what kind of conservatives we are, or who's a conservative now, or something in that vein. We did see. There is a passage by Father de Lubac of which I am fond. He has been noting that criticisms of the Church come both from its worst enemies and from good men; and that, in sum, they are the same criticisms. And he adds: "An arresting convergence!" We see, he goes on, some, "among them the best and clearest-eyed," drawn to the Church, in which they sense "the sole institution capable of giving, together with an answer to the problem of our ills, a solution to the problem of our destiny" (I am quoting from memory). Then comes a great passage: "But on the threshold—see what stops them: the spectacle that we are, we, the Christians of today—that spectacle

[49] Khrushchev's visit to Eisenhower in September, 1959.

repels them. It is not that they condemn us violently. It is, rather, that they cannot take us seriously." I would request that this thought be hung up also in the Church of the Laodiceans. The danger that *NR*'s handling of recent events incurred is in not being taken seriously. Its enemies could not ask for more. The logic of *NR*'s policy, as no doubt I have said to you before, is: War. If gentlemen hold that war is what is necessary, I, for one, wish they would say so simply, clearly, courageously, stating their reasons for believing so. It is not an easy position; it would take courage to set it forth at all. But it would be an intelligible position, and popular, I am told, with SAC [Strategic Air Command], though I doubt that it would be so with wider circles. But short of this forthrightness, shouts of "Russie go home!" and the like lack coherence, meaning, gravity. It is the *implications* of *NR*'s policy with respect to U.S. foreign policy that seem to me to need long and troubled threshing out. Otherwise, I fear a certain slaphappiness. In the long haul, it will do the magazine harm—not with the Left (what does the Left care about *NR?*), but with the serious Right. Count all this as the sound of empty gongs and tinkling cymbals, if you like. Yet I am sometimes right about these matters. But now I must get back to my school books, my graphs, my production-transformation curves.

And thank you for your generosity, kindness, patience.

As always,
Whittaker

Oct. 19, 1959

Dear Bill,

There's a check for three thousand dollars in this letter. Some time ago (longer than I like to think about), your friend lent it to me. We were pretty desperate then; and it is possible that his kindness saved my life. In any case, it gave me a great lift over a big reef. So you became one of the two or three people who, I consider, really helped me in a way I needed when I needed help. That was a rough time, but a great education. I got my belly full of people wishing me well and praying for my soul. I felt that my soul would get along well enough if only the bill collector could be satisfied (his cravings were wholly unsoulful); and I could be given some chance to reassemble the pieces of my life, which having at great effort been reassembled successfully once before, had been splendidly smashed to pieces by (and for the edification of) people who couldn't assemble a doghouse. I have never taken time or trouble to get at the precise injustice in that situation; I have never really wanted to. But there *was* one; or, if you dislike the word injustice, an irrationality in the situation. You can't have meant to give your life for the other animals, and not be made somewhat reflective when they.... But there's no percentage in that kind of reminiscence. It was a good education, and a necessary one. It told me wherein I was wrong, and it is one reason why I cannot bear to see a copy of *Witness* lying about. But, if that were all it told me, it would merely have reminded me of what I had known all my adult life, but had sought, in the name of transcendent values, to surmount for a while. It would have told me nothing new, and would have left me a cynic. But I am not a cynic, and never have been. I became a Communist, in part, in order not to be a cynic, or, to put it in other terms, because the cynic's suit doesn't fit me. The same temperamental setup that made me a Communist turned me against Communism and made me fight it (it's all set down in *Witness,* but nobody reads that part). So I didn't become a cynic now, either. I simply tried to stand on my own feet in a world which I accepted on its own terms. Of course, none (or few) are ever able even to begin to stand on their own feet without the help of others. And I think that the man who is capable of getting to his feet (or, more importantly perhaps, feels a demonic drive to do so) is incapable of feeling anything for the two or three who help him (it's always about two or three) but a kind of something that I won't try to put into words. A something he thinks about in the night when he stands alone on the hills and looks out and up. He thinks about it when he asks, as he does at such times and places, the question: What is man? Then, whatever answer he gives to the question, or fails to find for it, he thinks of the two or three; and he probably settles for that—for now, for what experience gave him as best. I think you know what, fumblingly, I am saying. I am saying: Thank you. I do not like to think, either, of the boat passing out of your friend's hands. I don't think it should. And I hope that, at least for a while, I may help him keep it afloat by floating back to him the bread he cast on the waters. (The Bible is, I suppose, the single greatest anti-intellectual book ever put together, but it is full of those magical simple phrasings—bread on the water, etc. It is full of them, of course, because it is, at its best, about simple life; because Job's question, the central issue, remains unanswered, and because Jonah does not lie, but says: "I do well to be angry." If only Christians could live up to Jonah. If only they understood the Bible!) Enough of this.

The letters keep coming in. Today, I got one from the wife of an Army man stationed in Turkey. It was mailed in Smyrna. After I had read it, I sat for a long while. Then I said to Esther: "I suppose I must reread that book some day." And, of course, she asked: "What book?" And, of course, I answered: *"Witness."* Nietzsche says somewhere that each book marks a stage that a man leaves behind him on his way to one higher. If it isn't so, there is not much in that man. I must reread that earlier book before writing the other which I now hope I shall live to write. There will be no discontinuity, but there should be more rigor; more mind, working more closely on reality. I believe that I am almost ready now to write it (I had to do a good deal of living first). But I have always known what the epigraph would be. It is: "Power (to his companion, Force, and to their prisoner, Prometheus): 'We have come to the last path of the

earth, in the Scythian country, in the untrodden solitude.' "
Aeschylus, of course.[50]

Affectionately,
Whittaker

Oct. 24, 1959

Dear Bill,

The postman honked once while I was dressing for school, and Esther hurried out and got your letter. To that I shall get back. First, I want to tell you about Esther. When I went downstairs to get the icon book, while you were here last, I overheard you say to her that she had a bad cough. Just before we left for Europe, you said how happy it made you that we both looked so well. Both of these times, I thought how often we know a reason for things, which is a perfectly correct reason, but still is not the whole, or sometimes even the real, reason. So I said to you, undoubtedly, that we were going abroad to show Esther Europe. And that was true. But it was also true that we were showing Esther Europe just then because I suspected, for cause, that she might have TB or lung cancer. I could not get her to go to a doctor, and I'm no good at the dictatorship of the proletariat. So I had to make a decision: should I take her to Europe before she knew anything for sure, and so could enjoy herself? Or should I take her after she knew, when it would be rather a funereal trip? Of course, the answer was easy in such terms. By the time we got back, Esther's cough was much worse. Still, she wouldn't go to a doctor. Rather by chance, one came to us and I seized the chance to have him examine Esther *in situ*. He heard something, of course, X-rays followed, and disclosed a shadow on the lung. There was an awful week (the week during which you came), when we did not know what the final diagnosis would be. It was not TB.

---

[50] WC never completed his book. In 1964, Mrs. Chambers and Mr. Duncan Norton-Taylor published *Cold Friday*, parts of which are fragments from the contemplated work.

Nevertheless, the shadow is of such interest that further tests are being run. Esther's own doctor has been away, but gets back in a day or so. When he does, I shall have to talk with him. For Esther is clearly not well. She has no energy at all, which is rather like saying of a rocket that it has no energy at all. She sits for hours on end in her chair, lacking the strength to do anything. It isn't fair to snow you under these clinical details. But this has been over us for about 6 months. I was convinced last May that something was radically wrong; but Esther, oddly, or perhaps characteristically, didn't really believe until she saw the X-ray. Then it hit her terribly hard. This, in turn, did odd things to me. I have lived so long with the idea of sudden death that I have got—not used to it; nobody gets used to it in the sense of all aboard the daisy chain. But I've had time to think it over, and weigh things, and brood upon the wisdom of the text: "Let no man say he is happy until the day he dies." It's too new to Esther. I suspect, too, that women in general are more tenacious of life than men, as, biologically, they should be. They aren't much as stoics, either; and can seldom delude or comfort themselves with concepts. This leaves them dreadfully vulnerable, and, if you happen to love one of them, it leaves you feeling rather helpless, helpless in an ultimate way. I don't want to leap too far ahead of the story. But there *is* a shadow in the X-rays; and Esther is not better since the TB threat was lifted; she is progressively worse. So there is something. I am believing at present that it is some bronchial virus residue about which doctors seem to know only a little more than the rest of us. But all this has long been unsettling us in ways that no doubt puzzle the few people who know us well enough to notice the variations from true north. It made me, as I said, slam through the Europe trip last summer. It decided how we should travel since I was determined that Esther should have no moment's concern about costs or pinching. So I kept our affairs in my hands in a way that is quite unusual in our house, and took charge of the show. This, too, is what made my illness in Rome and Florence so extremely unfortunate. This is why France et Choiseul seemed so special a haven when I was trying to let Esther do anything in Paris that the whim moved her to. And yet, to show you how ironies streak across ironies, I said to Tom Matthews recently how much we had liked France et Choiseul. He said: "I can't. That is where we stayed when Julie was dying." He knew nothing about Esther, of course. All this helped to unsettle me post-Europe, and, though I had made up my mind to return to college before we went abroad, it made me hesitate. In the week while we were waiting for the diagnosis, we discussed sending Esther to a well-known sanitorium near Cuernavaca while I completed this semester's work; after that, I would join her. So now you see what, all unknown, was actually taking place, not out of sight. We have spoken of this to almost no one (Esther doesn't like it discussed); and very few people know, and that is how I should like to keep it. But what is one saying? I believe Nora knows something—exactly how much I have forgotten. So more may know than I have supposed. I have also, in consequence, tentatively shifted another piece of schedule. I had meant to knock off biology (a required lab course) in summer session. One day, driving to school, I asked myself: "Why should I let my will to finish quickly take charge?" So I proposed to Esther that, instead, we should make reservations long in advance, fly to Europe the moment college ends next semester, and spend the summer in Italy. This had a magical effect on her spirits. Perhaps we shall do that. So, you see, that is how it is.

As for your escapade, I have always been afraid that you would drown yourself in a hurricane. But, of course, I subscribe to the view (with some qualifications) that each of us should be allowed to risk his hurricane after his own fashion and pleasure. How many hours (they must total years) I spent on the water, where now I would make no effort to go. How much I wrote about it, too; all destroyed, and all forgotten, so that, out of hundreds of lines, I remember only two:

I love those birds that wake in the night,
And sing, and go back to sleep again.

I presume I remember them because those are the only two
worth remembering. One night, rather late, Koestler and I
were discussing what our articulate fellows and we really are.
I said, *"Wir sind einfach paganische Dichter, und das ist alles."*
We are simply pagan poets, and that is all. K thought I was
a little drunk, and so I was.[51] Otherwise, I might not have said:
"pagan." But, of course, that is what we are, all of us, and that
is what equates us all: poets. It is true of K and Malraux and
Sperber and Milosz (who everybody thinks is so cerebral).
It is true even of Ruth Fischer who is usually credited with
writing the one great history of Stalinism. But what gives this
history its power is that it disguises a great love poem, which
this strange Isolde, physically unprepossessing and spiritually
cranky and sometimes spiteful, wove for her lover: it is her
Love-Death for Maslow. People feel the force of this, but that
is not how they read it. At its own level, *Witness,* too, is chiefly
a poem. I am more and more convinced that it is the force of
this that people feel; but few know it; they read into it the
meanings they choose. If you reread *Darkness at Noon* at this
late hour, you will see how true of it, too, this is. I reread it
recently. I came to the part where, after his breakdown,
Rubashov is permitted a few minutes of air in the prison yard.
Beside him trots the Central Asian peasant who has been jailed
because, "at the pricking of the children," the peasant and his
wife had barricaded themselves in their house and "unmasked
themselves as reactionaries." Looking sidewise at Rubashov in
his sly peasant way, he says: "I do not think they have left
much of Your Honor and me." Then, in the snow of the prison
yard and under the machine-gun towers, he remembers how it
was when the snow melted in the mountains of Asia and flowed
in torrents. Then they drove the sheep into the hills, rivers of
them, "so many that Your Honor could not count them all." I

---

[51] During the years I knew him, I never saw him drink.

cannot go on reading because I can no longer see the words.
To think that any man of my time could have written anything
so heart-tearingly beautiful, "wonderful, causing tears." This
is what makes K so precious to me; not the little man whom
so many people find cranky, and for whom one must sometimes
make allowances. But this pure creativity which is more
than, by taking thought, he could evoke: *O fons Bandusiae,
splendidior vitro.*[52]

What a great splurge this is. It is possible because today is
Sat. My last class of the week is done. I have a few hours
before I must dig in again. I have an A in Greek, which doesn't
count; any bright child could do as much. Economics gives me
trouble; chiefly graphs. I am in the odd position of understanding what the Lorenz curve and the production-possibility curves
represent, but not how to represent them. So far, my dish has
proved to be corporate structure and (to everybody's surprise)
the theory of accounting.

As always,
Whittaker

I think I have come on the key to the Russian mind, or at
least a clue to the reason why the Russian mind will always
remain elusive to the West. This requires a little background.
In our Russian course, we have got to the aspects of verbs.
There are two of these, the imperfective (which one learns first)
and the perfective. The perfective deals exclusively with completed action, indicated by structural change so special that
there are, in effect, two of every verb in Russian. Sometimes
the change is orthographic. More often, it includes (this is
rather like German—with a difference). And here comes the
clue to the thought process. One prefix is: *za*. Our instructor
counseled us to be careful to make a distinction between past
time, and past time with the use of *za,* since the use of *za* indicates that an action, which has been completed, is beginning.
Le voilà.

[52] O fountain of Bandusia, more splendid than glass.

Kempton should know that you can only read Dostoievski with the use of *za*.

Nov. 2, 1959

Dear Bill,

This is my resignation from *NR*. I have never taken any real part in editing the magazine; have contributed only some random and infrequent writing. It is now clear that, for some time, I shall be unable to do even that. So I must go.

It may not be possible for me just to slip away without, sooner or later, some questions being asked. Tactically, therefore, I propose (and I hope that, if only for its own sake, *NR* will for once heed something I say) that my name simply be dropped from the masthead without any comment whatever. It should take a while for the busy little eyes to notice that one of us is missing, and for the busy little tongues to ask why. If they do, the reason I have given, above, makes a perfectly adequate answer. It is quite unnecessary to amplify (I especially do not want it known that I have gone back to school). Nor, if questions are asked, is there any reason to rush to reply. By the time you get around to it, the matter should have lost its immediacy, if any, and be about as interesting as last week's boiled spinach. I beg *NR* to be guided by me in this procedure.

This is a retype of the beginning of a much longer letter. When I had finished writing it, I went upstairs and vomited. This is something that almost never happens to me; and, while it is an unpleasant detail to mention, it seems the simplest way to tell you that my action was not taken lightly or without its stresses.

As always,
Whittaker

As so often, I have held this letter a bit to reflect further. I needn't have. My course is the right one. It is only unfair to *NR* that I shouldn't have taken it sooner.

V

December, 1959, to October, 1960

Dec. 20, 1959

Dear Bill,

First day of Christmas break, and I am wild with liberty. I was still standing, by hanging on to the ropes, when the final bell sounded. Another second, and I might have dropped. But this letter has another theme.

I have been expressly requested to convey to you the thanks of a delighted reader of *NR*. First, some rather elaborate background to make them intelligible. Recently, one of your writers exposed a plot somewhat like the one mentioned by Dostoievski —"a vast, unnatural conspiracy of two students and a poet which shook society to its foundations." Your piece disclosed the cryptic corruption of the minds of language students by propaganda slipped into Russian textbooks. I own or have read all, or almost all, the books cited in the article, so that I can say that your writer's facts, so far as they went, were right. I thought that your writer made an obvious point, but, as sometimes happens with *NR* pieces,* missed a more important point. In fact, I thought his piece might better have been headed: How Not to Write Propaganda. Even if students had energy left from their struggles with Russian to get the message, it is so flagrant that only an imbecile could fail to know that this is propaganda. In general, I think, imbeciles lack the staying power to study Russian. Still, so far so good. But then your writer went on specifically to exempt from his charges certain texts which he lists. Let me translate a short lesson from one of these honorable exceptions. It would be unfair to say which one.

279

"Early in the morning, Comrade Volkov opens the window. After the rain, it is fine outside! The air is fresh, the sky is blue; there is not a cloud to be seen.

"Comrade Volkov lives and works on a collective farm. On the Kolkhoz, everybody has breakfast early. To take breakfast, Comrade Volkov enters a big, new building. This is the kitchen. For breakfast, Comrade Volkov is given black or white bread, meat and cheese. He drinks hot tea or milk. After breakfast, Comrade Volkov goes into the field. The day is hot: there is not a cloud in the sky!

"For lunch, he goes back to the Kolkhoz, and then again to work in the field without rest. In the evening, Volkov goes out with his comrade. They go to the Club. At the Club, there is a fine radio. There nobody is ever bored." ** That's it. I have no possible way of proving whether there is a propaganda intention, or not, in this passage. But if it is meant for propaganda, I must say: that is how propaganda *should* be written. First, grammatically, the passage is unexceptionable. It makes a number of important points. There is the adjective "hot" as applied to tea or to weather (two different adjectives in Russian). There are the distinctions among the prepositions: *k, b* and *na;* and the preposition *bez,* "without," which (mischievously, as so often in Russian) governs the genitive, not the accusative. There is the indispensable idiom: "There is not a cloud in the sky," where the word "cloud," for reasons evident only to the Russian mind, is again in the genitive. Etc., etc.

But what a scene we are presented with. As Russians say: "Pen cannot depict or tongue report its beauty." What more can we Simple Lifers ask than this full and tranquil collective life? A breakfast of black *or* white bread; meat and cheese is not in the American style, but it is first class among Russians. The choice of white bread is sheer frill. (Like most Slavs, I happen to hold that true black bread is preferable, any hour of the day, to almost any food ever devised by man.) Of course, Comrade Volkov works in the field *without rest* (*bez otdikha*). I never knew a farmer anywhere who didn't, since, sowing or reaping, they are usually racing the weather. Often they work long after dark, even in Carroll County, Md., and afterwards drop asleep in their chairs, too logged with fatigue for the delights of a night with comrades at the club, with its splendid radio, where nobody ever is bored. Is this not propaganda? I think, comrades, we must say that, decidedly, it is; at least in its effect.

Now I can get on with my mission of thanks. Among the exceptions cited by your writer was: *Essentials of Russian* by A. von Gronicka and Helen Bates-Yakobson. Prof. v. Gronicka is credited to Columbia. I have never heard of him otherwise; perhaps he is the well-known "grammatical fiction." Prof. Helen Bates-Yakobson is the head of the Slavic department at the George Washington University. Since she sometimes helps to supervise my exams, I have met and talked with her about the problems of teaching the linguistics of the *âme slave* [Slavic soul]. It is she who has asked me to thank you. And now I have done it. I hope you will not draw your writer's attention to this letter: There are trifles that wise men should keep among themselves for private smiling.

Vale,
Whittaker

* and others.
** I particularly like this last touch.

Jan. 12, 1960

Dear Bill,

John's alarm clock rang before five A.M. Since it waked me, I thought I might as well get up to give him the send-off, and, much more important, the hot coffee, without which nobody should set out on a 70-mile predawn drive to Washington. So it happens that I am about while it is still dark, on this day which I have long had in mind as one when I could write you a letter. It is the first day since before Christmas when I could. The Russian final is over; the great Greek test done (final to come). The feeling is, I imagine, something like what a man, who has been under water too long, feels when he surfaces. And like that, this is largely illusion: there is still a lot of swimming to do.

I was sorry about the Camus obit.[1] I should not have misled you by first misleading myself. I was physically staggering under my academic load, and I should have known that there wasn't a prayer of my writing anything. I thought your Camus piece came off very well (Jim, I suppose). It said what *NR* needed, editorially speaking, to say. Anything I might have said would have been out of line. This, and other things, convinces me of what I have been noticing: *NR* is much better off without me and one or two others. In terms of *NR* metabolism, we were indigestible lumps; and, if anything at all has been lost (questionable), the mixture is, in general, more uniform now. Frank Meyer is emerging clearly as the Voice. I am not being sniffy: this, I gather from stray *NR* readers, is just what they want to hear. And, technically, he writes it all well. It isn't my flapjack. But that is of no interest whatever. The fact is that this is what readers want. In addition, Mr. G[ary] Wills is coming along. In the end, I prophesy, he will pull ahead of Frank. Frank has worked himself into his shirt until the fit seems pretty perfect to the unpracticed eye. But, still, he had (has) to work at it; and there persists, if you have a sense of these things, a besetting, humanizing pathos. Of young Wills I think it can be said without undue unkindness: you shall declare the truth, and it will set you into a straitjacket of most elegant trim and fit. Wearing it, you can with all assurance point out (with a certain clinical unsparingness) the rags and loopholes of all poor, half-naked wretches wheresoe'er they be. Perhaps age may temper him. He, too, writes well; he, too, seems to me to be your man. The wonder of Jim is that, pursuing another quite different and self-contained orbit, he can make editorial harmony with these so different spheres. So you have the makings of a team or cadre; and I think *NR*

---

[1] WC had volunteered to write it, but it did not come in for the deadline.

reflects this. Unless my too hasty readings mislead me, *NR* shows a new editorial cohesiveness—a welcome change, since, in the past, the magazine's great defect was a tendency to ride off in too many directions at once. So I commend to you the organizing principle of (if you will permit from such a source) Lenin: *"Luchshe menshe no luchshe"*—Better less, but better.

When I came back from my Russian final, I stopped to pick up the mail. In it was your tear-out from the *Harvard Law Review*.[2] I was very tired (I had been studying since 3 A.M. that morning), and this evidence put me into a brown study, if not one of a darker shade. It seems to tell a great deal. No doubt, many others in the group were either unhappy about, or made uncomfortable by, the inclusion of No. 74. And perhaps the inclusion was governed by formalities, conventions, good enough in themselves and not easily breached. Still, I don't think we can stop just with that. Surely, there is something more to the inclusion. In fact, masses of people believe 74 to be, somehow, a wronged man, even when they don't suppose him to be wholly guiltless. This effect is intensified by time. Each day that passes makes the past less clear, more vague: the whole historical context has decisively changed. People simply can't remember. But that, I think, is only a surface manifestation. The fact is that masses of people *want* to believe him wronged and innocent. Quite unconsciously for the most part, they *want* to believe me wrong and wicked. It corresponds to a deep need in them. Koestler put his finger on it in the beginning: the parts were miscast. 74 looks like the American boy (at least if you don't look too closely)— clean-cut, "nice," probably played basketball. I look like some kind of intellectual—God only knows what kind. Even in my casual comment, there is a tone of mind that marks me off as different, automatically suspect; in the longhouse (probably on forged credentials) but clearly not of it. The American Boy should have been the one to try to rescue America and the

2 Including a picture of a reunion, class of 1929, Harvard Law School, the alumni neatly numbered for identification in the caption. No. 74 was Alger Hiss.

West—not that other. If, in fact, it wasn't that way, by necessity of belief they will force themselves to have it that way. It is when I look hard at this manifestation, much more than when I consider missile lags and such, that I cannot overcome a sense that the West will not win. America is dying of the American Boy, not only 74. This is what your tear-out reminded me of. They will get what they want, and it may well kill them. If I did not believe that men make their own history, I could say loftily: a judgment. Since I do believe that men make their own history (though not, we are reminded, just as they please), it is even worse. The result (judgment is an unnecessary concept) will simply parse the interactions of what really is, of reality. The consequence will be more terrible because quite merciless. What does energy know of mercy?

The afternoon of Jan. 1, I wrote you a few lines to note that you and your wife were the only two people from the world, out there, to wish us a happy New Year. I thought I should thank you both, and wish you the same.

As always,
Whittaker

Jan. 13. Since writing the above, I have read *Time*'s Camus obit. Very good, but a treatment off-limits for *NR*. If you are interested, and I think you should be, you might look at Hans Morgenthau's handling of the Charles Van Doren affair [3] in the *New Republic* (if I remember aright) of Dec. 12, 1959. It is paunchilly sanctimonious; you can hear the wheezing of organ bellows in the organ loft; and I, for one, cannot buy its ground premise without some long long thoughts. Nevertheless, this is one proper way to handle the matter; and, for those who can accept the premise, I think it is all well argued. How on earth did the *N. Rep.* come to run such a piece? See John Wain in the same issue.

[3] The TV scandal.

March 16, 1960

Dear Bill,

You have just done something kind for me, something that was so timely and word of which reached me in so odd a way, that I want to ramble back and tell you how it used to be.

In the village where I grew up, the Methodist Episcopal minister always lived on our street, a block above, or, later, next door, though across a wide lot, now a boulevard. The first I remember was the Rev. Mr. Glover; or, rather, I don't remember *him* at all. I remember his son, much older than I, who struck my interest because when an oil freighter was wrecked at Long Beach, young Glover went down, collected and sold the washed-up 10-gallon cans, and thus enterprisingly upped the Methodist Episcopal income. Best of all I remember Mrs. Glover, who was always especially kind to me, and her little girl; largely, I am afraid, because it was at her birthday party that I was sicker than I had ever been, and next day came down with bad scarlet fever, to the terror of all the parents whose children had also been partying.

Then there was another ME divine whose name I shall leave unsung. He was a big, loud-mouthed, assertive, fungoid man, whose unhappy wife regularly presented him with a baby as soon as she was able to totter about after the one just before.

In between this male ecdysiast and Mr. Glover, there came another. He was the Rev. Mr. Adams. I remember him very clearly—a quiet, thin, slightly stooped, white-haired man, of a mild but most dignified face; dressed in a dark suit, which I recollect as being longer in the jacket than the style was. From a distance, he made a great impression on me. I thought: this was what a minister should be. He had a wife, also quiet and dignified, just a blur in my memory, and a daughter, whom I thought of as grown when I was perhaps twelve. I have remembered her, too, for no reason I can put my finger on—some intangible *quality*. Her name was Josephine Adams. After *Witness* appeared, Miss Adams wrote me. It was a generous and rather moving letter. She had been caught by my evocation of Long Island in those years before the War (always the 1914 War). She had talked with Harold Shipway, who is glimpsed in *Witness* for a particular moment. His father had been Sunday School superintendent in Mr. Adams' church. Harold, never a particular friend of mine, was, nevertheless, the symbol to me of what a man and boy should be, beset by mongrels. So she wrote me.

Yesterday, she wrote me again. She had heard you on Mike Wallace's show (I didn't know he still had one). Wallace had asked you a question and you had answered with my name. Then she went on to express her pleasure at what you said. She went on to ask if she might send me *Up from Liberalism*, which she meant to ask you to autograph.

That is how I heard about it. Here I want only to touch on what you did and said. In the past, you have done and said much, a great deal, for which I have been grateful, and not good at saying how much. But there are moments when what is said and done is given an exceptional force by the moment's context, even if sayer or doer does not know it, does not know what moment it is he has brushed. I had reached one of those moments. I don't want to get too much into it; briefly, it was such a moment as one says in: "I am absolutely alone; I have given everything I had to give, and there is nothing." I do not wish to justify this moment or this feeling; only to note that it existed. You swept me out of this moment. I am grateful. I'm going to leave it there.

Some words to update our telephone conversation about Mr. Nixon. My rule is never to mention to anyone my contacts with him. I'm going to break it this once, for a reason, but I wish you not to mention what I shall say. Not long ago, I had lunch with him. He asked us down one Sunday, and we had a long talk. What was said? Except for two minor points, I could not say. I came away with a most unhappy feeling, neither the reason for, nor the exact nature of which, I have been able to explain to myself. I suppose the sum of it was:

we have really nothing to say to each other. While we talked, I felt crushed by the sense of the awful burden he was inviting in the office he wants. I felt dismay and a gnawing pity, which is pointless and presumptuous, since he seeks the office. He is asking to assume the first post of danger at the moment of the most fearful and (at least) semi-final stages of the transition from the older age to the new. If he were a great, vital man, bursting with energy, ideas (however malapropos), sweeping grasp of the crisis, and (even) intolerant convictions, I think I should have felt: Yes, he must have it, he must enact his fate, and ours. I did not have this feeling (I believe Ralph has it). So I came away with unhappiness for him, for all. Of course, no such man as I have suggested now exists? Apparently not. Mr. Nixon may do wonders; he may astonish us (and himself), a new *stupor mundi*. Then I shall have proved the man who, privileged to see the future close up, was purblind. I hope so. I hope, too, that he gets his chance, since that is his wish. But I could not help wondering too: Suppose he misses it? I cannot imagine what such a defeat will do to him. Yet I cannot bring myself to believe that his victory is in the bag. In short: I believe he is the best there is; I am not sure that is enough, the odds being so great.

As always,
Whittaker

An incident from my Greek class, which has left me in ill favor. We came on a Greek line of Diogenes': "Love of money is the mother-city of all the ills." Opinions were invited, and when my turn came, I answered with one word: "Nonsense." This was too vehement, but there was a reason. Behind me was sitting a junior, who manages on a scholarship or grant or something of the kind, and whose college life has been made a misery by poverty. He used to wait on tables in commons. Now he has a somewhat better job at the library. But he is caught either way; if he works hard at his job, his marks suffer. If he works hard at studying, his job suffers. He walks a perpetual tightrope, always threatening to pitch to one or the other side. As a result, he is always tired. I don't think I have ever seen him fully awake. All things considered, he is a pretty good student; but his sleepiness makes him an easy professorial butt. In addition, he is not a particularly personable youth. To say in the presence of such a case: "Love of money is the mother-city of all ills." That is why I answered: "Nonsense." So, at some effort, a line was dug out of Timothy: "A root of all ills is the love of money," etc., etc. This has Scriptural authority, of course. Again, I objected. Instead, I offered in Greek: "A lack of money is the root of many ills." I added: "The scarcity of natural resources is the root of most ills." Sickening to hear the same old misconceptions, half-thought-through, but offered as truth to the young. I thought I could speak with some freedom since there can scarcely ever have existed a man in whom love of money is so absolutely absent as in me: I can't even get *properly* interested in it. Oh, I also offered (while authority was being bandied) St. Thomas Aquinas': "Money is neither good nor bad in itself: it depends on what is done with it." But St. Thomas seems not to be in good standing. So, down the generations go the blinded minds—blinkered minds, at any rate. But I wonder what the impoverished junior thought about it. I did not ask. He, like the other Greeks who were doing most of the talking, is a pre-divinity student—pre-Flight, as they call it happily here.

March 28, 1960

Dear Bill,

The address you asked for is:

> Miss Josephine M. Adams
> 37 Clinton Ave.
> Lynbrook, L.I., N.Y.

I have told her you asked for it and may send her an autograph. So I hope you do.

I imagine you are on tour. I'll wait for your return for further talk.

As always,
Whittaker

—————— has just telephoned that —————— is fixed up very satis-factorily. Or so Esther tells me. For, at the first tinkle of the bell, I rushed outside to feed the fish in the pond—because they do not bark, and do not know the secrets of Washington.

June ??, 1960

Dear Bill,

You can scarcely know how much pleasure your visit gave us; how much we appreciated your making the effort to come here. There is only a handful of people we ever like to see. You are one of them.

As always,
Whittaker

Some days later. John got home for the weekend, and we were discussing ——————. John: But what's going to happen to him? I: Two possibilities, I think. He may be expelled as a trouble-some alien. He may be assassinated. J: Assassinated?! I: Yes, I think so. John: I hate to say this—but there's nothing that would delight him more.

October 22?, 1960

Dear Bill,

Out of my childhood, a nonsense rhyme:

> *Down in the cellar, dark, remote,*
> *Where alien cats your larder note,*
> *In solemn grandeur stands the goat.*
> *While wintry winds about him storm,*
> *He eats the coal to keep him warm.*

This occurred to me first, on discovering your lost letters, down in the cellar, dark, remote. But I feel sure that this wonderful verse, author unknown, must have some instant political application. Your missing mail is enclosed.

Also enclosed, my latest French composition. The ink and pencil corrections are mine: the red ink corrections are my professor's. Sometimes he has made again corrections I had already made. Apparently he does not recognize the sign for excision, at least as I make it. I mention this in order to commit the sin of pride. But I enclose the script for another reason. If you have the patience to get through it to the end (and the end is important), I think it will give you, more quickly than I otherwise could, a notion of my mood.

Thank you for many kindnesses to me, and your *patience* with me.

As always,
Whittaker

VI

April 9, 1961, to July 9, 1961

Shortly before Easter, Chambers expressed the wish to take a long drive south with Esther, and I suggested that they might join me in Charleston, and then drive to Camden, South Carolina, to spend the weekend at my mother's house. Initially he was excited, and we talked at some detail about the itinerary, which I plotted. A week before our scheduled departure, I had a telegram from him, cancelling everything. And he wrote me his final letter.

April 9, 1961

Dear Bill,

You meant to do something generous and beautiful, and we seemed to dash it back in your face. It was bound to seem that way; in fact, it wasn't that way. Weariness, Bill—you cannot yet know literally what it means. I wish no time would come when you do know, but the balance of experience is against it. One day, long hence, you will know true weariness and will say: "That was it." My own life of late has been full of such realizations: "So that was why he did that"; "So that was why she didn't do that"; about the past acts of people whom my own age (and hence understanding) has only just caught up with. There's a kind of pathos about it—a rather empty kind, I'm afraid; the understanding comes too late to do even the tardy understander much good. Anyway, we were too weary to go. At first, it had seemed something completely impromptu, simple, intimate with you. In fact, it wasn't, but we hadn't understood: then it was too much for us. We simply didn't have it. Incidentally, I think we spared you a lot of nuisance.

Our kind of weariness. History hit us with a freight train. History has long been doing this to people, monotonously and usually lethally. But we (my general breed) tried, as Strachey noted,[1] to put ourselves together again. Since this meant outwitting dismemberment, as well as resynthesizing a new lifeview (Grandfather, what big words you use), the sequel might seem rather remarkable, rather more remarkable than what went before. But at a price—weariness. People tend to leave Oedipus, shrieking with the blood running down his cheeks— everybody nicely purged by pity and terror, and so home and to bed. But I was about 23 when I discovered, rather by chance, that Oedipus went on to Colonnus. Camus must have been about nine while I sat reading the *Oedipus at Colonnus*. But each of us, according to his lights, was arrested in time by the same line—the one in which Oedipus, looking out from precarious sanctuary after long flight, sums up: "Because of my great age, and the nobility of my mind, I feel that all will be well." That is the Oedipus largely overlooked. Of course, I can say nothing of the nobility of my mind or even of Koestler's or Camus'; and I realize, too, that Oedipus spoke at a grateful moment of rescue. One cannot pretend to live at that height. And yet, to reach it even at times is something. One must have got rid of great loads of encumbering nonsense and irrelevance to get there; must have learned to travel quite light—one razor, one change, etc. And I suppose the "well" of the quotation is almost wholly a subjective value. And there remains the price— the weariness I mentioned which none of us complain about, but should take good care not to inflict on other people's lives. I did and I'm sorry about it. We're grateful too.

Something quite different which struck me—what seems to have been your desolation by [Malraux's] *Man's Fate*. But Hemmelrich goes back (supreme tenderness) to close the door left too hastily open on the bodies of his murdered wife and son. Tchen, about to throw himself and bomb under the automobile, believes that Pei (spared to life because Tchen acts

<hr>

[1] John Strachey, "The Strangled Cry," *Encounter*, November, 1960.

alone) will be able to write more meaningfully by reason of Tchen's act. Kyo takes the cyanide with the sense that the concept of man's dignity enjoins control over his own death. Katow, surrendering even that ultimate, divides his cyanide with those less able to bear man's fate; and walks toward the locomotive [2] through a hall of bodies from which comes something like an unutterable sob—the strangled cry. It may also be phrased: "And the morning stars sang together for joy." It may also be phrased: *"Il faut supposer Katow heureux,"* [3] as Camus wrote: *"Il faut supposer Sisyphe heureux."* For each age finds its own language for an eternal meaning.

As always,
Whittaker

"Where is Renoir's Girl with the Watering Can?" I asked the attendant at the entrance to the National Gallery.* I walked up the flight of stairs, turned left through two galleries, and spotted her near the corner. It was only 12:25, and I had the feeling he would be there at exactly 12:30, the hour we had set. I sat down on the ottoman in the center of the room. I could see through the vaulted opening into the adjacent galleries. I saw him approaching. It could only have been he, or Alfred Hitchcock. Five months had gone by since he had been at my home in Connecticut, but we were never out of touch; almost every Sunday afternoon I would call him, and we would talk, at length, discursively, and laugh together, between the strophes of his melancholy. (And every now and then—rarely, now that he was back at school—I would receive one of those letters.) The Sunday before, he told me he was to be in Washington on the 8th of June. I was surprised—he loathed Washington, and probably had not been there three times in ten years, although

---

2 Into whose furnace he will, by his executioners, be dropped alive.
3 One must suppose that Katow was happy.

---

* These lines are taken from an article in *Esquire* magazine, October, 1962.

he lived only two hours away. Perhaps, I wondered, one of those infrequent meetings with Mr. Nixon—though Nixon was in California now. Perhaps yet one more meeting with the FBI. I had told him I would schedule my own business for the same day. He asked me to keep the evening open, and we agreed to meet for a private lunch. "You've guessed what's up, haven't you?" he said, his face wreathed in smiles.

"I haven't the least idea."

"John!" he said proudly. We went off talking excitedly. His son would be married that afternoon, and I was to go to the wedding and the reception.

"Where shall we eat?"

"I don't know," he said—I couldn't, on the spur of the moment, think of the name of a single small restaurant in Washington which might be reasonably proof against Chambers' being recognized—we had had that difficulty so often in New York, when he used to come to National Review *on Tuesdays and Wednesdays. "I can't think of any place," he said helplessly.*

"I know!" I interjected. "We must eat at L'Espionage!" He smiled.

It wasn't open. We lunched somewhere, and talked and talked for the hour and a half we had. We walked then to the Statler and sat in the corner of the huge lobby. At that moment a reporter I had recently come to know approached me. I rose quickly and stood directly between him and Chambers, whose anxiety for the privacy of his son was intense (the press all but took over at his daughter's wedding seven years before, and the entire family had taken elaborate precautions to keep this wedding out of public view). The reporter talked on and on, but my taciturn answers finally discouraged him; we shook hands and he left. I turned around. Chambers was gone.

We met again at seven, in the blistering heat, at the church at Georgetown where a few months earlier John Fitzgerald Kennedy, Jr., had been baptized. Whittaker and his wife, Esther, slight and beautiful, with her incomparable warmth; a genial couple, old friends of the Chambers from Baltimore; with his

wife and sons, his steadfast friend Ralph de Toledano; the
bride's parents, a sister of the bride and a friend of the groom.
We went from there to a private room at the Statler, where we
drank champagne (for the first time in my life, I saw him take
a drink) and ate dinner. Whittaker was quiet, but I think he
was very happy. The bride and groom left. We got up to go.
After saying good night all the way around, I drew Whit aside
and made him listen to an irreverent story, which shook him
with silent laughter. I never knew a man who so enjoyed laugh-
ing. I waved my hand at him and went out with the Toledanos.
As we stepped into the elevator I saw him framed by the door,
his hand and Esther's clutched together, posing while his son-
in-law popped a camera in his face: a grim reminder of all those
flashbulbs ten years before. I never saw him again.

"Why on earth doesn't your father answer the phone?" I
asked Ellen in Connecticut on Saturday afternoon, a month
later. "Because," she said with a laugh, shyly, "Papa and the
phone company are having a little tiff, and the phone is dis-
connected. They wanted him to trim one of his favorite trees to
take the strain off the telephone line, and he put it off. So . . .
they turned off the phone." I wired him: WHEN YOU COME TO
TERMS WITH THE PHONE COMPANY GIVE ME A RING. *But he didn't*
call. The following Tuesday, I came back to my office from
the weekly editorial lunch—I had thought, as often I did, how
sorely we missed him there in the dining room. As I walked
into my office I had a call. I took it standing, in front of my
desk. It was John Chambers. He gave me the news. A heart
attack. The final heart attack. Cremation in total privacy. The
news would go to the press later that afternoon. His mother was
in the hospital. I mumbled the usual inappropriate things, hung
up the telephone, sat down, and wept. "American men, who
weep in droves in movie houses, over the woes of lovestruck
shopgirls, hold that weeping in men is unmanly. I have found
most men in whom there was depth of experience, or capacity
for compassion, singularly apt to tears. How can it be otherwise? One looks and sees: and it would be a kind of impotence

to be incapable of, or to grudge, the comment of tears, even while you struggle against it. I am immune to soap opera. . . . But I cannot listen for any length of time to the speaking voice of Kirsten Flagstad, for example, without being done in by that magnificence of tone that seems to speak from the center of sorrow, even from the center of the earth." *For me, and others who knew him, his voice had been and still is like Kirsten Flagstad's, magnificent in tone, speaking to our time from the center of sorrow, from the center of the earth.*

Epilogue

What is now known as the Hiss Case exploded across the nation's front pages on August 3, 1948. On that day, Whittaker Chambers—a short, stocky man in a rumpled gray suit—began a series of public disclosures which shocked the nation and finally led to prison and disgrace for Alger Hiss.

From the start, the case was a compound of ironies. To begin with, Alger Hiss's involvement in the Communist espionage conspiracy was no secret to official Washington. Nine years earlier, Premier Daladier had informed the American ambassador in Paris, William Bullitt, that according to French Intelligence reports Alger and Donald Hiss were Soviet agents. Shortly thereafter, Whittaker Chambers had told the story of a Communist cell in the government to Assistant Secretary of State A. A. Berle, who communicated the information to President Roosevelt and, in 1943, turned over careful notes of the conversation to the Federal Bureau of Investigation. Isaac Don Levine had labored in agonizing frustration to interest federal officials and newspapermen in the Chambers account. FBI Director J. Edgar Hoover had tried to budge the stubbornly antagonistic President Truman in 1945 and 1946.

So well were the Hiss activities and sympathies known that the *Christian Science Monitor* could write in 1946: "More than one Congressman, whenever the subject of leftist activity in the State Department is mentioned, pulled out a list of suspects that was invariably headed by Mr. Hiss." There was a second major irony in the case: Whittaker Chambers was called to the stand

by the House Un-American Activities Committee as a kind of
afterthought, yet he opened the door to the most sensational
and significant case in its history. Only because its chief investigator, Robert E. Stripling, recalled a two-year-old conversation with a high-ranking security official at State who had
described Hiss as "the Communist who runs the department"
was Chambers called—and then to buttress the testimony three
days earlier of Elizabeth Bentley, a former Soviet espionage
agent.

On that hot August morning when Chambers answered
"I do" to Acting Chairman Karl E. Mundt's "Do you solemnly
swear," the newspapers were far more interested in Miss Bentley's detailed story of a wide-ranging espionage apparatus, with
sources in almost every sensitive federal agency—an apparatus
for which she served as courier. The reporters covering the
hearing had no inkling of what Chambers would say—and in
this ignorance they were joined by most members of the Committee. At the press table there was a flutter of amusement that
a senior editor of *Time* should be on the receiving end of a
Congressional investigation. That amusement quickly changed
to astonishment—or bitter anger among the more politically
committed—once Chambers had moved past the preliminary
questions and into his prepared statement. . . .

That prepared statement was the opening gun of the Hiss
Case. To the fallible members of the Committee, to the hostile
press corps, and to a nation beginning to feel the first chill of
the Cold War, it understated what would be meticulously documented in all its terrible detail at later hearings, before a grand
jury, and at two trials. In a voice so low that reporters had
difficulty catching his words, Chambers began the long travail
of his witness:

> Almost nine years ago—that is, two days after Hitler and Stalin
> signed their pact—I went to Washington and reported to the
> authorities what I knew about the infiltration of the United
> States Government by Communists. For years international com-

munism...had been in a state of undeclared war with this Republic. With the Hitler-Stalin pact, that war reached a new stage. I regarded my action in going to the government as a simple act of war, like the shooting of an armed enemy in combat.

At that moment in history, I was one of the few men on this side of the battle who could perform this service.

I had joined the Communist Party in 1924. No one recruited me. I had become convinced that the society in which we live, Western civilization, had reached a crisis, of which the First World War was the military expression, and that it was doomed to collapse or revert to barbarism. I did not understand the causes of the crisis, or know what to do about it.... In the writings of Karl Marx I thought that I had found the explanation of the historical and economic causes. In the writings of Lenin I thought I had found the answer to the question: What to do?

In 1937 I repudiated Marx's doctrines and Lenin's tactics. Experience and the record had convinced me that communism is a form of totalitarianism, that its triumph means slavery to men wherever they fall under its sway, and spiritual night to the human mind and soul. I resolved to break with the Communist Party at whatever risk to my life or other tragedy to myself or my family.... For a year I lived in hiding, sleeping by day and watching through the night with gun or revolver within easy reach. That was what underground communism could do to one man in the peaceful United States in the year 1938.

At this point, it became obvious that Whittaker Chambers was not scratching in the kitchen middens of the Communist Party. To those with any knowledge of Communist organization, the brief description of his break was an overt confession that he had once been a part of that complex alliance of Red Army Fourth Bureau (Intelligence), Soviet secret police, and the Comintern. Only the faceless men of espionage risk death when they "surface"—the technical term for resuming a place in society. As Chambers continued to read his statement, he carefully underscored this point in a manner which would alert U.S. security forces and serve notice on the men he named:

> I had sound reason for supposing that the Communists might try to kill me. For a number of years I had myself served in the underground, chiefly in Washington, D.C. The heart of my report to the United States Government consisted of a description of the apparatus to which I was attached. It was an underground organization . . . developed, to the best of my knowledge, by Harold Ware. . . . I knew at its top level a group of seven or so men, from among whom in later years certain members of Miss Bentley's organization were apparently recruited. The head of the underground group at the time I knew it was Nathan Witt, an attorney for the National Labor Relations Board. Later, John Abt became the leader. Lee Pressman was also a member of this group, as was Alger Hiss, who, as a member of the State Department, later organized the conferences at Dumbarton Oaks, San Francisco, and the United States side of the Yalta Conference.
>
> The purpose of this group at that time was not *primarily* espionage. Its original purpose was the Communist infiltration of the American government. *But espionage was certainly one of its eventual objectives.* Let no one be surprised at this statement. Disloyalty is a matter of principle with every member of the Communist Party. . . . [Emphasis added.]

In the course of the somewhat disorganized questioning that followed, Chambers described how the underground apparatus operated, where it met, and who its members were. He told how, under orders from J. Peters, leader of the underground activities in Washington, members of the apparatus who "were going places in the government" were detached for security reasons and how, from that point on, they did not meet as a group. It was his assignment, Chambers testified, to be the link between these men and J. Peters. A direct inquiry from Chief Investigator Stripling brought in the name of Harry Dexter White, who in the 1940's became Assistant Secretary of the Treasury and Secretary Henry Morgenthau, Jr.'s most influential adviser. White, though not a member of the original cell, was "going places" too—and he was assigned to Chambers.

If there was any focusing of attention on Alger Hiss, it was the Committee's doing. Chambers could testify more fully about him because, by his own account, the two men had become close friends. By 1948, all the men named had left government employ, but Hiss had moved on to the ultrarespectable position of President of the Carnegie Endowment for International Peace. . . .

From an investigative standpoint, the hearing had demonstrated the continuity of two Communist underground groups—one operating in the 1930's and the other during the war. Harry Dexter White had not only worked with Chambers, he was an integral, though remote, part of the Bentley apparatus and known to its members as "one of us." Miss Bentley's testimony had, however, admittedly been hearsay—the shop talk of espionage. Chambers could nail the accusation home. But it was the mention of Alger Hiss that sent the jungle into an uproar. The late Elmer Davis filled his nightly newscasts over the American Broadcasting network with protestations of Hiss's innocence and countercharges that the Chambers testimony was an attack on the New Deal, and a Republican plot. The New York *Times* inveighed against "false accusation"—seemingly unaware that until all the facts were in it might itself be falsely accusing Chambers. Liberal cartoonists and commentators had a field day with the tarbrush.

On August 5, Alger Hiss made his triumphal appearance, at his own request, before the Committee. The hearing room was packed with friends and well-wishers, and at the press table the reporters waited expectantly for the flat denials which would destroy Whittaker Chambers. Urbane, smiling, and patronizing, Hiss took the stand and read as categorical a statement as the Committee had ever heard. "I am not and have never been a member of the Communist Party. I do not and have never adhered to the tenets of the Communist Party. I am not and have never been a member of any Communist front organization. I have never followed the Communist Party line, directly or indirectly. To the best of my knowledge, none of my friends is a Communist. . . . To the best of my knowledge, I had never heard of Whittaker Chambers until in 1947, when two members of the Federal Bureau of Investigation asked me if I knew him. . . . So far as I know, I have never laid eyes on him. . . ."

Then he rapidly ticked off the names of the other members of the apparatus supplied to the Committee by Chambers: "I have known Henry Collins since we were boys in camp together. . . . Lee Pressman was in my class at the Harvard Law School. . . . Witt and Abt were both members of the legal staff of the Agricultural Adjustment Administration. . . . Kramer was in another office of the AAA and I met him in that connection. I have seen none of these last three men I have mentioned except most infrequently since I left the Department of Agriculture. I don't believe I ever knew Victor Perlo. . . . The statements made about me by Mr. Chambers are complete fabrications." Curiously, he did not deny the flat assertion of the Committee that the Communist connections of these people were a matter of common knowledge. He did not even feel "qualified" to "testify absolutely" that his brother Donald was not a Communist—and even about his wife, Priscilla, he watered down his answer by stating that "so far as I know" she was not a member of the Party.

Before the hearing had ended, the Committee began to flounder. Mundt noted plaintively that he was puzzled as to why Chambers "should come before this Committee and discuss the Communist apparatus, which he says is transmitting secrets to the Russian Government, and he lists seven people—Nathan Witt, Lee Pressman, Victor Perlo, Charles Kramer, John Abt, Harold Ware, Alger Hiss, and Donald Hiss . . ." The witness was so much in control of the situation that he interrupted Mundt loftily to correct him. "That is eight," he said and later, ominously, "I wish I could have seen Mr. Chambers before he testified." Representative John Rankin, who had been most enthusiastic over the Chambers testimony, switched completely. "After all the smear attacks against this Committee and individual members of this Committee in *Time* magazine, I am not surprised at anything that comes out of anybody connected with it." (Laughter.)

By the hearing's end, Committee members were busily apologizing for have inconvenienced Hiss and he was graciously accepting their apologies. Reporters and spectators rushed to Hiss, shaking his hand and congratulating him. Among the few in the room who abstained were Representative Nixon and Chief Investigator Stripling. In a memorandum prepared for this writer, Nixon described the reactions of the Committee to the morning's reversal.

> I would say that 90 per cent of those who attended the hearing, including 90 per cent of the press, were convinced Hiss was telling the truth. The impression Hiss had successfully conveyed was that the name Chambers and a picture of Chambers meant nothing to him whatever and that this was simply a case where he had been indiscriminately smeared by a man he had never known before. Hiss on that day was a convincing witness because the Committee had no facts on which to cross-examine him which would in any way shake his story.
>
> Immediately after that hearing the Committee went into executive session and virtual consternation reigned among the members. Mundt, along with all the members of the Committee except myself, said that it was quite apparent the Committee had been taken in by Chambers and that unless the Committee was able to develop a collateral issue which would take it off the spot and take the mind of the public off the Hiss Case, the Committee would suffer a great deal of damage. [Representative F. Edward] Hébert insisted that the only way to handle the problem was to send the file containing the testimony of Chambers on August 3 and the testimony of Hiss on August 5 over to the Attorney General and to ask him to determine who was lying. I objected to that decision, and Stripling sided with me. I insisted that although the Committee could not determine who was lying on the issue of whether Hiss was a Communist, we could at least determine which of them was lying on the

issue of whether Hiss knew Chambers. I suggested that we immediately go to New York, contact Chambers, and get him in executive session to tell everything that he knew about Hiss. Stripling suggested that there was a witness in the Bentley Case who also lived in New York and that the Committee might interview him at the same time.

The Nixon strategy was at once simple and ingenious. He hoped to pump dry the Chambers well of memory, to get on the record every single fact which could be known only by a close and long-standing friend. If these minutiae were later corroborated by Alger Hiss and/or the Committee's investigators, it would establish that Hiss was lying when he carefully denied knowing a man *named* Whittaker Chambers and, by a rule of law governing testimony, tend to impeach his other denials. If, on the other hand, Chambers' account of his personal association with the Hisses turned out to be fiction, the case would collapse. Acting Chairman Mundt and the Committee reluctantly agreed to allow Nixon to pursue this course, though the pressures for an immediate whitewash of Hiss were very great.

At that moment, the Nixon plan called for considerable courage. Even friends of the Committee were dubious. Nixon recalls that right after Hiss's first appearance, he was told by Mary Spargo—a reporter on the Washington *Post*—"Here's a chance to win some liberal support by repudiating Chambers and clearing Hiss." When Nixon demurred, she said, "Well, go ahead. But I warn you, you'd better be right or you're a dead duck." Antagonists of the Committee were already blasting away. Dean Carl B. Spaeth of the Stanford University law school, Francis Sayre, who represented the U.S. at the United Nations, Clarence Pickett of the American Friends Service Committee, former Secretary of War Robert P. Patterson, Senator Herbert H. Lehman, Acting Secretary of State Will Clayton, Ralph Bunche, Chairman H. H. Fisher of the Hoover Library, Mrs. Eleanor Roosevelt, and many others had written

Hiss deploring the investigation and pledging their faith and support.

The Committee's decision to allow Richard Nixon to continue the investigation had one effect: from that point on it was his show. For better or for worse, he was inexorably tied to the course of the inquiry. It made him a national figure, and it might have destroyed him. For the friends of Hiss—left, right, or center—never forgave him. But it was not all opposition. Very early in the investigation, Bert Andrews, bureau chief of the New York *Herald Tribune,* saw a good story and moved in as an unofficial adviser to Nixon. The Andrews role in the Hiss case has been exaggerated, but there is no doubt that his moral support of Nixon was a tremendous factor. Kenneth G. Crawford and Samuel Shaffer, both of *Newsweek's* Washington bureau, ran full stories.

From this point on, Richard Nixon took control of the Hiss Case. With the full, able, and dedicated backing of Robert Stripling, Research Director Benjamin Mandel, and the Committee staff, he helped make the investigation a classic of its kind—careful, thorough, and unbiased. On August 7, in Room 101 of the Federal Courthouse on New York's Foley Square, Nixon began his questioning of Chambers. In the cold print of the official transcript, Nixon's language seems harsh and uncompromising. And, in a sense, he was too. His purpose was to get at the facts and to do so he used the techniques of cross-examination. Step by step, he took Chambers along the old dry path of his former associations with Hiss. With Representatives Hébert and John McDowell breaking in now and then, Nixon bore in to elicit the details of Hiss's home life, the nicknames used by Alger and his wife, Priscilla, the kind of car they owned—an old 1929 Ford with a hand windshield wiper—that Hiss had bought a new Plymouth in 1936 and turned over the old car to the Communist Party.

Chambers told the Committee about Hiss's personal habits, boyhood anecdotes ("I remember he told me as a small boy he used to take a little wagon—he was a Baltimore boy—and walk up to Druid Hill Park, which was at that time way beyond the civilized center of the city, and fill up bottles with spring water and bring them back and sell it"), Priscilla Hiss's background and where she came from, that she was a Quaker. In the course of this testimony, Chambers casually mentioned one episode which was to be the clincher for many people. To a question by Mandel, "Did he have any hobbies?" Chambers answered: "Yes, he did. They [the Hisses] had the same hobby—amateur ornithologists, bird observers. They used to get up early in the morning and go to Glen Echo, out on the canal, to observe birds. I recall once they saw, to their great excitement, a pro-thonotary warbler."

"A very rare specimen?" McDowell asked. "I never saw one," said Chambers—and most Americans had never even heard of the species. When Hiss later corroborated the fact that he had seen such a bird and more than ten years later was as excited about it as he had been when the incident happened, it was a dead giveaway.

For Nixon, and for the Committee, the secret session in New York was a clincher. It was obvious that Chambers was not talking of a man whose life he had studied, but of a onetime friend. There was just too much about Hiss that was not on the public record—some of it not known to any of his friends. In the nine days between this hearing and Alger Hiss's second appearance before the Committee, Nixon continued his marathon inquiry into what Chambers knew and what his motives had been. He even made several trips to the Chambers farm in Westminster. "On these occasions," Nixon later said, "I asked Chambers innumerable questions concerning his relationship to Hiss and his answers to them were in all cases forthright and convincing." On the matter of motive, Nixon realized what was gradually seeping into the minds of some of the less biased reporters: In destroying Hiss, Chambers was also destroying himself.

On August 16, when Hiss took the stand in the Committee's hearing room in the Old House Office Building, he could sense a different atmosphere. The members had studied the

Chambers testimony. Nixon's hunch had turned into conviction. The staff had checked out every fact at that time susceptible of proof and had found that Chambers was telling the truth. Hiss's former arrogance now turned to wariness, and the change in manner was not lost on the Committee. As Nixon led Hiss step by step to corroborate what Chambers had said about him, his wife, and his home life, the witness began his long retreat from the categorical statement that he had never seen Chambers. "The face," he said in typical government jargon, "is definitely not unfamiliar." He also very carefully repeated that he had never known a man *"by the name of Whittaker Chambers."* But this gambit no longer impressed the Committee. Thereupon, Hiss changed his tactics. Aware that Chambers had furnished damaging details of their past association, he launched into a pettifogging attack on the Committee, accusing its members of bad faith. His charge that the testimony he was giving would be leaked to Chambers, giving him "ex post facto" knowledge, was quickly demolished when Stripling and others pointed out that Chambers had been the first to supply the incriminating details and that Hiss was merely corroborating them.

At this point, Hiss made what lawyers have since called his most serious error. He grudgingly identified Chambers, subject to confrontation, as one "George Crosley"—according to the Hiss account a free-lance writer to whom he had supplied public information and sublet an apartment, and whom he had befriended in 1934 and 1935. This gave him the opportunity for confirming part of the Chambers story, for explaining how Chambers came to know so much about him, and for avoiding the charge of perjury. But it also placed on him the onus of pinning the "George Crosley" personality on Whittaker Chambers—something he was never able to do. And it also trapped Hiss in a major lie which was to be his undoing. This trap was of Hiss's own making. For having been warned—reportedly by a friend in the Justice Department—of Chambers' comments on the old Ford, Hiss had to tailor his story to fit his purported dealings with the "deadbeat" Crosley.

Suddenly turning voluble, Hiss testified that he had sublet his apartment to the "Crosleys," that until their furniture arrived he had put them up in his new home, and that he had "thrown in" the old Ford which he no longer needed since he had a new Plymouth. The Ford, said Hiss, "had been sitting out in the streets in the snows for a year or two. I once got a parking fine because I forgot where it was parked. We were using the other car." He set the date for these transactions at July, 1935, certain that the date of transfer could not be traced. The date, and the unnecessary detail, lived to haunt him as the hearings progressed.

It was not until several days later that the Committee realized the importance of the car testimony. What jolted them most was the brief exchange about the prothonotary warbler which Chambers had casually mentioned. When Hiss admitted to an interest in ornithology, Representative McDowell asked casually: "Did you ever see a prothonotary warbler?"

> HISS: I have right here on the Potomac. Do you know the place?
> THE CHAIRMAN (sharply): What is that?
> NIXON: Did you see one . . .
> HISS: They come back and nest in those swamps. Beautiful yellow head, a gorgeous bird.

The Committee dropped the subject. But the balance of the scales had shifted definitely and irrevocably. Subsequent outbursts of righteous indignation by Hiss that the Committee equated the value of his word with that of Chambers, which but eleven days before would have given the Committee some pause, merely led to acrimonious debate. The Committee made it clear that it was not going to be impressed by Hiss's efforts at proclaiming innocence by association with famous men or by his anger that the testimony of a "self-confessed former Communist" and "self-confessed traitor" was being taken seriously. The session wound up when Hiss and the Committee agreed

EPILOGUE 311

that a confrontation between the two principals should be arranged. But before this, Hiss had been damaged further by his reluctance to take a lie-detector test.*

The qualified admission by Alger Hiss that he had known Chambers as "George Crosley" changed the focus of the investigation. The newspapers still continued their litany of "Who is lying, Hiss or Chambers?" but the public—through leaks to the press from Committee members—now knew that at least part of the Chambers story was true, and that Hiss had been less than candid in his first appearance before the Un-American Activities investigators. Repeated attempts by President Truman to discredit the inquiry as a "red herring" and the anguished outcries of much of the liberal community only served to stimulate the public interest. In accordance with its promise to Hiss—and its own desires—the Committee arranged for a secret confrontation of the two men. On August 17, Representatives McDowell, J. Parnell Thomas, and Nixon met in executive session in Room 1400 of New York's Commodore Hotel. Hiss was sworn in and Nixon stated that since the case "at this time" was "dependent upon the question of identity," Chambers had been asked to appear. Hiss said he would "like the record to show" that he had just learned of the death of Harry Dexter White and that "I am not sure that I feel in the best possible mood for testimony." He also vigorously protested a New York *Herald Tribune* story reporting that "the Committee had asked me yesterday if I would submit to a lie detector test."

There was some bickering over "leaks" from the Committee, and then Nixon asked Staff Investigator Louis J. Russell, "Will you bring Mr. Chambers in?" What followed was startling. For though Hiss had repeatedly demanded an opportunity to meet his antagonist face to face, he kept his back turned to the door,

---

* In his August 7 testimony, Chambers had agreed readily to such a test. The idea had been suggested by Bert Andrews to Nixon. Much was subsequently made of Hiss's refusal in later testimony to agree to submit to the lie detector. Recent experiences with the polygraph machine, however, have indicated its general unreliability, and today law enforcement officers concede that its major value is as a psychological device, not as a scientific instrument.

not even turning his head as Chambers walked in. In his book *Witness*, Chambers describes how ten years before, he, Chambers, a hunted man after his break with the apparatus, had pleaded with Hiss to give up his Communist faith. At that parting of lives and loyalties, Hiss had wept. Now his stony refusal to look at his accuser was perhaps the most damning evidence against Hiss, for it wordlessly conceded that he did not need to look at Chambers to determine whether he was the "deadbeat" Crosley. Clearly, he *knew*.

And then the comedy began. For Hiss's sole interest seemed to be in the state of Chambers' teeth. He demanded to know the name of the dentist who had worked on the Chambers dentures. He put such stress on this that Nixon was constrained to ask: "Mr. Hiss, do you feel that you would have to have the dentist say just what he did to the teeth before you could tell anything about this man?" Hiss dropped the subject. Nixon and Stripling then took Hiss over the ground of the so-called sublet of his apartment to "George Crosley" in July of 1935. Hiss amplified his previous account. As he told it, the rental had been $75 a month, he had thrown in a six-year-old car as part of the deal, and he had lent "Crosley" money but had received only a rug in payment. These new details about the car were, at the time, unimportant. Returning to the identification of Chambers, however, Hiss still refused to be categorical. With the Committee's permission, he moved to his own questioning.

> HISS: Did you ever go under the name of George Crosley?
> CHAMBERS: Not to my knowledge.
> HISS: Did you ever sublet an apartment on 29th Street from me?
> CHAMBERS: No, I did not....
> HISS: Did you ever spend any time with your wife and child in an apartment on 29th Street in Washington when I was not there because I and my family were living on P Street?
> CHAMBERS: I most certainly did....
> HISS: Would you tell me how you reconcile your negative answers with this affirmative answer?

CHAMBERS: Very easily, Alger. I was a Communist and you were a Communist.... As I have testified before, I came to Washington as a Communist functionary.... I was connected with the underground group of which Mr. Hiss was a member. Mr. Hiss and I became friends. To the best of my knowledge, Mr. Hiss himself suggested [that I live in the apartment] and I accepted gratefully.

HISS: Mr. Chairman.

NIXON: Just a moment. How long did you stay there?

CHAMBERS: My recollection was about three weeks. It may have been longer. I brought no furniture, I might add.

HISS: Mr. Chairman, I don't need to ask Mr. Whittaker Chambers any more questions. I am now prepared to identify this man as George Crosley....

STRIPLING: You will identify him positively now?

HISS: I will on the basis of what he has just said positively identify him without further questioning as George Crosley.

But the icy calm was now gone. As Chambers repeated his accusation and made his own positive identification, Hiss rose, white-faced with anger, and advanced toward his accuser. "May I say for the record at this point," he said violently, "that I would like to invite Mr. Whittaker Chambers to make those same statements out of the presence of this Committee without their being privileged for suit for libel. I challenge you to do it, and I hope you will do it damned quickly." This was a fatal error, forcing the issue and leading to his trial and imprisonment. But he felt sure that if Chambers possessed documentary proof of espionage, he would have made it known to the Committee. And he was confident that without such proof, Chambers would either run from repeating the accusation where it was not privileged, or be unable to defend a libel action.

Hiss's mistake in judging Chambers and in reading his character was not shared by others who witnessed the unfolding of the Hiss Case. After the Hiss indictment, James Wechsler wrote of the first confrontation in the *Progressive:* "There are those who believe that Chambers was in effect imploring Hiss to acknowledge the degree of guilt already ascribed to him—mere association with the Communist ring—so that it would not be necessary to unfold the papers which presumably damaged both men, transforming the case from the level of Communist affiliation to the more desolate plane of espionage. According to this view, Hiss misinterpreted Chambers' initial failure to produce the documents as assurance that he never would; and Chambers was equally confident that Hiss, correctly understanding his gesture, would never sue for libel." The case, then, would have ended inconclusively. But other factors were at work. It was a Presidential election year and issues were scarce. The House Un-American Activities Committee, moreover, was under strong attack, in part to counter the impact on the nation of the Hiss-Chambers case, and its chairman, J. Parnell Thomas, had been accused by Drew Pearson of accepting kickbacks.

The general political situation was best summed up by Kenneth G. Crawford, then assistant Washington Bureau chief for *Newsweek,* several days after the first confrontation:

> The political potential of the spy investigation is dawning slowly on strategists in both parties. They now believe the country is talking about it to the exclusion of almost every other public question. Republicans are a little worried about the bumbling nature of the House Committee, even though it has been strengthened by Nixon and Mundt.... Drew Pearson's exposé of Thomas, made possible by the defection of a former employee with large bundles from Thomas's files, is making the chairman even more of a liability than he used to be.... Some of the Dewey people are talking about this kind of deal: appoint a Senate Foreign Relations Committee to make a detailed study of the influence of Hiss and associates on Roosevelt foreign policy; a Senate Banking subcommittee to follow through on Harry Dexter White's German pastoralization policy, particularly that Communist-packed Treasury mission that went to Germany after the war at White's instigation and under his protection.... Democrats meanwhile are seeing how far out on a shaky limb Truman's "red herring" statements have got him. Some of them advised him to get off

the limb after his first press conference statement but they have made no impression on him.

He has now repeated the red herring comment ... at two more press conferences. The White House people ... are still talking wistfully about a Presidential Commission to study the whole problem of Communists in government with such figures as General Eisenhower, Judge Hand, etc., to give it the necessary stature. I understand that the President himself is beginning to doubt the wisdom of his line—that the Hiss break shook him a little. All the President saw in the thing up to the time Hiss started changing his story was a successful attempt by the Republicans to rob him of the political advantage he thought he had got from the special session of Congress. He still feels more or less that way about it but has wondered out loud to a friend today. ... At yesterday's press conference, Truman said no American secret ever was leaked to the Russians.

But the case had moved beyond President Truman's soul-searching. It was now a race between the House Committee and the Administration, between the facts and the cover-up. While House Committee investigators were checking on Hiss's testimony—looking into leases, car sales, etc.—the pro-Hiss forces were seeking to minimize the admissions of the August 17 hearing. It was merely by a normal lapse of memory that Hiss had not immediately recognized Chambers. The serious accusation, that Hiss had been a member of a Communist underground, was still at issue. The cocktail circuit was rife with rumors, all dutifully reported, that Chambers had invented the story of Communist involvement out of malice and for obscure motives. It was necessary, if these theories were to be substantiated, to negate the Chambers account of a meeting in 1939 with Assistant Secretary of State Berle during which he disclosed details of the Soviet apparatus. Perhaps, it was said, Chambers was once a Communist. But if he had told Berle of an underground group in the government, why was nothing done about it? Had he mentioned Hiss at that meeting? Had the meeting actually taken place? Or was the Chambers testimony part of a Republican plot against the New Deal?

The answers to these questions were an important part of any further investigation. And the Committee wanted answers. Before the public confrontation of Hiss and Chambers, the Committee wanted its own corroboration, and it called Isaac Don Levine, who, according to Chambers, had been present at the 1939 meeting with Berle, to affirm or deny. Levine had fought the Communists for years (*Newsweek* had described him as the "dean of anti-Communists"), and his liberal and pro-Communist enemies had always been overwhelmed by the solidity of his information. On August 18, Don Levine laid it on the line. He told of his meeting with Chambers in June, 1939, of the conversations they had, of attempts to get the story to President Roosevelt, and of the meeting on September 3 with Berle.

"The picture which emerged by midnight was quite appalling," Levine told the Committee, "and I think Mr. Berle was very much shaken by the various names of the Soviet agents that Mr. Chambers disclosed. Mr. Chambers furnished, in addition to the names, descriptions and characterizations of the various persons which served to provide a background and give an authentic and authenticating character both to his narrative and to the answers to the questions which Mr. Berle then propounded. I think it was sometime between midnight and one o'clock when we left [Mr. Berle]. When I got to my hotel, after I took leave from Mr. Chambers, tired as I was, I jotted down all the names that I could recall on a sheet of hotel stationery."

NIXON: Can you tell us whether the name of Alger Hiss was mentioned in that conversation with Mr. Berle?

LEVINE: Both Hiss brothers were mentioned. The name of Alger Hiss and the name of the other Hiss.

NIXON: There is no question that those names were mentioned?

LEVINE: There isn't any question, because I made a record at the time and I am looking at it now.*

* The Levine notes, written on hotel stationery, were not only made available to the Committee but were heavily quoted in a series of articles for *Plain Talk*, which Don Levine was editing at the time of the hearings. He also allowed the press to inspect them.

Isaac Don Levine's testimony was a blockbuster, demolishing the ugly and carefully disseminated gossip that Chambers had been coached by the Committee and/or the Republican Party. It even jarred those who professed to believe that the Chambers testimony was a sudden aberration, a Johnny-come-lately effort to "get into the anti-Communist act." Yet the doubt persisted in the minds of many, particularly the Washington press corps, which only knew of the Commodore Hotel confrontation from Committee leaks and the planted rumors of the Hiss camp. Even after Hiss had invented "George Crosley," the *Christian Science Monitor* continued to work on a story which was to feature a compendium of laudatory statements by prominent people, all defending Hiss's integrity and vouching for his loyalty.*

On a hot, heavy August 25, Alger Hiss and Whittaker Chambers had their public confrontation. It was steamy in the caucus room of the Old House Office Building, but 1,000 spectators sat tensely in the wilting heat (another 300, held off by Capitol police, waited outside). They knew that this was the moment of crisis, that it was either win or lose for the protagonists in what had become a titanic drama. Hiss surveyed the scene wryly from a small table at one end of the Committee bench, calmly chatting with his lawyer and smiling at friends. At the other end of the bench Chambers sat impassively. Only the Committee members and staff knew that they had finally come up with hard, documented proof that Hiss was lying about his relationship with Chambers—and corollary, though circumstantial, evidence that the former State Department *Wunderkind* was associated with the Communist Party.

It started out quietly and easily. The only ominous note was the quiet assertion by Chairman Thomas that "as a result of this hearing, certainly one of these witnesses will be tried for perjury." This put Hiss on notice, and from that point on he began bickering with the Committee, playing semantic games,

* "I feel entirely convinced," said Mrs. Roosevelt, "that if he had been a Communist I certainly would have caught something to make me suspicious."

arguing over unessential and irrelevant points, and attempting to put the Committee on the defensive by falsely stating that he had been deprived of copies of the transcript of previous hearings—then being forced to concede that they had been furnished to him as promptly as possible. Even the *Manchester Guardian's* Alistair Cooke, whose sympathy for Hiss was abounding, admitted that these petty and pettifogging tactics did not sit well with those who had admired his seemingly frank performance of August 5. The crowd in the room was disposed to sympathize with Hiss's accusations of bad faith against the Committee, but as these were demolished one by one, the mood changed.

In quick order, Hiss identified Chambers as the "George Crosley" he had known until "sometime in 1935." Chambers identified Hiss and said the last time he had seen him was "about 1938." But after some fencing, the Committee got down to the issue which broke the Hiss Case wide open: the disposition of an old 1929 Ford which Hiss claimed he sold to "Crosley" in the summer of 1935. It had been said that Hiss was caught unaware by the close questioning he received on this subject from the Committee. The fact is that he knew his original story was punctured, that the Committee had checked auto registrations. Hiss was therefore faced with the need to qualify or deny what he had previously said, without seeming to do so. But he was impaled by the very detailed and graphic account in his earlier testimony, and his tactic was to develop a progressive loss of memory.

The story of the car may seem petty, in view of the later espionage disclosures. But it is significant as an example of proper investigative procedures—and because it forced Hiss's most ardent adherents to concede that at the very least he was hiding something. It is very difficult to boil down the massive detail involved in the car story and requires some recapitulation of earlier testimony. These are the essentials:

In admitting that he knew Chambers, Hiss had been compelled to come up with a legitimate story of the background of this association. He was handicapped by not knowing just how much of the Chambers testimony would be susceptible of proof. To explain Chambers' knowledge of his homes, he had invented the story of having sublet his apartment. But he had improvised just a little rapidly about the Ford. When the Committee had asked him if he had owned such a car, he had assumed that Chambers must have told the members of its ultimate destination.

In executive session testimony, he had tried to rid himself of this albatross by stating that he had given it to Chambers as part of the sublet arrangement, in May or June of 1935. This required that he acknowledge possession of his new Plymouth as of that date—but Hiss had embroidered this by swearing that the old Ford had stood on the streets "in the snows" for one or two years. During the public confrontation, he retreated from the flat assertion that he had thrown in the car as part of the sublet deal. He may have done it before, during, or after the time that Chambers had occupied the "sublet" apartment. And he wasn't quite sure whether or not he had sold it or merely allowed Chambers the use of it. He was no longer certain that any legal transfer had taken place at the time, though he had previously so testified. Though he had been categorical about having had the Plymouth during the one or two years the Ford had sat in semi-abandonment, he now became vague.

Painstakingly, though sometimes impatiently, clambering over the obstacles Hiss threw in its way, the Committee demonstrated that (1) Hiss had bought his Plymouth in September, 1935, months after he testified that he had given, sold, or made available to Chambers the old Ford; (2) it was not until July, 1936, long after he insisted he no longer had any association with Chambers, that the Ford had been transferred, and the document with his signature was there to prove it; (3) the sale had been made to one William Rosen, who had given a false address and subsequently took the Fifth Amendment when questioned about the transaction; (4) the transfer, consummated by a reputable motor company in Washington, had been so handled that there would be no record. Caught in the net of his own lies, Hiss tried to explain that he might have given Chambers the car after September, but he could hardly make the Committee or the public believe that he would have presented a car to a man who had "welshed" on the rent and on a a number of small debts, had been a "fourflusher" and was by that time repugnant to him. He denied that he had ever said he sold the car to Chambers and sat grimly on the stand as Nixon read pointedly from his August 16 testimony. Yet he continued to argue and was rewarded by the sardonic laughter of the audience which had once applauded him.

His only recourse was to lash out, to counterattack by again challenging Chambers to repeat the Communist accusation where it was not privileged, and to lay the groundwork for the anti-Chambers smears by demanding to know whether his accuser had ever spent time in a mental institution or been convicted of a crime. These questions did not endear him to the Committee. Its members had heard every friendly witness reviled as insane or crooked and spotted Hiss's intent. When questioned as to his motives for raising the insanity issue, Hiss said blandly that it was based on hearsay—someone whom he could not name had told someone else that Chambers had once been committed. Hiss's efforts to deny any other intent except the desire for knowledge further impeached him with Chief Investigator Stripling. For immediately after the first hearing, Hiss and his counsel, William Marbury, had said to Stripling that Chambers was a "psychopathic case—he is crazy"; and then proceeded to pass the word on to friendly reporters.

Hiss's final effort to impress the Committee with his innocence came when he listed a virtual *Who's Who* in government, then asked the Committee to get the opinions of the dropped names as to his loyalty. But the Committee had its answer for that—and right from Hiss's mouth. How, the witness was asked, could they know? Their testimony would be as worthless, Hébert pointed out, as Hiss's that he had no way of determining whether or not Lee Pressman, Nathan Witt, and the others named as his colleagues in the apparatus were Communists. From that point on, it was all downhill for Hiss. As Samuel Shaffer, *Newsweek's* Capitol correspondent, remarked, "After the first public hearing, many in the audience pushed their way up to Hiss to shake his hand and congratulate him on his impressive performance. After the public confrontation, he and his lawyer pushed their way out alone."

Clearly, the Committee had scored heavily. Though it had not proved that Hiss was a Communist, it had demonstrated conclusively that he was lying—that there was something murky in his past which he could not admit. Students of Communist subversion and espionage, studying the record, felt without a shadow of a doubt that Hiss and Chambers once were part of the same apparatus. All the telltale marks were there. The Washington press corps was badly shaken. The more ardent Hissophiles still argued that the last word hadn't been said, that an explanation existed. But for the most part correspondents felt a sense of betrayal. They had accepted every word of Hiss's as gospel truth, using him as a stick with which to beat the House Committee on Un-American Activities, and he had let them down. Behind the scenes, a new strategy was evolved: to minimize the importance of the Chambers disclosures and to rehabilitate Alger Hiss.

Perhaps, it was argued, Hiss had flirted with the Communists in the 1930's and then lied about it in the "Red-baiting, witch-hunting" Cold War era. To admit even a passing acquaintance with a Communist put a man in jeopardy, the Elmer Davises insisted, and Hiss was foolish enough to lie in order to protect his position. He may even have been sentimental enough in the Depression years to donate his old and useless car to some Communist Party organizer, but this was no more reprehensible than contributing to a Communist front with noble purposes or sending money to the Spanish Loyalists. This thought was comforting for those who had been shocked by Hiss's performance before the House Committee. It conjured up a picture, romantic and idealistic, of a young man concerned over the world's problems. The next step for the Committee, therefore, was to probe this aspect of the case—and the most logical witness to question was A. A Berle, who had heard the Chambers story in 1939.

On August 30, the House Committee called Berle, put him under oath, told him he could smoke if he wished, and asked him to speak his piece. It was a difficult moment for Berle. He was fully aware that anything he might say could hurt the electoral chances of President Truman. As chairman of New York's Liberal Party—though still a Democrat—he was already deeply involved in the 1948 election. On the other hand, he still bore the scars inflicted on him by the Acheson-Hiss group in the State Department during his tenure. And he knew from direct knowledge the laxness of department security procedures and the refusal of the Foreign Service to tighten them. That this dilemma was on his mind is not conjecture. Prior to his testimony he had discussed it fully with some of his colleagues.

"I would like to say," Berle began, "that I am testifying from recollection about something that happened nine years ago. If there are any discrepancies in detail, please lay it to faulty memory and not lack of desire to tell the story." The testimony that followed was long, inaccurate both in detail and in broad outline, and deprecating. Its net effect was to play down the importance of Hiss in the State Department hierarchy, to cast doubt on the Chambers and Levine testimony, and to minimize the seriousness of the case.

Describing the meeting in August, 1939, Berle did "not recall that Mr. Levine accompanied Mr. Chambers." Moving on to Chambers' disclosures, Berle said that he had been told of a group of "sympathizers who might be of use to [the Communist Party] later in the United States Government. This was not, as [Chambers] put it, any question of espionage. There was no espionage involved in it. He stated that their hope merely was to get some people who would be sympathetic to their point of view. With that in mind, apparently a study group of some sort had been formed of men who were interested in knowing something about Russia and Russian policy and the general Communist theory of life. ... He mentioned Alger Hiss, Donald Hiss, Nathan Witt, and Pressman. ... In one respect, what he told me omitted something that he has told you: He did not make *the direct statement that any of these men were members of the Communist Party.* They were apparently, from what I then gathered, men who were sympathetic to their general point of view." Berle said he considered this a "pretty grave matter" but that Chambers had refused to "bear witness."

Berle was "disturbed" enough by learning of this innocuous "study group" to look into the then position of the two Hiss boys. "According to my recollection, neither of them had any position that amounted to very much in the State Department. ... Alger Hiss was doing some relatively unimportant work in, I think, the legal department"—he was in fact top assistant to Assistant Secretary Francis Sayre—"... *but neither was in any position* where he either had access to confidential information or where he had much *to do with policy."* Nevertheless, he checked with Dean Acheson, who gave the Hiss boys a clean bill of health. So, too, had Supreme Court Justice Felix Frankfurter. He was worried, Berle added, because confidential information handled by the Acheson-Hiss group consistently leaked to columnist Drew Pearson—but this was not "a fatal crime" since other government officials leaked information to the press.

Berle's final remarks, in effect, summed up the views of those who believed that Hiss's only sin had been to show some interest in Communism. (Berle felt constrained at one point to say, "Well, I am not counsel for Mr. Hiss.") "I have had some experience with the men who have been in [the Communist apparatus] and then got out of it. They sometimes tend to exaggerate a little the depths of the experience they had. They have obviously been through a violent emotional experience, and I gather that part of the Communist apparatus is designed to impress the people in it with the all-powerful quality of it, probably exaggerating their own importance. ... I should question whether their actual importance, except in a few limited areas in Washington"—which he did not specify—"was as grave as they would like to make out. . . . I am by no means clear that Hiss would have been taken into the Communist Party unless things had gone along further than they apparently did. *Sympathizer, possibly, but to be taken into the fold, it is a pretty exclusive and secret organization, that Communist Party, and I recall that Chambers did not make any direct statement to me then.*" (All emphasis in Berle testimony added.)

This wrapped up the case. Berle did not inform the Committee that he had taken notes of his 1939 conversation with Chambers, typed them himself, and turned them over to the FBI in 1943. Had the Committee so known, it might have secured copies of those four incriminating pages and allowed Berle, in the lawyer's phrase, to refresh his recollection. Those notes were headed "Underground Espionage Agent," and there was nothing in them about a "study group." In fact, they detailed espionage operations, listed the names of men in key government positions (Sol "sends weekly reports to C.P." from the Treasury), identified underground couriers, told of the theft of Navy secrets in 1937, and indicated that Chambers had understated rather than "exaggerated" in his testimony before the Committee. Of Alger Hiss, the notes stated: "Ass't to Sayre —CP—1937 / Member of Underground Com.—Active." Of Donald Hiss, "Member of C.P. with Pressman and Witt."

Some indication of what may have been going through Berle's mind is suggested in a memorandum sent by the *Christian Science Monitor*'s New York Bureau to the home office:

FROM A THOROUGHLY RELIABLE CONTACT.

ACCORDING TO THIS INFORMANT BERLE HAS SAID PRIVATELY THAT CLASSIFIED MATERIAL WHICH HISS WAS HANDLING WAS REACHING THE RUSSIANS. IT WAS CODED STUFF. BERLE TOOK THE HANDLING OF THIS MATERIAL OUT OF HISS' HANDS AND THE LEAKS STOPPED.

THIS, OF COURSE, IS PARTLY CIRCUMSTANTIAL, AND IT RAISES A NUMBER OF QUESTIONS, THE CHIEF ONE BEING: WHY HAS BERLE NOT TOLD THIS TO THE COMMITTEE?

325

... THIS SEEMS TO ME THE MOST DAMAGING PIECE OF INFORMA-
TION AGAINST HISS I HAVE HEARD. IF CLASSIFIED MATERIAL WITH
WHICH HE WAS PERSONALLY CHARGED WAS REACHING THE RUSSIANS,
THEN HIS MEMBERSHIP OR NONMEMBERSHIP IN THE COMMUNIST
PARTY WOULD APPEAR TO BE MERELY AN ACADEMIC QUESTION.

The memorandum is dated September 2, 1948 ("9/2/48"), just three days after Berle had testified. It should be noted that the Berle testimony followed an appearance by Whittaker Chambers on *Meet the Press* during which he had said, in answer to a question by Washington *Post* reporter Edward Folliard, "Alger Hiss was a Communist and may be now." No immunity protected this accusation, and it threw the gauntlet at Hiss's feet. It took Hiss a month and the impatient prodding of friendly newspapers like the Washington *Post* ("Mr. Hiss himself has created a situation in which he is obliged to put up or shut up") before the threatened libel suit was filed in Baltimore—a period in which Hiss and his lawyers were studying every scrap of testimony taken by the Committee. In this context, what Berle said under oath may have been responsible for the assurance with which Hiss instituted his "daring suit" (to quote Chambers).

From that point on, the House Committee on Un-American Activities faded into the background. It could probe no further without interfering in a pending litigation. The transcripts of the hearings were forwarded to Attorney General Tom Clark for study and possible action. But no one expected that the Justice Department would do anything more than file them away. President Truman was still describing the hearings as "red herrings" and predicting that the Committee was dead and would not have its mandate renewed. In the newspapers, the Hiss case was receding into the editor's limbo of "no public interest." The Committee believed that it had rested its case, at least partially vindicated, and that the libel suit would result at best in a standoff if Chambers defended himself successfully.

It had no way of knowing that in the law library of William

Marbury, Hiss's attorney, the wheels were grinding relentlessly toward a denouement as unexpected as it was dramatic. For with the Justice Department clearly loath to act against him, Hiss had decided to move in for the kill. From the nature of the questioning at the pretrial sessions in Marbury's office, it became clear to Chambers that "Hiss was determined to destroy me—and my wife—if possible." A sense of self-preservation, and rising anger, impelled Chambers to act. He had carefully skirted the outright charge of espionage on the assumption that Hiss would realize his own danger and not press too hard. But the time for squeamishness, for protecting Hiss, was past. Chambers journeyed to Brooklyn to retrieve a package of papers he had entrusted to his nephew at the time of the break with the apparatus. He was no longer quite certain what was in the package, secreted in an old dumbwaiter shaft, but he remembered vaguely that it included "some papers in Hiss's handwriting." When he brushed aside the accumulated grime of years and examined the contents, he found typed copies of 47 documents, five rolls of microfilm, four incriminating memoranda in Hiss's handwriting, and five in Harry Dexter White's handwriting. "When I saw what I had," Chambers said to this writer later, "I was amazed."

At the next pretrial hearing, Chambers produced the documents—secret and confidential messages from U.S. ambassadors to the State Department—copied on what would subsequently be proved was Hiss's typewriter. The Justice Department was called in, the papers sealed, and everyone concerned enjoined to keep the matter secret. This was on Novembr 17. On December 1, a Justice Department source informed a United Press reporter that the "investigation of the celebrated Alger Hiss-Whittaker Chambers controversy" was being dropped. On the same day, columnist Jerry Kluttz wrote in the Washington *Post* that "some very startling information" had been turned up by the Justice Department.

Nixon was aboard the S.S. *Panama,* en route through the Caribbean to California. But two wireless messages interrupted that leisurely trip. The first, from his administrative assistant William Arnold, informed him that there were serious developments in the case. The second, from newspaperman Bert Andrews, confirmed this and asked if the Committee would reopen its investigation. Nixon wired back, instructing Stripling to advise him on the new evidence and informing Andrews that new hearings would be held if they were "necessary to prevent Justice Department cover-up." Events were moving to a crescendo. Stripling, unable to get confirmation or denial, was successful to a point. Chambers admitted that he had withheld evidence from the Committee, but refused to elaborate. To do so, he said, might put him in contempt of court. The following day, at Nixon's direction, Stripling served Chambers with a subpoena calling for any documentary proof still in his possession. That night, Committee investigators drove with Chambers to his farm. In a scooped-out pumpkin were the five rolls of microfilm.

This hiding place was the source of much gleeful comment from the pro-Hiss forces, and held up as one more indication of Chambers' zany mind. It was not until later that Chambers explained why he had hidden the microfilm there. Hiss investigators had been prowling about his farm, and a scooped-out pumpkin in a patch seemed—and was—the least likely place they might search while he was out of the house. But the case had gone past the stage where jeers could prevent full disclosure. Before the microfilm had been turned over to the Committee, "informed sources" at the Justice Department had let it be known that they were planning to indict Chambers for perjury. The morning after the microfilm had been delivered to the Committee—developed and enlarged to proper size, it gave Stripling a four-foot stack of documents—a federal grand jury was hastily convened in New York, and its first act was to subpoena Chambers.

On December 5, Nixon was picked up in mid-Caribbean by a Coast Guard plane and flown back to Washington. Operation Whitewash was in full swing, and Nixon moved to block it.

On December 6, he and an angry Committee rushed to New York to question Chambers. They were met at Pennsylvania Station by U.S. Attorney John McGohey, who accompanied them to the Commodore Hotel, pleading that the Committee drop out. But none of the members had any faith in the Justice Department's motives. Quickly, the members and McGohey were shouting at each other, pitching accusations, until Stripling threw open the window and said, "We might as well let them hear about it on Fifth Avenue." This ended the curfuffle, but it did not satisfy the Committee that an impartial investigation would be pressed.

On December 7, the Committee obliterated once and for all the contention that the typed and microfilmed documents were of no importance or that they might have been copied by Hiss in the line of duty and then somehow stolen by Chambers. Former Undersecretary of State Sumner Welles told the Committee that some of the documents were still too secret to release to the public and said that the distribution within the State Department would have been "extremely restricted," to be "kept under lock and key." He also noted that whatever the contents of the documents, to have delivered them to a foreign power would have broken our most secret codes. Assistant Secretary John Peurifoy went even further. To make verbatim copies of the documents would be "a very unusual procedure." Of the four memoranda in Hiss's handwriting, Peurifoy said, "I would regard anyone making notes of what I have seen here, in personal handwriting, and taking them out of the Department, as violating all security regulations."

> HÉBERT: Would there be any reason for an individual to make a memorandum such as you have just looked at, in his own handwriting?
> PEURIFOY: No, sir. Not in my judgment.
> HÉBERT: You would have to assume that he did it for some ulterior motive?
> PEURIFOY: I think that is right. Under the Yardley Act . . . a

person would be liable to a $10,000 fine, and I think up to ten years' imprisonment, for doing such a thing.

Most damning was the secret testimony of former Assistant Secretary Sayre—not only Hiss's superior but a close personal friend. First he stated that only he, Hiss, and two secretaries of unquestioned loyalty had access to files which were always kept locked, destroying Hiss's alibi that the handwritten memos were prepared as part of his work.

> NIXON: Did Mr. Hiss (as he claimed) have as one of his duties the paraphrasing of these documents and bringing them back to you in this way?
> SAYRE: The answer is "No."
> NIXON: ... Do you agree there was nothing important or nothing wrong with turning this stuff over?
> SAYRE: I violently disagree, not only because of the substance of these cables, but because they were in highly confidential codes.... The other point is that some of these cables reveal sources from which information was obtained.

This ended the long debate. It was certain now that Hiss had lied and Chambers had told the truth. Despite the opposition of the Truman Administration and the hostility of the press, the House Committee on Un-American Activities had demonstrated, dramatically and effectively, that Communists in government systematically looted the nation of its secrets. The Communist conspiracy was not a figment of fevered or sick imaginations. The Committee could write *Q.E.D.* and proclaim its finest hour. The rest was police work, and the FBI, allowed to perform its functions free of the political interference of a political Attorney General, brilliantly gathered together the evidence. On December 15, Hiss was indicted for perjury involving his denial of passing secret documents to Chambers. ("I hope that nobody anywhere will ever refer to this case as a red herring," Mundt said, but President Truman disappointed him.) On January 21, 1950, after two trials, Alger Hiss was convicted. Two years later, before the Senate Internal Security subcommittee, Nathaniel Weyl testified that he had known Hiss in the Communist underground. And even after the courts had closed the case, evidence continued to pour in, corroborating Hiss's guilt.

Skeptics can look back and wonder at the words of John Sherman, a member of the Communist apparatus, who was asked by the House Committee on Un-American Activities if he had known Alger Hiss and Whittaker Chambers. He took shelter behind the Fifth Amendment when Chambers was mentioned. But he was forthright in his response about Hiss.

"I would not know him from Adam," Sherman said. He was speaking the exact truth—for he had known Hiss in the underground under the cover name of "Adam."

RALPH DE TOLEDANO

Index

A

Abramovitz, Alice, 183
Abt, John, 304
Acheson, Dean, 323
Acme Boot, 134
"Adam" (cover name), 330
Adams, Josephine, 144, 285–86, 288
Aeschylus, 154, 218, 269–70
Agee, James, 106, 163, 167, 168, 186
agents of influence, 169–70, 302, 316, 322–23
agriculture, 56, 239
air travel, 195, 212, 222, 250
"Air-Conditioned Auschwitz" (Chambers), 101
alcoholic beverages, 273, 297
Alcorn, Meade, 220–21
Alpbach, Austria, 251
"amalgam" (Communist rhetorical device), 35
Amerasia case, 93
American Mercury (magazine), 244
Americans overseas, 132
Amor, Mrs., 95
anarchism, 52
Anderson, Thomas, 168
Andrews, Bert, 307, 311, 327
angels, 238
anger, 37, 182
anti-Americanism, 257
anti-Communism, 26, 28, 38, 129–30, 266, 316, 317
antisemitism, 205
Antonov-Ovseenko, Vladimir 180
"Architects of Disaster" (*National Review* feature), 91

Stein, Gertrude, 67
Stein, Sol, 125
Stevenson, Adlai E., 79
stoicism, 29
Strachey, John, 294
Stripling, Robert E., 300, 302, 305, 307, 312, 320, 327, 328
"study group," 322–24
style (literary style), 116–17
Suez crisis (1956), 104, 107
suicide, 50, 210, 252
"surfacing" from espionage work, 301
Switzerland, 238–39, 250

T

Tamuz, 263–64
taxation, 245, 249
Taylor, C. Marshall, 117
teachers and teaching, 190
tears (crying), 297–98
technology, 230–31
teeth, 312
telephones, 106, 297
television, 218, 236
terrorism, 53, 183
Tet Offensive (1968), 14
Third Party Movement in U.S., 65
"third rail . . . just above," 17
"Third Rome," 89, 173
Third Rome (Chambers), 265
Thomas Aquinas, Saint, 104, 288
Thomas, J. Parnell, 311, 314, 317
Thomism, 184
Thompson, Craig, 93
"Tigers do not sharpen pencils," 67
Time (magazine), 89, 121, 148, 284, 300, 305
time, history and time, 200
Tito (Josip Broz), 109, 110
"Toasted Susie is my ice cream" (Stein), 67
Toller, Ernst, 158
Tolstoi, Leo, 135
Tory politics, 55